EXILE ON FRONT STREET

EXILE ON FRONT STREET

MY LIFE AS A HELLS ANGEL

GEORGE CHRISTIE

SIDGWICK & JACKSON

First published 2016 by Thomas Dunne Books, an imprint of St Martin's Press

First published in the UK 2016 by Sidgwick & Jackson
an imprint of Pan Macmillan
20 New Wharf Road, London N1 9RR
Associated companies throughout the world
www.panmacmillan.com

ISBN 978-1-5098-4032-8 HB
ISBN 978-0-283-07266-6 TPB

Copyright © George Christie 2016

9 8 7 6 5 4 3 2 1

A CIP catalogue record for this book is available from the British Library.

Designed by Kathryn Parise
Printed and bound by CPI Group (UK) Ltd, Croydon, CR0 4YY

Visit **www.panmacmillan.com** to read more about all our books
and to buy them. You will also find features, author interviews and
news of any author events, and you can sign up for e-newsletters
so that you're always first to hear about our new releases.

To my wife, Nikki, and my children Moriya, Aubree, and Finn.

My story is, most of all, about you.

And to the memory of my son Georgie, may the wind always

be at your back. Rest in peace.

People confuse the outlaw and the criminal. Some outlaws commit crimes, but the real outlaw isn't a criminal by trade. He's someone who refuses to live by society's established norms of behavior. He has an internal code and answers only to his own sense of honor and right and wrong. The outlaw doesn't conform; he rebels. He doesn't accept; he questions. In the end, the outlaw might change and adapt, but he bends for no man and won't let his life be defined by someone else. Jesse James was an outlaw, but so was Albert Einstein. I've been many things—father, son, husband, leader, brother, and friend—but through it all, I was always an outlaw.

—GEORGE CHRISTIE

EXILE ON
FRONT STREET

INTRODUCTION

I hadn't planned on writing a book when I quit the Hells Angels. After more than three decades as president of the Ventura charter, peacemaker and spokesman for the club, I was perfectly happy to step down, quietly run my businesses, be the best husband and father I could be, and ride off into the sunset.

Then the club leadership did what they're so good at doing—they turned on me. My former charter, a bunch of guys I had looked out for like they were my own blood and had called "brother," voted to change my status two weeks after I quit. All of a sudden, I was officially "out bad, no contact." Given some of the characters who wear the patch in good standing, that's a low bar. It's the worst label in the outlaw motorcycle club culture. It's reserved for rats, hopeless drug addicts, and other low-lifes who have disgraced the patch.

To make matters worse, tough talkers inside and outside the club spread the lie that I had been kicked out, ignoring that I quit first. It gave all kinds of people—many of who had never even met me and didn't know me—license to spout a lot of nonsense. In the outlaw world, they call it being put out "on Front Street." It means you're exposed and un-protected, a target for anyone from law enforcement to your former club brothers to complete strangers. So anybody with an ax to grind tried to rewrite history, saying I had been expelled in disgrace. Some spread the particularly dangerous lie that I had cooperated with law enforcement. Never mind that four months after I quit, I was indicted and wound up doing a stretch in federal prison. Had I rolled on anybody, I wouldn't have done a day.

"Out bad" versus "stepped down" may seem like a difference without a distinction. But it's important to me. I left on good terms having done my best for a club I loved and given it absolutely everything I could. Those terms were changed after I left, by people with their own agendas. They've done their best to tarnish my name and reputation ever since. Simple as that.

I won't lie. It stung. It was a pure betrayal. At a point I thought, "Enough is enough." The sad truth is that you can stand silent only so long until people take your silence as an admission of something. I've found that the more I keep quiet, the more people put words in my mouth. So I wanted to set the record straight. That's when I decided to write this book.

A man's measure is a lot more than the most obvious parts of his life. My story goes well beyond the Hells Angels. As the best Hells Angels like to say, "The man makes the patch, the patch doesn't make the man." That's why I also wanted to reveal the man behind the patch and put the lie to some simplistic and offensive stereotypes about the men who ride motorcycles as a life rather than a hobby.

You could say I was born and raised to be an outlaw. As a member of an isolated immigrant culture, as a surfer, and even as a Marine in the Vietnam era, I lived on the edges, always belonging to outsider groups. So the denim vest of an outlaw motorcycle club member fit comfortably right from the start. Unfortunately, what it means to be an outlaw has changed since the early days. When I first became a Hells Angel, the idea was to share a love of motorcycles, freedom, and partying—to live as you pleased, not as society dictated—with a bunch of rowdy, like-minded individuals. These days, the life is something much different. A lot of club members rarely ride. The Hells Angels Death Head patch is currency. *Brotherhood* has become just another overused word.

The story of how the outlaw culture and I got from then to now is complicated. The best I can do is to write the simple truth, as brutal as it may be. A lot, both good and bad, happens over forty years spent in the outlaw world. Especially if you're a family man, as a lot of outlaws are. The personal side is often a surprise to people who meet me. That's another part of what I'm hoping to explain, the reality beyond the dramatized fiction. Undercover cops and informants who have written about the club paint members with one brush. In those books, we're one-dimensional criminal scum. Most outlaws who write about the life are just as bad. According to them, we're heroic freedom fighters living only to ride, feeling no pain, misunderstood by the rest of the world, and endlessly and unfairly persecuted by law enforcement. Like all of life, the outlaw truth can't be written in black or white. It's infinite shades of gray.

Gray being gray, others may remember differently. But this is all the absolute truth as I recall it. Throughout this book I've made every possible effort to re-create conversations and events faithfully. I've researched crucial events, asked others who were there. I've sifted through police records, court transcripts, and newspaper articles. If I've failed to be accurate on any point, it isn't for lack of trying or a desire to deceive. I mean no disrespect to anyone, but I'm also not trying to be diplomatic. I've never been one to worry about what other people think, and I'm not going to start now. I don't owe anybody anything. I started out to write this book knowing that I was going to step on some big toes. I don't care. I just want this to be an honest accounting. The real story, my story, scars, flaws, and all. No regrets.

That means talking about all I've done as a Hells Angel. Honestly, I've been ready to kill for the club, for nothing more than a piece of fabric sewn on another piece of fabric. That willingness is the price of admission. But I also want to explain what I've done outside the club. I've been a devoted father, trying to support my children as best I could. I was a dedicated martial artist, bike builder, and businessman. I wasn't always the best husband to my first wife, and every day I put the lessons I learned in that relationship in practice making my second marriage successful. I've lost one child, and I'm working hard to ensure I never bury another.

Both those aspects of my life—inside and outside the club—have been affected by law enforcement. That's a gray area as well. I remain friends with a lot of local cops. Many people I've come across in law enforcement maintain a sense of decency and common sense. They gave me some basic respect and I gave it back. (Something many in the club never liked about me.) The feds are another matter. Sometimes, especially at the federal level, agents and prosecutors blur the line between outlaw and cop. They are driven individuals who are often more about the win than they are about any sense of right and wrong. That part of my story is a cautionary tale for any freedom-loving American. Love or hate outlaws, the legal system in this country needs fixing. Outlaws, like a lot of people on the margins, are canaries in the coal mine when it comes to the erosion of constitutional rights.

Really, though, it all comes down to this. I was a Hells Angel for forty years. I belonged to the red and white. I vowed my allegiance to a group of brothers who were, at the best of times, a second family to me. At a point, though, I changed, the world changed, or the club changed. Probably all three. I found myself riding a road down which I was no longer willing to take my wife and young son. That doesn't change the first and most important truth. I loved being a Hells Angel. It was a dream from a young age, and I don't regret it for a minute. So many days I felt like a god, drunk with freedom and power, riding a motorcycle I'd crafted with my own two hands with that winged skull on my back. I was part of something bigger than me, something that stretched around the world. I may be exiled now, to that ugly, lonely place we call Front Street, but

I'm the same man I was. I have my differences with certain members, but I love the club to this day, and I'll always hold dear the memories of my time as a Hells Angel and the bond of my closest brothers. That's something nobody can take away from me. Not law enforcement. Not the people who look at my tattoos and scowl thinking they know all about me. And not my enemies in the club and their puppets.

As an outlaw I never saw myself as a criminal. At times we made up the rules as we went along, but so did our forefathers. Sadly, in the end we failed. We became the people we had rebelled against. I discovered that if I was going to remain a true outlaw, I would have to do the unthinkable. This is my story.

1

I was born in Ventura, California, but I was raised in Sparta.

My grandparents on both sides were Greek immigrants. In the fifties, Ventura had a tight-knit Greek community that was suspicious of outsiders. There was Us and there was Them. Cops, courts, politicians, were Them. Anybody who wasn't Greek was Them. We took care of ourselves. Greeks owned a lot of the local businesses. Restaurants, machine shops, five-and-dimes. My grandfather was a cobbler. The Greek attitude was "Who needs them?" You have a problem? Take it to AHEPA (American Hellenic Educational Progressive Association) or Daughters of Penelope. As I would later discover, the outlaw culture had the same outsider perspective. That was one of the things that ultimately attracted me to the outlaw lifestyle. The unwritten rules were familiar.

But to a kid, the Us-versus-Them thing was confusing. My grandparents on both sides had changed their names. Vlassopoulos became Blacy. Chrispikos became Christie. If it's Us, why change your name unless you were ashamed? I also knew early on that people in town looked down their noses at Greeks. We weren't respectable society.

I was overweight, something else that made me an outcast. Food is love in a Greek house, and there was lots of love in our home. My dad was a fantastic cook, and I was pudgy until I started high school. Being Greek and heavy made me a target, though I was only physically bullied once. It was the first time I used my fists and my temper to solve a problem. But the experience lit a white-hot anger in me that would eventually die down, but never go out. To this day I despise bullies. Of course, you don't need to be bullied to be an outcast. Kids made fun of me and refused to have anything to do with me.

That was a big part of why I hated school. It didn't help that anytime I read more than a couple sentences letters would jump around and change shape. Numbers would become letters or vice versa. A *b* would become a *d*. It was frustrating as hell. It would be a long time before anybody put the word *dyslexic* to it. At the time, I was just written off as lazy. Outside of school, I spent most of my time with my family. My mom and dad were fun and devoted parents. I always knew that I was loved unconditionally. Laughter was the sound track of the Christie house. My mom loved a good laugh, a joke, and the holidays. That's how we came to have a talking Christmas tree.

When I was six, my mom told me our Christmas tree would talk if my cousins and I were good. So we'd sit politely around the tree, draped in jewel-colored lights and glittering tinsel, and do our best to behave. The pine smell filling the living room, the tree would come to life: "How are you girls and boys tonight?" We'd stare in wonder. Then it would say, "I see little Jimmy there. Are you still picking on your sister?" Jimmy's eyes would get huge and he'd shake his head no. If I'd been a smarter six-year-old, I might have thought it a little weird that our Christmas tree had a Spanish accent. Up in the rafters talking down through a disconnected heating vent was Chubby, the Mexican woman who lived next door. But that tree kept a whole neighborhood full of kids polite and well behaved throughout the holidays.

Although my mother, father, and I lived in Camarillo, I spent most of my time in Ventura at my grandparents' house. Pappoús Blacy owned a small shoe repair shop right behind the tiny two-bedroom clapboard house he shared with Yiayiá. Pappoús was lord of the clan, feared as much as loved. His nickname was the Governor. He had no formal education to speak of, but he was one of the wisest men I've ever known. He was a short, barrel-chested Greek, with a confident, imposing presence. He wore dark-framed glasses and a brown fedora, and he was built solid, as if he were rooted to the earth and nothing was going to move him if he didn't want to move. Yiayiá was the flip side of the coin, just as strong as Pappoús, but sweet, gentle, loving, and unbelievably kind.

They made Ventura special for me, but the town itself was a kid's paradise. If my cousins and I weren't begging quarters off Yiayiá (Pappoús had cut us off because our tab with him got too large) to buy cherry Cokes at the corner drugstore soda fountain, we'd head down to Ventura's long wooden pier to fish off the side. Nobody had money, but there was still plenty to do. My happiest childhood memories involved that combination of Ventura and family.

My dad eventually bought a diner, the Frontier Café, where I worked on and off until I graduated high school. Sometimes, after a morning of surf fishing, my mom, dad, and I would scout out other family-run restaurants to see what they were doing with their menus and what might work in our restaurant. We called ourselves "the three Gs"—George, Georgia, and Georgie. One Sunday we had lunch at a local Italian place, an old-school trattoria with checkered tablecloths and empty, straw-wrapped, potbellied Chianti bottles used as candleholders, draped in a hundred coats of red wax. The owner came and sat with us, talking in broken English about how his business was doing. When we left, he walked out with us. As we were saying our good-byes, a low rumble grew into a thunderous roar that shattered the quiet afternoon. A biker pulled up at the stoplight about twenty feet from us. It was the first time I had seen an outlaw up close. It was 1955. In school, most of us had buzz cuts and wore pressed trousers. This guy wore a denim jacket frayed where the sleeves had been cut off, and blue-black jeans crusted with road grease and dirt. His Ray-Bans were pushed up high on his forehead, holding back a wild mane of black hair. He seemed like a magician, controlling everything around him. People on the sidewalks were frozen in the moment. As he idled, the pipes quieted, and I could hear the distinctive rattle of the clutch basket ringing out. He just sat there on that hand-built Harley bobber. Then, in perfect sequence, he lowered his sunglasses with his left hand, cracked the throttle with his right, pushed the suicide clutch with his foot, and jammed the jockey shifter into first. He reached up over his shoulders to grab the handles of his "ape hanger" bars, gave it the gas, and shot across the intersection. It seemed like he disappeared in a blink, leaving just echoes and a memory etched in my mind.

The restaurant owner broke into a tirade. "Look at him, worthless. Goddamn animal." The man spat into the street and looked down at me. "That's your America."

I thought, "You bet it is." It was hands down the most amazing thing I'd ever seen. It wasn't just a kid's fascination with something shiny and loud. Deep down I realized that this guy wasn't playing by anybody else's rules. He was doing his own thing and saying to hell with anyone who didn't like it. Nobody was going to bully him, and he didn't need anyone's approval. He was in control. To an unpopular, chubby, little Greek kid, that seemed like a magical idea.

As the years went by, society kept pushing me in the direction of the outlaw, even as my parents and grandparents kept me grounded. Surfing became a part of that push-pull. Living so close to the beach, I was inevitably drawn to the sport. My parents thought it would be a good, wholesome way for me to spend my time. We had moved to Camarillo from Anaheim right before I started junior high school partly because the Anaheim schools had a lot of juvenile delinquency. So my parents were keen on my being involved in something positive.

I bought my first board for $40, with a little financial help from my mom. It was a butt-ugly olive drab, but it felt like I'd latched onto something, an identity I could own. I started hanging out at the beach every day, picking up techniques and learning how real surfers behave.

Surfing changed everything. I loved the water anyway, and surfing wasn't like other sports. You didn't need a team or a lot of gear. It didn't require special talent, size, or huge muscles. You just needed to practice. Nothing replaced time spent on the waves. I was also a natural from the start, and it felt so great to find something I was good at, something that I could claim as mine.

A waitress in my dad's restaurant had a son who was an avid surfer. My dad asked her if her boy would take me out and give me some pointers. She was all for it. But her son, John Schoemer, wasn't as thrilled. He was seventeen to my fourteen, and I'm sure his idea of surfing didn't involve dragging some kid along. But among surfers—like among bikers—how you handle yourself is everything. Perform, honor the code, and you earn acceptance. Once he and his friends found out that I could hold my own on the swells and respected the way things were done on the waves and on the beach, I became one of them. It was a first for me, being a part of a group outside of the Greek community. The other guys were older and some of the roughest characters in Oxnard. The leader was a Samoan named Doodie Juarez, 220 pounds of pure muscle. He was an artist on a surfboard and a legendary fighter. After a day of surfing, he and his friends loved to drive down to Point Mugu and get into fights with the Seabees from the Point Mugu Naval Air Station. Long days spent shredding waves were followed by long nights drinking dollar jugs of wine around bonfires on the beach.

Surfing was my introduction into an outlaw brotherhood. The average person didn't know real surfing culture. It wasn't the clean-cut, corny world of Beach Boys songs and Annette Funicello movies. Surfers were athletes, but they weren't jocks. They were outlaws. Like any outlaw group, they had a pecking order, with the toughest dog at the front of the pack. You had to regularly prove yourself. We had turf. Surfing a new beach without knowing the regulars meant somebody was going to dump you in the waves and throw you a beating on the beach when you came in. Just as a Harley and a leather jacket don't make you an outlaw club member, owning a five-foot piece of fiberglass and foam won't make you a surfer. You have to know and respect the code.

Being part of that group didn't mean leaving my parents behind. They stayed involved with whatever I was interested in, and that included surfing. My dad read my issues of *Surfer* and knew almost as much as I did. So he understood when I told him I had to have a Dewey Weber board.

My first board had become an embarrassment and the butt of jokes. Dewey Weber was a legendary surfer who had started making a line of boards that defined surfer cool. A surf shop in Hermosa Beach sold the boards. My dad agreed to drive me there and let me pick one out. I was just about to turn fifteen, and—much as I loved him—I did not want to be seen with my old man. I made him promise to stay in the car while I went inside. It was the hippest surf shop I'd ever been in, with Technicolor boards lined up along the walls and a fire pit right in the center. Walking through the door, I was stunned to find Dewey Weber and Harold "Iggy" Ige warming themselves around the pit, still wet from the morning waves. These were my idols. They were rebels, gods. I was trying to comprehend finding myself in the same surf shop as these two when I heard a voice boom out from behind me.

"Hey, Dewey! You think we can find this gremmie a board?"

True to form, my father's promise was a fake-out. He had waited about ten seconds and then followed me into the shop. *Gremmie* is surfer slang for a total novice, someone who wouldn't know one end of a surfboard from the other. My dad knew this. He also knew who Dewey Weber and Harold Ige were.

"Iggy! How are those waves breaking?"

I tried to pull my head down into my body like a turtle. But as luck would have it, although Dewey Weber was considered a pure surfing outlaw with his wild shoulder-length hair and scraggly beard, he was also a class act. He came over and talked to us like we were old friends. He asked me about my stance and what kind of board I wanted. I got my

Dewey Weber board, I met the man himself, and I went to sleep that night one very happy kid.

Thanks to a summer spent surfing every day, I started high school in great shape. Hanging out with the Oxnard guys also gave me a "fuck everybody" attitude. I promised myself that I would never again care about what people thought of me. That attitude played well in high school. People wanted to be my friend. Kids asked me to hang out. They wanted to talk to me in class and invite me to parties. Anyone might have thought it was a big break.

It just pissed me off.

Those were the same kids who had made fun of me when I was that overweight Greek kid in the back of the classroom. I hadn't changed. I was still me. I was still Greek. My parents still loved me. But suddenly, because I was thinner and had an attitude, I was cool? It was hypocritical bullshit, and it made me unreasonably angry.

I still struggled with schoolwork and I got to know the principal, Mr. Killingsworth, all too well. He was a former wrestling coach, built like a tank with a big round head, jowls, and a crew cut. He looked just like a bulldog. The look matched his attitude. Without meaning to, he taught me lessons that had nothing to do with math or history. The biggest was to never trust authority figures. I learned that one after I took a standardized intelligence test with the whole school. It was easier than most tests because it was mostly diagrams and puzzles, or simple multiple-choice questions. No big sections of text to give me a headache, and no writing. I didn't know what the point was, but it was a nice break from the dull routine of regular classes. A couple days later, I got called into the principal's office. I walked in to find my parents sitting in two chairs with an empty stiff wooden chair right between them. I was in trouble; I just didn't know why. Mr. Killingsworth looked angry.

"Sit down, George."

I sat between my parents, facing him head-on.

"Do you know why you're here?"

"No."

"We want to know where you got the answers to the test."

"What do you mean?"

"You cheated on the test. I want to know where you got the answers."

"I didn't cheat."

I looked at my parents, and for the first time in my life, they weren't backing me up.

"Then explain to me how you managed to score at the top of the test, but your grades are all C's and D's? Can you explain that?"

No, I couldn't. We went round and round. How did you cheat? I didn't cheat. Of course you did, until my mom finally chimed in. "My son says he didn't cheat, he didn't cheat."

Killingsworth gave up. No apology. To him, there wasn't even the possibility that I wasn't lying. Another of Them looking down his nose at me. It left a bad taste in my mouth, but I learned. People were going to make up their minds before they even had the facts, without giving me a chance. The truth didn't matter. It wouldn't change their opinions.

That was part of what made school like doing time. I felt most like myself when I was hanging out with other surfers. Friday nights we'd kill time in the lemon orchards, drinking beer and smoking. Then we would cruise the town looking for parties. Normal teenage stuff. I got to know the local cops, who made us empty many beers into the gutter. I never got into serious trouble. But my attitude, and who I hung out with, earned me a reputation.

That's why my cousin Chrissie came to me for help. Her friend Cheryl Sanderson was having a problem with a senior at school. He was harassing Cheryl with aggressive sexual comments. He was just another bully. This guy had a crush on this pretty, petite, quiet redhead with her nice Dentyne smile, cute freckles, and pixie nose. But like any bully, the only way he could express his feelings was to intimidate her. Greek kids are taught to respect women. So after Cheryl told me some of the things he had said, I agreed to talk to him. I found him in the hall and we set up a meeting after school, in a far corner of the practice field. I wasn't calling him out and I didn't think we needed to fight. I just wanted to straighten the guy out with a little lecture. Kids gathered, though, expecting action.

"Look, man, you have to quit talking shit to her. It's not cool. Keep it up and we'll have a problem."

He seemed to get the message. He wouldn't look me in the eye, but he said, "Sure, no problem."

As I turned to walk away, he sucker punched me in the head. I went ballistic. There's no temper like a Greek temper. He was bigger than I was, but I spun him around and hit him hard enough to knock him down. I put my weight on his back, holding him facedown. I locked his arms behind him. It had rained recently, and there were big puddles everywhere. I pressed his face into about two inches of water. He struggled, but with me on top of him, he wasn't going anywhere. The other kids freaked out. They thought I was going to drown him. After half a minute, I let him up. I left him with a warning that if he ever crossed paths with Cheryl or me again, he'd wind up swallowing a lot more than some muddy water.

Word spread. Cheryl thanked me for my help. It was the first bond between us, a hatred of bullies. I would ultimately discover that she had skeletons in her closet that made her desperate to maintain control over her life. It was an obsession for her, being in control. I hated feeling out of control myself, so I kind of got it. We became friends even though we didn't travel in the same circles. I still hung out with surfers.

One of them, Vaughn Lammars, became one of my best friends. Vaughn picked up the nickname Birdie Bighead because he was skinny and had a big head. He wasn't much of a surfer, but he was funny and social, and he knew everyone worth knowing and was a kick to be around. Bird was the first in our group to ride motorcycles and would introduce me to the outlaw culture.

Another friend, Danny Brucker, fanned those flames. Danny's father owned a company that provided cars, motorcycles, and related props to the movie business. The family lived on a huge ranch in Somis, where I learned to ride motorcycles. Danny's old man stored a football field's worth of amazingly cool cars and bikes. The most famous were displayed in their museum, Movieworld Cars of the Stars. Danny drove a different set of wheels to school every day. One day it would be a 1942 coupe from some gangster movie. The next, he would pull up on a perfectly restored Indian Scout, with its Indian-head front fender and wide buckhorn handlebars. These beautiful customized rides were courtesy of Dick "Woogie" Woods. He was a mechanical genius and a customizing artist who worked for Danny's father. Dick was also a founding member of the Question Marks, a Southern California outlaw motorcycle club.

In my junior year, I bought a brown 1953 Ford sedan and painted it taxicab yellow. Anyone who rode in it had to sign the white headliner. It was a hit with the girls, and I wound up dating several. That's when I picked up that Cheryl was interested in me. She never missed a chance to ask about who I was dating or to tease me about my "girls." Normally, someone like Cheryl would have seemed unattainable. She was one of Them. She came from an upscale WASP family with a big, beautiful house in the best part of East Oxnard. But once we started dating, the differences didn't seem to matter. Eventually we started talking about the future. It was the norm in the midsixties. A lot of people got married right out of high school. It seemed natural that we were a couple and would stay a couple. But I was a kid. I wasn't thinking about the future; graduation was as far down the road as I could see. Whatever my future held, it would have to wait. Our relationship would have to wait. There was a war on, and I was about to become a Marine.

2

Joining the military was a given. The way I was raised, you didn't wait for your draft number to come up. My parents were both veterans. I grew up knowing that you did your duty as part of being an American. So in high school, about twenty-five of us cooked up a plan to join the Marines as a group. We had the mistaken idea that the experience would be easier if we went through it with people we knew. The Marine Corps recruiter could not have been nicer. Sure, we could go through basic training and do our service as a group. Of course we could specify where we were assigned.

You might say we were a little naïve.

In the spring of 1965, Vietnam was just heating up. The draft was in full swing, and the military was processing a lot of recruits. Our recruiter slotted us into a reserve unit and told us we would probably be activated. We didn't yet know much about what was going on in Vietnam. Our induction date was set for February 1966. That was fine with me because it left the summer and holidays for surfing, partying, and Cheryl.

It didn't take long for Cheryl to crowd out everything else. She was a loner and didn't make friends. She didn't want to go out with a big group, but she didn't want to be alone either. That put me in a bind that I'd wrestle with for as long as we were together. I liked to see her happy, which, in retrospect, she rarely was.

Somewhere in the summer of 1965, we decided to get married. There was no down-on-one-knee moment. We just came to the conclusion that we should be engaged, and that we'd get married after boot camp. Cheryl wasn't thrilled that I was enlisting. I don't think she worried that I'd die in a jungle somewhere. She just hated that the Marines had control of me, which was what she wanted.

We were through the holidays before I realized it. It seemed like weeks, not months, had passed when I found myself on a rattling bus ride down I-5 to San Diego with my friends and fellow Marine recruits. The bus was the bone-jarring shadow of a school bus, with a rusted floor and seats barely held in place by loose bolts. But it was a fun ride. Everyone was nervous and excited, joking like all young guys do when they're on edge. One of us had been assigned to connect with the Marine Corps recruit depot when we got to San Diego. He went inside the bus station to use the pay phone while the rest of us stood around smoking, eating burgers, and drinking milk shakes. A couple minutes later, he rushed out white as a sheet.

"Throw the food away, throw the food away."

"What are you talking about, man?"

He was obviously scared. "Just do it. And put out your cigarettes."

We ignored him.

A drill sergeant rolled up in a Marine bus. This guy was all over us, yelling for us to get our asses on the bus, knocking food out of people's hands. After a short ride to the Marine Corps depot, he hustled us off the bus, screaming at us again. We were supposed to assemble along a line of yellow footprints on the blacktop. There weren't enough. Guys began fighting over footprints. It was chaos by design. The sergeant kept screaming about how worthless we were, telling us in graphic detail what he was going to do if we didn't find some footprints to stand on. Guys were getting smacked on the head. Nobody was smiling now.

The rest was a blur. Throw your civilian clothes in a pile and get a uniform. Get in line to get your head shaved. Turn out and get reassigned. Get to mess. Get to quarters. Line up. Drill. When they started putting guys in different platoons, we figured out the recruiter had fed us a line of shit. We weren't going to be kept together, but that was the least of our worries. Each of us was doing whatever he could not to be the one getting yelled at or hit.

I watched guys in boot camp change overnight. Kids that came in weak turned into hard-core Marines. Big, husky guys broke down in tears. By the end of the first day, we were marching in cadence chanting how much we wanted to kill Vietcong. The most important thing was your rifle. We were all assigned an M14, and it became an extension of your body. Sometimes you slept with your rifle.

Closed communities, whether the Greeks, the Marines, or the Hells Angels, share a few basic codes of conduct. One of the most important is that you don't break rank. You wear the same uniform, you're family. Fights stay inside the family. I knew this rule well from being a surfer. Halfway through boot camp I got into it with guys from another platoon. I was walking to mess hall when they clustered in front of me.

"You're walking on our dirt."

It's a test of your mettle, just like fistfights during club runs would be when I prospected for the Angels.

"Go fuck yourself."

A kid at the head of the pack swung on me. He was taller, but skinnier and slower than I was. I dodged the punch and counterpunched him twice in the face. He tried to grab me, but got a knee to the gut for his troubles. A look of surprise spread across his face. I was quicker and tougher than he expected. He ate another punch and I drove a hook into his ribs. His buddy, trying to help him, clipped me over the head with the wood stock of his M14. He opened up a wide gash on the crown of my head that started gushing blood.

Everyone froze. I put my hand over the cut and could tell it was deep.

My hand came away covered in bright red, glistening blood. I looked him in the eyes with a snarl because I was furious. You don't use a weapon on a fellow Marine.

"You fucking asshole."

I headed to the medic station. As soon as I was finished getting stitched up, two MPs were waiting to talk to me. They put me in a room and grilled me.

"Who did this? Who started the fight?"

"What fight?"

"You know what fight. Who hit you?"

"Nobody hit me. I banged my head on my rack."

"The hell you did. You better start talking, Marine."

If I hadn't talked to cops as a Greek kid, I wasn't going to talk to MPs as a Marine. What were they going to do? Head wound aside, it worked out well for me. Now I was known as someone who wouldn't rat out another Marine. It upped my bar. A couple days later, a staff sergeant pulled me aside and suggested that I "go regular," transfer to an active unit. He patted my shoulder and said, "We need guys like you over there." I understood that he meant Marines who would back up other Marines, not just look out for themselves.

I considered it. I was young and green enough not to know what I wanted to do with my life, and the Marines seemed like a good potential career. I thought I'd be good in the field. On my next leave, I told Cheryl that I was thinking of going active, and she hit the roof. I could see the panic in her eyes; she didn't like the idea of me in a war zone. I let it go because I knew that I would probably be activated anyway, at which point the decision would be out of our hands.

Home on leave, I drifted back to spending time with Bird. He had left surfing behind and become a full-time outlaw. He was a window into the culture, and I liked what I saw. He had a lot of fun. He lived in his mom's house in Camarillo Heights and was customizing an old Indian Chief in his bedroom. Still wearing my Marine uniform, I went over to see how the bike was coming along. Bird told me he wanted to introduce me to a friend of his who lived out in Oxnard. You enter the outlaw world one person at a time. Once you're solid with one guy, he lets it be known to others. The more people vouch for you, the more accepted you become. I'd always been social, and being a people person played into the culture.

Dick Woods and Danny Brucker had told me stories about David Ortega. He was a Question Mark, a real outlaw, and he seemed like a good person to know. But it didn't go so well right out of the gate. David opened his door and immediately got uptight at the sight of me in my uniform. He got in Bird's face.

"What the fuck, man? You bring a cop to my house?"

I jumped in. "I'm no cop, I'm a fucking Marine."

"Look like a cop to me."

But we both knew I'd passed the first test. In the late sixties, everyone foolishly believed that cops weren't allowed to lie to you. The myth was, a cop had to say he was a cop if you asked him. So as far as David was concerned, I wasn't a cop, but that didn't mean I was cool. He led us out into the alley behind his house and rolled a thick joint. This was the second test. He eyeballed me with a smirk on his face.

"Marines smoke pot?"

"This one does."

He lit up the joint and passed it to me. I took a toke and passed it on. David loosened up and we started talking about bikes. It was a nice enough afternoon, but I had no inkling that this shaggy-haired, barrel-chested, gruff Mexican dude would become one of my closest friends and brothers. By the time I was out of the Marines, David would be on the back end of a three-year stint in San Quentin for possession of marijuana, and we'd both be radically different people.

Marine reserve service was easy. I had to give the Marines two weekends a month and fifteen days in the summer. That freed me up for a more or less normal life. I took a job with General Telephone & Electric (which would eventually become Verizon) as a cable splicer. I was just another working stiff, waiting to see what happened with the war. I was becoming less enchanted with the idea of participating in it. I'd started reading about Che Guevara and Malcolm X. Revolt was everywhere. My sports hero Cassius Clay had changed his name in 1964 to Muhammad Ali, and he refused to serve in the military. My opinions and outlook were evolving as I waited to see what would happen with my future and the war.

In the meantime, Cheryl and I got married on June 3, 1967. The ceremony was held in a high-society Santa Maria church her parents had joined just so we could get married there. I'm not a fan of hypocrisy and it struck me as bullshit, this stiff traditional wedding with all the fanfare. I was killing time in the parking lot beforehand, smoking a joint, when I started thinking, "You don't have to do this. You can get in your car and drive away right now." As things worked out, it was an omen, one I would have been wise to heed.

We spent our honeymoon in a quaint, comfortable motor lodge up the coast, nestled in the mountains just outside Santa Cruz. The rooms were plain but clean, and they all had a hell of a view of the sunset out over the coast. Somebody had arranged for champagne, even though neither of us was twenty-one yet. We'd never gone all the way, and I convinced Cheryl to smoke a joint with me to lighten things up. I could see she was tense, but the pot hurt more than it helped. When we finally got undressed and started to get physical, she freaked out and began crying hysterically. I had to get a washcloth and put it on her head. It took me the better part of an hour to calm her down. I loved her and wanted to help her, but I had no clue what was going on. I felt helpless. As a young guy, it was only natural for me to think, "What did I do?" That set the tone for our relationship. Cheryl would never like sex. I would come to understand something had happened in her past, and it left her with bad associations with anything sexual. Sitting on the edge of the bed, listening to her sobbing in the bathroom, I couldn't possibly have figured out that I had just opened up a deep, dark closet that would haunt our marriage. Even if I had understood, I didn't have the tools to deal with it. All I knew was something wasn't right and it felt like my fault.

We set up house as soon as we got back from the honeymoon, renting an apartment in Camarillo for $150 a month. Cheryl had a job as a parts inspector for SenTec, a military contractor. With two paychecks we did well. Before long we upgraded to a happening two-bedroom bungalow in downtown Ventura. It had funky detailing on the inside, with arched passageways, two fireplaces, and, most important to me, a sizable garage. GT&E needed people to work graveyard, and I volunteered. The third shift paid more money, and it left me free to go surfing or to hang out with Bird during the day. Cheryl and I didn't see much of each other during the workweek, setting a pattern that would play out for our entire marriage.

I was still putting in my reserve weekends and was designated a rifleman, the core of frontline Marine infantry units. My unit began advance combat training, including infiltration and close-quarters combat. Everyone was being prepped for activation, and we trained with guys rotating out of Vietnam, using a mock-up site known as Vietnam Village. That was where my problems with the Marines really began.

The war was making less and less sense to me. Protesters were everywhere, and my uniform and haircut got as many scowls and muttered comments as it did smiles. To make matters worse, a corporal just back from a tour in Vietnam started showing everyone some disgusting photos. One was of a pile of heads, and another showed a necklace made out of ears. This guy wouldn't stop running his mouth about it. It sickened me. He was laughing, flipping through the photos. Like death was nothing. Like these weren't people he was laughing about. Finally, I had enough.

"What does that make you? That make you a man? 'Cause it makes me sick."

That lit his fuse. "You're no fucking Marine. What are you, a fag?"

"No, I'm a man. And next liberty, if you see me, you better cross the fucking street."

It knocked him for a loop, someone standing up to his bullshit. Later, I would see it for the fear and confusion it really was. But there in the moment, I felt like this guy embodied everything wrong with the war, the Marines, and the country. It was the first of many signs that I didn't fit in the military.

Away from the Marines, and partly because of my military experiences, I kept moving toward the outlaw lifestyle. It was time to buy my first motorcycle. At that point, no outlaw would consider buying a new motorcycle. Besides, you couldn't buy a custom bike; you had to build one from the ground up, out of the carcass of an old "basket case." It was a point of pride that separated the outlaws from the argyle-sweater-wearing weekenders in Honda ads.

I had a friend named Leon who knew what I was looking for. He called me one day to say he'd found the perfect bike out in Simi Valley. He agreed to drive there with me to check it out. Leon was an older guy, a legitimate outlaw. He had even pulled a denim cutoff vest out of his closet with the original tiny "bumblebee" Death Head patch worn by the first Hells Angels in Berdoo and Frisco. He had been an Angel and had left the club on good terms.

The bike was a well-worn, rode-hard 1957 Harley-Davidson panhead. It was a straight-leg hardtail frame—no shocks or springs between your butt and the road. The owner's widow was selling it because she had no use for a bike without a husband. I agreed to pay $200, left her $150 on deposit, and came back a week later with the rest of the money and a borrowed pickup to haul the bike home.

I worked on that motorcycle whenever I wasn't splicing cable for the phone company or sleeping. I worked on it even when there wasn't really anything to do, just to spend time with it. Cheryl came to hate it, but it was everything I'd dreamed of since I had seen that outlaw on a street corner in San Fernando Valley, shattering the still of the late afternoon with his straight pipes, modified to amplify.

That distinctive sound is part of the adrenaline rush and pure emotion of owning a Harley. But ironically, there is something incredibly peaceful and meditative about actually working on your own motorcycle. After a while, the motorcycle comes to be more than a simple machine. You develop a connection to it. You become intimate with each and every part. You understand it in a way you only understand a close friend. The sounds it makes when things are right, and when they're wrong. The particular feel of the frame under your weight, and the proper snap of the throttle as you rev the engine. This simple interaction, between flesh and metal, machine and man, was at the core of what I believed being an outlaw meant. This unspoken thing was understood between men when somebody said about you, "Yeah, he's an outlaw." It was the first and most crucial thing that drew us all together, me and my brothers. It wasn't about cars, or hot rods. It was motorcycles. We ate, slept, and breathed them. We nurtured them. It was what we lived for, to fly recklessly down the road on the machine you had built, your mouth closed tight against the bugs, the deafening white noise of the wind in your ears, bouncing in almost poetic rhythm to the tires on the road. A feeling of true and complete freedom. Unattached. Answering to nobody. Later on, when that stopped being a feeling shared among all the men in the clubhouse, when the life stopped being primarily about motorcycles and living your way on your terms, that was when the brotherhood began to fall apart.

Cheryl could never understand that connection, and it was another part of the ever-growing wedge that would ultimately drive us apart.

The machine is just one part of being an outlaw. If you're going to live in an extreme culture, something different from nine-to-five polite society, you'll be tested all the time. It was true of surfing, it was true of the Marines, and it was especially true in the outlaw world. Among outlaws, somebody is always ready to get over on you, take advantage of the slightest perceived weakness. If I had any doubts about that, they were erased early on.

I'd done all the mechanical work I could do on my bike, and the next step was to get it painted. Originally it was red and white (ironically, the Hells Angels' colors), and I wanted a traditional outlaw black look. I took the bike apart so that the frame, tank, and other parts could be custom-painted. I had no experience painting bikes, so Bird hooked me up with a couple of guys running a bike-painting business out of the cluttered garage of a tract house in Port Hueneme. I talked to one of them, we agreed on a price, and I left the parts with him. But a week later, I got a call from Bird, who had eyes and ears everywhere in the outlaw world.

"Hey, man, these dudes aren't going to give you your bike back."

"What do you mean?"

"They think you're a trick. They're going to rip you off. When you come to get it, they're not going to give it to you. They'll just part it out and tell you, 'What bike?'"

I found it hard to believe, that someone would underestimate me like that. I called the painter and asked him how my bike was coming. He gave me a runaround about ordering paint, giving things time to cure, how he was backed up. I hung up and thought, "Damn, Bird's right." The outlaw world was a little bit like the Old West. Somebody was always poking you to see if you were soft. A lot of outlaws were stand-up, but others saw the culture as an opportunity. It was by definition outside the law, after all. People didn't call the cops. You didn't sue somebody.

You might call those guys *brother*, but you'd have to always be aware that they would take whatever they thought they could get. It was up to you to stay one step ahead of them. One of the cold realities of outlaw life is that, unless you want to be a target, you make it known that you'll punish anyone who tries. Every man decides for himself how he's going to face challenges to his reputation. For me, that usually involved a shotgun.

I drove over to settle things. I got out of my car and walked up the driveway and into the garage cradling a High Standard 12-gauge, pump-action, short-barrel shotgun in my left arm. The guy had his back to me and turned around when I was about ten feet from him. He visibly stiffened.

"How's the paint job coming?" We both pretended not to notice the gun, which took some doing because a shotgun is a hard thing not to notice.

"Good, good. We should have it done by this weekend."

"You know what? I think I'm just going to take it now. How about you put it in my trunk?"

He didn't raise much of a fuss. I drove off with my bike unpainted, but with all its pieces intact. Bird heard about the whole thing from the painter himself, who called me "that dirty motherfucker." Like I was the one who had tried to put him in a trick bag. It cracked Bird up and left me with a nickname I wouldn't shake until I became a Hells Angel: Dirty George.

The good thing about a nickname is that it gives you instant recognition and a reputation among one-percenter clubs. The *one-percenter* designation comes from a piece of postwar history. A few motorcycle clubs full of hard-drinking ex-servicemen had taken over the town of Hollister, California, and gone a little wild at an American Motorcyclist Association (AMA) rally over a long Fourth of July weekend in 1947. Locals were appalled at the drunkenness, lawbreaking, and generally rowdy behavior. The papers picked it up coast-to-coast, and the AMA wrote off the incidents as the fault of "outlaw" bikers who represented "one percent" of the otherwise law-abiding population of motorcycle riders. Outlaw bikers proudly owned the term, eventually creating 1% patches for the front of their vests. By the end of the sixties, the only true one-percent clubs were the Hells Angels' California charters, the Gypsy Jokers in Northern California, the Losers from Monterey, the Question Marks of Oxnard, the Straight Satans in Venice Beach, and Satan's Slaves from San Fernando Valley. Everybody knew everybody, by their bikes and their reputations. Once I got my bike painted and back together,

Easyriders magazine did a spread on me, my shotgun, and my bike, titled "Ain't that Dirty George?"

Much as I was becoming an outlaw, Marine training still took up a good part of my time. Training got more intense as rumors spread that we were going to be activated. Meanwhile, thanks to nightly news coverage from the front lines, nobody had any doubts about what waited for us in Vietnam. A lot of Marines—me included—were now completely disillusioned. I knew I would probably have to go, but like most of my fellow Marines, I no longer had any desire to fight.

I was opposed to the war, but my bigger problem was with authority. Everyone in the command structure seemed to be another version of the bullies I'd hated so much growing up. It went beyond making tough Marines. Many officers, noncommissioned and otherwise, were just sadists. There was a reason behind the epidemic of officers getting "fragged" (blown up or shot by soldiers under their command), much more so than in any other war in the nation's history. Insubordination and a lack of discipline were everywhere on base. The drug abuse that would decades later be captured in movies about the Vietnam War actually got its start during initial training and deployment. I lost count of how many exercises I went on with Marines who were obviously drunk or high. And not just on pot. Many of us were dropping acid.

Most of that went unpunished; people in command either weren't noticing or didn't want to see. But some rules were set in stone. At the top of the list was willful insubordination. You simply never squared off with an officer, even a noncommissioned officer. I knew that rule as I struggled to deal with a gunnery sergeant who had it in for me. I never knew what about me set this guy off, but he rode me constantly, and I'd give it back any way I could. It's hard to write up a Marine for being a wiseass, and I can clown somebody with the best of them. But sarcasm didn't get me anywhere because this guy was a bully, and bullies are never satisfied.

We took part in a large-scale amphibious-landing exercise at Camp Pendleton, with senators and VIPs watching from bleachers. This high-profile event had a lot of flag-waving and speeches. As soon as we hit the beach and the gate dropped on our amphibious-landing vehicle, the proctors listed the gunney as KIA, and he was removed to food service. I ridiculed him mercilessly at chow, ribbing him that he couldn't even make it off the beach without getting himself killed. After that, he upped his game, calling me out for bullshit no one else had to deal with. The other Marines split into two camps. One group thought he was our only hope of getting through Vietnam alive and that I should let everything slide. The other group hated this guy every bit as much as I did.

I'm easygoing. That's why people are always surprised when my temper flares. It happens when something builds up too far, and it happened with the gunney. I had just had my fill of this guy. We were on the rifle range with four guys standing on the firing line between him and me. At a break in the shooting, I told the guys to clear the line, and they stepped off. Suddenly the gunney noticed what was going on.

"What the fuck are you doing, Christie?"

"We're going to settle this now." I held my rifle down at my side, like a sidearm. "Draw."

"What? Are you crazy?"

"You want to prove how tough you are? Draw."

It was way out of line. My anger had gotten the better of me because he had pushed and pushed and pushed. I was so damn frustrated. He could see I was serious and it really shook him up. He probably wasn't much older than I was, and virtually no respect was left for rank in camp. It could all have gone sideways and changed my life in a moment. Instead, he ran off the firing line and left the range.

I calmly unloaded my rifle and addressed nobody in particular, "I told you he was full of shit."

But there was no shaking him. He was in my face as soon as we returned to barracks.

"I'm putting you on report, Christie."

I felt the rage rise again as we began yelling at each other nose to nose. Then I dropped a bomb. "Fuck you. You better watch your six, gunney, because when we get to 'Nam, you're going to be the first one I shoot."

His eyes went wide. It was any officer's worst nightmare, to get in a forward theater of combat knowing that members of your own platoon hated you so much that they would cap you during a firefight. I knew full well that I'd crossed the line in the biggest way possible, but I was so mad I didn't care. There was no taking it back. I got my gear, and even though training wasn't over, I went home. I missed a platoon meeting and figured nobody would care. I was wrong. I soon got my activation orders in the mail, telling me to report to Camp Pendleton.

Cheryl was beside herself. I had more to worry about than being activated, though. I knew damn well that there was still a price to be paid for threatening an officer. That sort of thing doesn't get swept under the rug. So even though I said my good-byes to Cheryl and my family, I figured chances were good I'd be spending the rest of my service—and then some—in the brig or in the highest-risk posting in Vietnam.

I showed up at Pendleton just about holding my breath. A couple hours later I was ordered to report to Long Beach Naval Hospital for evaluation. I knew that I was in a world of shit, and my imagination ran wild as I went to the hospital and waited to see a psychiatrist. I had no idea whether I'd be locked up as a head case, arrested and sent to Leavenworth, or just cleared and shipped out to the front lines. There wasn't a good option from where I sat. All I knew was that I had royally fucked up.

As soon as the psychiatrist asked a couple of questions, I saw a light at the end of the tunnel. I realized that if I played it right, I might get out of the jam. He was asking things like "If you died and came back, would you rather come back as an eagle or a dove?" I took my time because the answers would be crucial in determining what came next. He was particularly interested in drugs. Were there a lot of drug users in the platoon? What kind of drugs did people use? Were they using on duty? Did I use drugs? He wasn't looking for me to give up names, just information. I told him I smoked pot and had dropped acid. I told him that there were a lot of drugs on base. I figured I wasn't telling him anything that wasn't common knowledge. He took a lot of notes.

Eventually, he got around to the firing-range incident.

"What if he had raised his rifle, gone ahead and drawn? Would you have had a shoot-out with him?"

"I didn't have to worry about that. I knew he'd never raise his rifle."

"But hypothetically."

"I can't answer that. I knew what he was going to do the minute I did it. He wouldn't do anything. He just wasn't going to."

"But how could you know?"

"Because of how he acted. He's always been full of shit." I wanted to say, "Because I'm an outlaw. Because I live in the outlaw world and you have to know the bullshitters when you come across them." But I decided to bite my tongue. I answered everything as best I could. In the end, he sent me back to Pendleton, where, after waiting around for a few more hours, I was told to go home.

I didn't hear anything for three days. Then I opened the mailbox to find my discharge papers—a general discharge under honorable conditions. A step down from an honorable discharge, but far above a dishonorable discharge. I wouldn't be going to the brig or to Vietnam. And the only person who was happier about it than me was Cheryl.

3

A few days after I received my discharge, I answered the door to find two Naval Intelligence investigators in suits standing on the front step. They were no-nonsense and uptight, and I realized that I might still be subject to prosecution. They didn't come right out and say what they were after, but it eventually became clear that it was just a general exit interview. They asked questions and took notes. Like the psychiatrist, they focused on drug use. I still wouldn't give them names, and they didn't push. As they were leaving, one said, "You know, this isn't the end of your life. You still have a future. Keep that in mind."

Two weeks later, two more investigators showed up. They asked about my background, and the firing-line incident. We got onto the subject of my work for GT&E. One of the guys told me the Department of Defense was hiring, and that my communications experience might get me a job. I was shocked. The Marines had just shown me the door, and here these guys were talking about how I might get a job with the DOD.

The DOD paid higher than civilian companies did, and the benefits and job security couldn't be topped. The investigators gave me the idea that I had a shot, so I went down to Point Mugu and filled out an application and the security-clearance paperwork. A month later, I got called in for an interview. A week after that, I was offered a job at more than double what GT&E was paying. I gave my notice that day.

I went to work as a communications troubleshooter for the Pacific Missile Test Center, with security clearance to classified sites at Point Mugu, Port Hueneme, and even the high-security facility on San Nicolas Island. I liked the work and was good at it.

Outside of work, I moved deeper and deeper into the outlaw life. Like so many young guys at the time, I was completely disenchanted with America as this great, shining ideal. I had grown up buying into the American dream. You worked hard and were rewarded, and everybody played fair. We were God's country. We were "good," and anyone who opposed us was evil. But the older I got, the more I learned, read, and talked to people, the more I realized how far the truth was from the dream. Our government was clearly lying to us, from Vietnam to Watergate. Everything was messier and more complicated than the black-and-white story we'd been sold. So much nonsense had been stuffed down my throat, "facts" that turned out to be lies. I was frustrated and jaded. I wanted to turn my back on all of it and slam the door behind me. I consciously wanted to let go of what I saw as fake and a lie and to live a different life. Being an outlaw was a response to all that, an answer of sorts. The outlaw world promised what we all felt was real freedom. It was authentic, the exact opposite of the lockstep, mindless conformity of Arrow shirt ads, freshly mown lawns and polite Sunday-afternoon backyard cookouts. By the early seventies, all of that seemed plastic and phony. I knew there would be consequences for living against the grain, just as every outlaw does. But to me, the price was well worth it.

I spent more and more time with the Question Marks, riding as a friend of the club. I wasn't ready to commit to them because I didn't get the sense that they were committed to themselves. The Question Marks were a mess. Dick Woods, the figurehead founder who had designed the club's logo and hand-drawn the patch onto foul-weather jackets for the first members, had been stabbed in a fight with the Hessians. He was trying to help some Satan's Slaves recover a motorcycle the Hessians had stolen and got rat-packed in a bar. It was a serious injury, and he basically retreated to a cabin in the hills. Other members had been in bike wrecks or just drifted away. The remaining core couldn't keep their bikes running and weren't all that up for partying. Even David Ortega had to keep a low profile because he was on parole.

I was young, full of energy, and I absolutely loved being on my bike. So when the Question Marks weren't up for action, I headed to San Fernando Valley to party with the Satan's Slaves. I spent entire weekends with them. It developed into what seemed like a natural pattern for Cheryl and me. I was more social than she was, and she gave me no reason to stay home. It was familiar for her; her father had been a traveling salesman and was regularly gone for days at a time. It became our uneasy "normal" and would be for as long as we were together.

Even though we were spending less and less time together, Cheryl and I both assumed we'd have a family. Despite our nearly nonexistent sex life, she got pregnant. Our daughter, Moriya, was born in August 1971. I camped out on a stiff vinyl bench in the fluorescent-lit hospital waiting room for hours, trying to figure out what it would mean to have this child in our lives. How do you balance the outlaw's notion of freedom against the responsibility of a father? I'm not sure I ever figured that one out. I just trusted that I'd make it all work. After what seemed like forever, a nurse brought out this tiny, swaddled bundle. I don't think there's any way to prepare for becoming a parent. It's overwhelming. I looked down into that round, little face, into those jet-black eyes, and was overcome. The way she looked back at me, it felt like a connection, and it's a connection that I still feel to this day.

It didn't take long for the three of us to fall into a routine. I was making good money with the DOD, so Cheryl quit her job and stayed home with Moriya. I loved my daughter, but those were different times and the outlaw culture has its own way of doing things. Being an outlaw isn't a hobby. If you're in, you're in all the way. Clubs and the life come first. You wrestle with it. Your family wrestles with it. But you have to accept that the commitment is complete and then balance your two families as best you can.

The Slaves were picky about who they let hang around. The Hells Angels were the unquestioned kings of the outlaw world, but even they held the Slaves in high regard. They were classic outlaws. Make a small slipup, a minor violation of their social code, and they would beat you senseless, take your bike, and that was the end of it. God help you if you came around wearing a denim cutoff. Someone would slice it off your back with a bowie knife and you'd wind up on the receiving end of a boot stomping (denim cutoffs were what club prospects wore, so in the Slaves' eyes you were posing). You had to know what not to say, when to be quiet, and when to stand up for yourself. Really, though, they just wanted to flip society the bird, party, and ride motorcycles. Exactly what I wanted. They weren't looking for trouble, but didn't avoid it either. If you were in the way of their having fun, they'd just go through you.

Smackey Jack was the most infamous Satan's Slave. He was out there even for a biker. He had a reputation for pulling out people's teeth when they pissed him off. He carried a pair of pliers with him, along with a brown leather bag of trophy teeth tied to his belt. Legend had it that Smackey Jack had even drunkenly pulled one of his own teeth and offered it to a bartender in exchange for a drink.

The time I spent with the Slaves was an education. I learned how club life works. Even beyond their unity as a club, I admired how the Slaves handled themselves. They were confident enough that they didn't need to start something just to make a statement. They weren't the Hells Angels, but they never played second string to anyone. They already had a solid-gold reputation and weren't going to waste time or energy trying to add to it. I would have prospected for the Slaves had they asked. It was just a case of crossed wires because I would later learn that they were waiting for me to say I wanted to become a member. Over time, though, I became as close as an independent can be to a club. Part of that was riding with them on runs.

Runs in the outlaw biker world are a combination of wild party, camping trip, and networking opportunity. They provide the chance to see and be seen and to meet a lot of connected people in one long weekend. Clubs use runs to test newcomers and weed out losers. You learn who's who, and if you pay attention, you quickly figure out where the power lies, and how different clubs conduct their business. Runs were always held at large campgrounds as far as possible from civilization and law enforcement. A club or group of clubs would take over an entire area of a KOA park or campsite. The most common run sites included Bass Lake, about thirty miles south of Yosemite, and the Lake Isabella and Kern River Campgrounds, east of Bakersfield. At these locations deep in the mountains people didn't bother you. And cops had a hard time keeping tabs on anyone out in the wilderness.

Over the next few years, I went on many runs with the Slaves. They gave me legitimacy because we were seen together so much that people considered me *affiliated* (the term for someone officially attached to a club). I got a lot of street cred for simply being accepted by the Slaves.

I was checking in with Cheryl from a gas station on the road to Bass Lake when she told me to get home quick because she was in labor with our second child. We had waited several years before trying again, so that Moriya would be out of diapers and fairly independent. George Christie III was born a few hours after I made it back to Ventura, on April 22, 1976, my mother's birthday. My parents were with me when I met Georgie for the first time at the hospital. I'm not sure who was more proud, me or my father, knowing that the name would be carried on.

As soon as we got the baby home, Moriya hovered over him, mothering him. She was, from the start, protective of Georgie. She would look after him well into adulthood. Moriya has always had a natural motherly instinct, but I think it was also a survival response. Cheryl was increas-

ingly about Cheryl, and I was gone a lot of the time. If Cheryl wasn't ignoring the kids, she was dominating them. We had very different
parenting styles, which was obvious whenever I stayed home for a stretch.
Cheryl had been raised in a strict and dysfunctional house, a "spare the
rod, spoil the child" environment. Although she never opened up about
it, I always suspected Cheryl had been abused as a child. I think it forever
colored our relationship and affected the kind of parent she was.

Harsh punishment was a foreign concept to me. I'd been raised as an
only child in a Greek house. The Greeks fight childhood fears and terrors
with comfort and hugs. They treat bad behavior by isolating the kid until
the bad behavior stops. My parents never hit me; they gave me time-outs
decades before time-outs would be recognized as time-outs. Whatever
was haunting her, Cheryl was a rigid disciplinarian. Her answer to her toddler's tantrum was to hold Moriya's head under the kitchen-sink faucet,
cold water running full force. When Georgie was afraid of the dark, she
forced him under the covers, ignored his pleas, turned off the lights, and
closed his door. I'd go in, turn on the Winnie-the-Pooh night-light,
calm him down, sit on the edge of his bed, and talk him to sleep.

"You can't just stick a kid in the dark and expect him to get over it."

"That's how I'm doing it."

"That's not how we're doing it."

"You want to do it your way, fine. You'll need to spend a lot more time
at home."

And that was it, the point of almost everything that went on between
Cheryl and me. She wanted to—needed to—control me. It wasn't that she
wanted me to stay home because she liked to do things with me. It wasn't
that we lived in a bad town and she wanted her man around at night.
Thanks to the DOD, we had bought a beautiful house on an acre of property in a safe, upscale neighborhood of Oak View. She wanted me to be
there because that meant she was in control. That would always be the
most important thing to Cheryl.

A month after Georgie and Cheryl were home and settled, I took off on a run to Kern River with the Slaves. There, John "Old Man John" Noble, the Hells Angel who would become my mentor, changed my life. Several Angels charters were at the run, including a few Los Angeles members (known in the club as LACO, for "LA County"). Old Man John, an old-school outlaw, was the LACO president. I had met him a couple times before and liked him instantly. We had both done time in the military and were both in the culture for the same things—fun, motorcycles, and brotherhood.

John was in his late fifties, but didn't look a day over sixty-five. A trucker by trade, he had the weary, ragged look of someone who has logged too many miles in a rickety rig on poor roads. His face was deeply lined, and he covered a good part of it with a scruffy gray beard. He was six foot and then some, with hands as big as oven mitts and the thick build of a blue-collar workingman. He usually wore a leather kepi hat, the standard issue for Civil War foot soldiers. He probably owned no more than a single pair of jeans at any one time. I never saw him without a half-smoked cigar clenched between his teeth, even when he was riding.

I could tell John saw something in me. He looked at most of the guys in his charter as his sons, and that's how our relationship would play out. By the time I got to the Kern River Campground, John had already asked around about me and gotten a strong recommendation from both the Slaves and the Question Marks. I was standing at the edge of the bonfire when he ambled up alongside me.

"Hey, George, got a minute?"

"Sure."

He took the cigar out of his mouth and looked into the fire. "I was wondering what you would think about prospecting for us."

Joining any outlaw motorcycle club is a long, tough process that involves three stages, each with its own challenges and tests. You start as a hangaround, something I'd done informally, riding with the Question Marks and the Satan's Slaves. It's a chance for everyone in the community to get to know you and what you're about, and for you to learn written and unwritten rules. The first formal stage in club membership is *prospecting,* essentially a long period of hazing where you prove your worth and dedication to the club. I didn't have to think about Old Man John's offer. Club membership was where I was headed anyway, and the Hells Angels were the elite, not just in California, but in the country. For that matter, worldwide. They asked precious few to join, and it was a privilege when they did.

"Yeah, absolutely."

"Okay, good. You need to make the rounds of the LA members. Make sure everybody knows your intentions. Then I'll throw it up for a vote, but I don't think you'll have a problem."

"Thanks, John."

My head was spinning. I had always known I would join a club, but I hadn't figured on joining the club of clubs. I spent the rest of the run talking to the Angels who were there. Over the next few weeks, I visited the houses of all the LA members at least once. A prospect vote has to be unanimous, and I made sure that everybody was comfortable with me. I was officially voted in as a Hells Angel prospect in the last week of August 1976.

The LACO charter had a rule then that new prospects had to steal a bike and donate it. Like a lot of rules, it made no sense to me. So I proposed what I believed to be a fair and diplomatic solution. Prospects normally stole bikes even the owner didn't want, broken-down basket cases that the club would sell for at most $500. I offered a compromise in a clubhouse meeting.

"Look I'll give you five hundred dollars. Let's call it an initiation fee. If I get caught stealing the bike, by the time I bail out, get a lawyer, pay a fine plus time, it's going to cost me a lot more than five hundred dollars."

I didn't care about the money. The issue to me was that I didn't respect or like thieves. I think stealing is a dangerous and low business. I made that point as well, telling everyone, "I think it's a bad message for us to send to the outlaw community." Some members got bent out of shape, saying that I was ruining "tradition." Like any other organization, every motorcycle club always has people who do whatever has been done before without ever questioning it. I managed to persuade Old Man John and the established members to accept a $500 "initiation fee." The stolen-bike policy faded into history. From that point on, LACO prospects just laid cash on the counter.

Prospecting was my least favorite part of joining the club. Nobody likes prospecting. You get to wear a cut (the vest-and-patch combination that identifies you as a member of a motorcycle club), but with only a partial patch. Club patches have three parts: a downward-curved "rocker" at the top that identifies the club name, a middle graphic that shows the club logo (the Hells Angels' is a winged grinning skull in profile, called the Death Head), and a bottom, upward-curved rocker that identifies the member's location. So I had this red-and-white *California* on the bottom of my vest, and everyone in the outlaw world knew at a glance that I wasn't a full member. It felt incomplete.

A prospect's time is not his own. If I wasn't at work, I was at the beck and call of any member, or sweeping the clubhouse, cleaning up empty bottles, and emptying ashtrays. The time commitment was the hardest part because I was straddling two worlds. I had one foot in the unforgiving outlaw club culture, and one in the straight, suburban world working a high-paying, secure job with the DOD. I had a great house and a growing family. But in my way, I was as preoccupied with my own goals, my agenda, as Cheryl was with hers. We both knew that my joining the club meant even more of my time would be spent away from home. She didn't like it, but I didn't put it up for a vote.

The only upside to prospecting is the people you do it with. My closest friend became Craig "Jesse" Kuhn. Jesse and I became prospects at the same time. At first, we kept our distance and sized each other up. Jesse had been raised in upstate New York and then moved to Florida. Florida was Outlaws territory, and that club had the state sewn up. The Hells Angels were at war with the Outlaws. That meant that anybody from

Florida was subject to suspicion as a possible infiltrator. Old Man John told me to keep an eye on Jesse, which ironically led to Jesse and me becoming the closest of friends.

Jesse was all attitude and solid muscle, built like a pit bull. He was short and beefy, and everything about him—neck, wrists, hands—was thick. He shuffled a little like a boxer when he walked, and his hands were naturally curled into loose fists, as if he were always ready to throw a punch. Which he was. If he didn't know you well, you'd never see him smile. Like many outlaws, Jesse loved to fight. Unlike many, he was exceptionally good at it. I had no problem fighting, but I preferred to use my head whenever possible. I tried to counsel him to take it easier. He'd come up on the East Coast, where fighting first and asking questions later was accepted by everyone, including cops. But it would get him in trouble in California. At our best, we balanced each other out and developed a respect for each other's strengths. Jesse and I were also avid bike builders—there was nothing on a bike that Jesse couldn't fix—which cemented our friendship. He absolutely loved old Harleys and really dug what I had done with my flathead.

Hells Angels prospects have to do whatever a full-patch member asks, as long as the member doesn't ask a prospect to do something the member wouldn't do himself. Outlaws being outlaws, there's a lot of latitude in how members treat—or mistreat—prospects. No matter what, prospects have to be available 24-7, which played havoc on my making it to work on time, much less having a home life. Along with the other prospects, I set up for parties and runs, maintained security around the clubhouse, and cleaned up after meetings and runs. Prospects learn quickly never to reveal that they're good at something. If you're a talented mechanic, you'll wind up working on every member's bike. Let it slip that you're a good carpenter? You'll be building bookshelves and backyard decks for every member in the charter.

Prospects stick together to handle all the bullshit. We called it the "prospects' union." Even prospects from other charters would help you out. It was a lifesaver when a member made an unreasonable demand that he expected you to fumble. One day I was sitting in the clubhouse when Tall Paul blurted out, "You know what I want?" He wasn't speaking to anyone in particular, but as I was the only prospect within earshot, I knew he was talking to me. And I knew I was about to hear some outrageous order.

"I want a burger. I want a really good burger, you know? I think . . . I want one of those Hippo burgers. Yeah, that's it. That's what I want. A Hippo burger."

Hippo Burgers (the full name was Hippopotamus Hamburger Restaurant) was a famous joint on Van Ness in San Francisco. They did, in fact, make incredible hamburgers. Unfortunately, they were in San Francisco. I wasn't about to ride six hours just to buy a hamburger and cart it six hours home. But I had a good friend who was a Frisco prospect. I called the guy, who agreed to pick up the burger, wrap it in a few sheets of aluminum foil, box it up, and take it to the airport. United had just started running shuttles to LA from San Francisco every half hour during the day. My buddy bought a ticket, checked the box with the burger in it, and sent it on its way. I headed to LAX and picked up the burger at baggage claim an hour later. I got a real kick out of seeing Paul's face when he opened the box and found a burger wrapped in the restaurant's signature paper with pink hippos all over it.

Fighting is also a part of prospecting because it's a part of club life (inside and outside the club). A fight is a way for a member to test that a prospect can hold his own in a situation such as a bar brawl. It's called *holding your mud*. There was always the question "Can this guy hold his mud?" The worst that happens in these fights is that someone gets knocked out. The prospect is expected to fight back against a member who starts a fight. No grudges, no hard feelings. Members—and especially officers—are supposed to know when to say enough. You don't seriously hurt a prospect, just like you wouldn't hurt another member. Kicking, elbows, head butting. All okay. Weapons aren't. (In fact, when full-patch members fight each other, they'll get fined if they don't take off their rings first.) But on one run, LACO's sergeant at arms, Ray Glore, got into it with one of the hangarounds. Ray had been drinking. Like all bullies, he was a mean drunk. The hangaround quickly got the better of Ray, landing jabs and crosses at will. Ray was bleeding from a split lip and a cut on his cheek. His legs were wobbly. He pulled out a knife and stabbed the kid, collapsing the hangaround's lung. I rushed him to the hospital. That formed my opinion of Ray, and I wasn't alone.

Even if they don't break the spirit of the rules, members often take it too far with prospects. Outlaws being outlaws, and booze and drugs being a staple of biker events and clubhouse life, members often make some ridiculous demands. You walk a fine line between doing what you're asked to do and establishing yourself as a strong-willed, smart person who isn't anybody's bitch and will be an asset to the charter. You can push back, but you have to choose your battles carefully. My battle was Boots and Patches.

Boots and Patches was a raunchy club legend. On a big run with lots of prospects in attendance, a member would yell it out. It meant that all the prospects had to strip down to their boots and vests—nothing else—then empty the latrines into a big ditch and have a rope tug-of-war over the waste. I knew what Boots and Patches was, but I'd never heard it called or seen it happen. Then late one afternoon on a run at Bass Lake, a member shouted it out. He was drunk, high, or both, and I just stood there as he walked up to me.

"Get those pants off, prospect."

"I'm not going to do it."

"The hell you're not."

"I'm not. Unless you do it."

"I'm not the prospect."

But we both knew the rule. Don't ask anyone to do what you won't do.

"Tell you what. You get the members together and I'll get the prospects. We'll all do it, members against prospects. Losers eat shit."

He got furious. But I was willing to fight over it. I wasn't going to strip down in front of dozens of people and wind up sprawled neck deep in shit. I wasn't going to put my brothers in that position either. There was no need for it. The outlaw life draws a lot of extreme personalities, and some of them, especially when they climb the chain of command, want to impose ridiculous nonsense on other people. There's a lot of playing "top this." It can get stupid real quick. Being a fairly reasonable guy, it's a part of club life I never appreciated. There's a lot of wild fun to be had without trying to make guys take off their pants and pull one another into a ditch full of waste.

When the prospects saw that I wasn't backing down, they weren't about to strip either. Ultimately, the more sober senior members realized that there was no good argument to be made, and only potential members to be lost, so they let it drop. Boots and Patches died an overdue death on that run. No prospect ever stripped down (except of his own accord) again.

4

Before undercover cops, confidential informants, and rats created chaos inside one-percent clubs, prospecting periods were short. These days, a potential Hells Angel has to prospect for at least a year so that background checks and other tests prove that he's not a cop or an informant. In the seventies, it was different. I spent four months prospecting.

Getting your patch is the biggest thing that will happen to you as a club member. They call the date your anniversary, and it's celebrated every year just like a birthday would be. I became a full-patch member on December 26, 1976.

Prospects never know when they'll get their patch, but I had a clue. The day after Christmas, Old Man John called and told me to get the clubhouse ready for a meeting at eight that night. John said, "Make sure you're riding your bike, prospect." We both knew he didn't need to say it. I always rode my bike, even in the dead of winter. But he was tipping his cards. A prospect wouldn't be voted in if he showed up in a car; somebody would say, "I'm not voting for him. He's not even riding." So I told Cheryl I was leaving, kissed the kids good night, and rode my bike to the Glendale clubhouse, through a winter chill that had sharp teeth.

Jesse, me, and a group of other prospects and hangarounds stood at the front edge of the yard, waiting for the meeting to get going. We clustered around a fifty-five-gallon drum filled with burning two-by-fours, stomping our feet, holding our hands out to the fire, and trying to ignore a night that was as cold as it gets in Southern California.

One of the new prospects, Fat Mike, summed up everyone's feelings: "What the hell do they need to meet in the middle of the holidays for? Jesus, don't they have something better to do?"

Everyone added his two cents to the general grumbling as the guys passed around a pint of whiskey. I passed because I didn't drink. I had never been a big drinker and don't have an addictive personality. Partying and then having to pay for it the next morning never made sense to me, and I didn't like the idea of getting crazy stupid at any time. I just didn't have a taste for booze, which set me apart from most outlaws. But nobody ever complained—it just meant more for everyone else.

Suddenly the clubhouse door slammed open and a voice shouted, "Christie, get your ass in here." I sprinted back to the clubhouse and into the meeting, closing the door behind me. It was quiet as a library, everyone looking deadly serious. John was staring daggers at me. After an uncomfortable minute or two, he broke the silence.

"Well, prospect, you been thinking about this, about joining us. You've been around for a while so it's time for you to stay or go." He leaned forward. "You sure this is what you want to do? Are you really ready to commit to the club, make this your whole life?"

"I think I've proved where my head's at."

"Yeah, you have. I just want to make sure you don't get confused between us and your other family." He was telling me that the Angels came first. Would always come first. I knew that and had understood it ever since I had started riding with the Question Marks. I had made my choice years before.

"I'm not confused, John."

"Well then, I guess this guy needs a cut." Tall Paul stood up, took off his vest, and threw it at me. "You can wear this one to Berdoo." The meeting broke up into a mini-riot, guys mock fighting me, punching me, people shouting. Finally, John crept up behind me and lifted me up off the floor in a bear hug and a cheer went up. Then they called in the prospects and hangarounds. John put his arm around my shoulders. "I want to introduce you to our newest member."

Everyone congratulated me. Any tribe survives by growing, and a new member is always good news. The only one who took it badly was Jesse. He looked crushed. We had become prospects at the same time, and I knew that he'd hoped he would patch in at the same time. His problem was the Florida connection, a stigma that a little time would erase. He'd get patched in a few weeks later.

Berdoo was where any new members in Southern California went for their patch. Berdoo was the first Hells Angels charter and maintained a strong sense of history and tradition. By the time I became a member, Southern California had a distinct identity from the northern part of the state, where the Oakland Hells Angels were getting most of the press. Berdoo was the closest clubhouse to the unofficial Southern California seamstress, Betty. Betty was a legend. She sewed the patches by hand, and having her sew it onto your cut was an honor. She lived in a quiet, lower-middle-class neighborhood on the outskirts of San Bernardino. Because a lot of wannabes regularly tried to get ahold of fake patches, a Berdoo member had to accompany you to Betty's, to verify that you really were a Hells Angel. So, after a raucous party at the Glendale clubhouse, four guys rode down with me to the Berdoo clubhouse. Riding fast through the cold only makes you colder, and by the time we arrived, the exposed skin on our faces was numb. It didn't bother us because Berdoo had a warm reception waiting, and we partied into the early morning. We crashed on the sofas and the floor of the clubhouse, and at nine the next morning, we rode over to Betty's.

The small yellow tract house was packed in close to its neighbors, all trim front yards and homes. There was a strict protocol. You didn't swear, smoke, or get rowdy. Betty was a quiet, religious woman. Her house had a small sitting room in front. We filed in, trying not to track dirt onto the rug. We stood around, awkward in the neat-as-a-pin room. Betty disappeared into her little workshop behind the waiting room, and we listened to the whir of the Singer sewing machine rise and fall as she attached the top rocker and Death Head to my denim cutoff. It felt like forever, standing in that silent waiting room. When she finally came out and handed me the cut, I just stared at it for a minute because it almost didn't seem real. Short of seeing my children for the first time, I'd never been so happy.

Betty gave us a stern reminder to ride quietly until we were out of her neighborhood. I made it a block before I dropped down a gear, cranked the throttle, and filled the morning air with that unique, deep-throated roar. I don't think I dropped below eighty on the way back to the Glendale clubhouse. That was the start of a several-day party. I limped home a little worse for the wear. Cheryl was pumped for a fight as soon as I walked through the door.

"Have a good time with your buddies?"

"I got my patch." I showed her the cut, which I was still wearing. "I can come and go as I please now."

"Good. Now maybe you can start spending some time around here."

"Well, actually, I'm going to Oakland tomorrow and I don't know when I'm going to be back."

If looks could kill, I would have been a dead man standing.

Ten of us from LACO made the trip up I-5 on New Year's Eve 1976. I was excited because it would be the first time I'd ride a distance flying the Death Head, and the first time I'd be a full member at a club celebration. There was no better way in the world to tour the Bay Area, the center of the universe for the Hells Angels. Not only was Oakland a base of power, Frisco was a close second and the oldest charter behind Berdoo. Charters in the Bay Area were also a lot closer geographically than they were in Southern California. A twenty-minute ride in any direction would put you at the doorstep of a different clubhouse.

The Hells Angels grew from a handful of charters to hundreds of charters and thousands of members worldwide. Composed of strong-willed, independent, confrontational men, the club has always had to balance members who were by their nature fiercely independent and rule breakers, and the needs and rules of the charter to which they belonged. That same tension exists between individual charters, which develop their own distinct personalities and have their own ways of doing things, and the club at large. Charters operate independently and send representatives to regularly meet and vote on clubwide issues. Some charters were stronger than others. The oldest charters retained the most power, and Oakland founder Ralph "Sonny" Barger had shrewdly built Oakland into the center of power in the club.

Oakland was a big charter with more than twenty-five members, and they threw epic parties. We made it to the Oakland clubhouse just as the New Year's party was heating up. The clubhouse was in a gritty industrial neighborhood, on Foothill Boulevard, a wide road that paralleled the freeway. The building had a half-height gray brick façade and a gigantic Hells Angels sign over it. As we rolled up, bikes were everywhere. On the sidewalk, in the back, on the street. I could hear the sound of the party above the noise of my pipes as I threaded through a tangle of motorcycles parked randomly at odd angles to the curb.

Although Sonny was behind bars, finishing a stint for drug possession, plenty of legendary Hells Angels were still in the area. The first person I ran into on my way toward the front door was Paul "Animal" Hibbits. Paul and I had gone to high school together and had both spent many happy hours tearing around the Bruckers' ranch. But standing out in front of the clubhouse, he was less than warm to me. Animal joined the club right out of high school and was a player in Oakland. He gave me a quick hug and then let me know that he expected a lot out of me. He basically told me that because we were from the same town, what I did—good or bad—reflected on him. Never mind that he was a year younger than I was. That was just how the club hierarchy worked. As we talked,

I watched police cruisers roll by. They drove slowly, but never stopped, much less got out. People were running out the front door and lighting rolls of firecrackers. The local cops wanted no part of this wild scene.

The first thing I saw as I made my way through the clubhouse door was a card table set up in the main room. A group of members sat around it playing high-stakes five-card draw. A few thousand dollars were in the pot, and the players were ignoring the commotion around them. There were Albert Lee "Big Al" Perryman, Marvin "Mouldy Marvin" Gilbert, and Jim "Jim Jim" Brandes. Every single one a Hells Angels legend. Everybody who was anybody in the outlaw biker world was at the party. I didn't leave until the next night, and the party was still going strong.

Animal let me crash in his room at the clubhouse and catch a few hours of sleep in his bed. But I was buzzing from adrenaline and eager to hit up all the Bay Area charters. The next stop was Richmond. I'd spent some enjoyable time on runs with the Richmond president, Angelo Borburia. Angelo had a reputation as his own man and had led Richmond through the aftermath of a scandal involving a murder and an informant. I liked Angelo because he was a straight shooter. He would prove to be a great guy to have in my corner.

Richmond was known as a discreet charter. They kept to themselves and didn't air their business with the rest of the club. They were not a friendly bunch, but seemed to like me. I unwound in the empty Richmond clubhouse, waiting to meet up with Angelo. He walked in looking stylish with his long hair done in twin braids Willie Nelson–style. He was taller than me, good-looking, and had the strut of a true leader. He had a quiet confidence about him.

He stood in front of me with a big smile on his face and dropped a plastic sandwich bag full of white powder onto the coffee table. "Hey, man, you ready to party?"

"That's why I'm here."

He shook a little coke out of the baggie and cut up a generous row of lines on the top of the coffee table. He rolled up a $20 bill to make a straw and handed it to me. "After you."

We sat there talking, listening to Big Brother and the Holding Company's album *Cheap Thrills,* and doing some of the best coke I'd ever had. Suddenly Angelo jumped up. "Oh, hey, man, I've got a gift for you."

He disappeared and came back a minute later with a small black box that he handed me. I opened it to find a silver ring with the German SS insignia. Angelo gave a ring just like this to select guys in the club that he thought embodied what it meant to be a true Hells Angel. There was a saying in the club: "Hells Angels aren't made, they're born." In Angelo's judgment, a few guys were born to be Hells Angels. When they found their way to the club, they became the best Angels. That's what the ring meant. Even though I wasn't a big fan of Nazi memorabilia, it was a huge honor. It stunned me. A Hells Angels president had given me this incredibly meaningful gift, and I was completely blown away.

"Wow, Angelo, I don't know what to say."

"How about 'Thank you,' for starters?"

"Thank you. Thank you, brother."

"C'mon, man, let's take a ride. I have something I want to show you."

He gathered up his bag of coke and we headed out on our bikes. I followed Angelo's back wheel onto the 580, and across the Richmond–San Rafael Bridge. I was puzzled where we could be going because it was almost midnight and there wasn't a San Rafael charter. We were going the opposite direction from any charters. We finally rolled off the freeway and wound through a dark warehouse district, pulling up in front of a plain building that looked like just another industrial space. But 20 Front Street was much more than just another warehouse. I followed Angelo through the door and found myself face-to-face with a skeleton sitting at an electronic keyboard, a cigarette stuck between his teeth and his rib bones wrapped in a button-down, paisley, short-sleeve shirt.

"What the hell?"

Angelo wore a wide smile. "That, my brother, is the most dangerous job in showbiz."

I drew a blank.

"Keyboardist for the Grateful Dead." It was a well-known punch line. The band's keyboardists famously met untimely ends. I knew that because I was a huge Dead fan. All at once, I connected the dots. This was Club Front, the Grateful Dead's recording studio. We went through another door into one of the sound rooms. Standing in the booth on the other side of the glass was Jerry Garcia—the genius behind the Grateful Dead. He was tinkering with a chord progression on his guitar. A chunky, shaggy, bearded guy with laughing eyes and a wide smile stood next to the sound engineer. I immediately recognized him as Lowell George, lead guitarist and mastermind of Little Feat, another one of my favorite bands. Jerry came out of the booth and Angelo introduced us. Jerry was a quiet, unassuming guy, kind of a normal hippie character. He was soft-spoken, and everything about him seemed gentle, from his always-smiling eyes to the way he spoke. Lowell and Jerry went back into the booth and kept working on a riff that Jerry would use on the next Dead album.

It was yet another surreal moment in a trip full of them. Every half hour, these two musical giants came out of the booth and did a few lines of coke with Angelo and me. Then they went back to work. Although watching somebody fiddle endlessly with three or four chords would otherwise be as exciting as watching paint dry, I was high, amped, and in the presence of two guys whose music I had loved all my adult life.

Angelo and I rode to San Francisco at a little after four in the morning. We ended up at the Frisco clubhouse. If Oakland was the most blue-collar, working-class clubhouse—it looks like a union hall inside—Frisco was the most psychedelic, bohemian clubhouse. Unlike the bunker look typical of most Hells Angels clubhouses, Frisco's was tacked onto the back of a brown, two-story clapboard house. The furniture was overstuffed and comfortable, and there were all kinds of unusual decorations and memorabilia, including a complete Harley attached to the wall as a memorial plaque for a fallen member. I crashed on the comfortable couch, incredibly happy as I fell into a deep sleep in seconds.

The next afternoon, Angelo picked me up for a ride down to the San Jose clubhouse, where I got a chilly reception. San Jose has a reputation as the most suspicious Hells Angels charter. It would be a long time before any San Jose member was even cordial to me. Mostly, other members never saw them, and they only got involved with the club at large during officers' meetings and clubwide votes.

My New Year's trip stretched out to almost a week, and I blew through my DOD sick days. But it was so exciting to be in the midst of so many brothers under the patch that it was easy to forget there was a regular, workaday world going on around us. I almost didn't want to come home, but I had my "other" life to slip back into. That life meant the comedown of getting back to work at the DOD.

Being a Hells Angel and an employee is a challenge. It's why so many Angels wind up working for themselves. Unless you are a trucker, mechanic, bartender, nightclub bouncer, or businessman, you're probably going to have a hard time balancing work and the outlaw life. It's part of the reason why many Hells Angels turn to illegal activities. You need money to support yourself. It's just reality. Most employers, especially in the sixties and seventies, wanted to see short hair, a button-down shirt, and a get-along attitude. That's not a Hells Angel.

Not surprisingly, the Department of Defense was particularly conservative. My long hair and scruffy beard already set me apart. I didn't have problems at work because I was good at my job. But I also didn't push it. I didn't ride my motorcycle to work, and I certainly wasn't going to wear my cut onto a naval base. So every morning I'd ride to the house of a friend I worked with, park my bike in his garage, and leave my cut on the bike. Then we'd drive to work together in his car. I'd do the whole thing in reverse at the end of the workday. It wasn't perfect, but it kept me under the radar. But somewhere down deep, the outlaw in me realized it was a house of cards that wasn't likely to remain standing.

5

As a young Hells Angel, I wanted to be on my bike all the time. I was full of testosterone and had an appetite for action. I wanted to announce to the world that I was one of the outlaw elite. I never wanted to take my patch off. That's also the official line. Angels are expected to put even casual club gatherings ahead of everything else, including family. So I didn't think twice when Jesse called me to tell me some members were heading to a swap meet at the Great Western Exhibit Center in Anaheim. I had only been home from work for a couple hours when I headed out. It was nothing new for Cheryl. She understood that my leaving on a Friday night meant I would be home Sunday afternoon, even if she would never be totally comfortable with the routine. She would always be conflicted between loving the power the Hells Angels brought us—the looks we got on the rare occasions we were out together, the obvious deference we got from other bikers—and hating being left behind, the one not in control.

I was glad to ride away. I was raised to cherish family, but I was being pulled in two directions. Routine, the sameness and predictability of suburban life, drove me up the wall. All the little worries that cropped up, along with Cheryl's endless nagging and digs—or worse, her aggressive silence—got inside my head. It felt like a physical need, an overwhelming itch to get out and moving. Sometimes, it wasn't even a matter of going anywhere. I'd just get on that motorcycle, and everything that was eating at me would melt away. I'd hit the freeway, open her up to some crazy high end, and mentally flush everything out. Ride fast on a good road and it only takes a few miles to fall into a calm road trance. You're on autopilot, capable of registering cars coming into your lane and street signs, but not much else. It's an incredible feeling, almost like a drug. Knowing I had that outlet sitting in the garage would somehow quench the thirst, helping me limp by until the next time I could jump on the bike and go. It became my Zen.

So I wasn't thinking about Cheryl, the kids, the DOD, or anything else by the time I pulled up at the clubhouse to meet Jesse. I was just happy to be riding with the last flare of the setting California sun casting a fading light across my Death Head. Jesse was as amped as I was. We were looking forward to a weekend of partying. The last thing we expected was to stumble across half the damn Mongol nation.

Angels from LACO, Dago (San Diego), and Berdoo met up in the parking lot of the Exhibit Center, each bike cocked at an identical angle, lined up in a row. We had just walked through the entrance when I spotted the first Mongol patch—a black-and-white rendition of a bare-chested wild man with a topknot and shades riding a raked chopper. I didn't think anything of it. The Mongols were small change in the outlaw biker world, not one of the "big four"—Hells Angels, Outlaws, Bandidos, and Pagans. Like all outlaws, though, they lived in the long shadow cast by the Death Head. That particular Friday it didn't matter. There was bad blood that I learned about only later. It was the fuse on a powder keg.

Chester Green had been a Richmond Hells Angel. He testified against fellow member Bill Moran in a murder trial. The club tossed him out in bad standing. To protect himself from blowback, which might reasonably have included a bullet to the head in some dimly lit parking lot, he joined the Mongols. Changing clubs wasn't done in the outlaw world. Legitimate clubs wouldn't take another's cast-off. But his brother, Bud Green, was already a ranking Mongol. Bud, as I found out later, was living with the ex-wife of a Los Angeles Hells Angel, a tall guy with a solid, wiry build and a face that was all sharp angles. When he got pissed, his scowl told the whole story. So we all knew something was burning him up. We just didn't know what.

In the days before the Internet made everything available, swap meets were where you could find bits and pieces you couldn't get anywhere else. Older bikes broke down all the time. Swap meets were a lifeline for inexpensive replacements and aftermarket gear. A lot of the stuff was hot, but nobody asked questions—especially when you finally found that valve cover for your 1942 ULH eighty-inch flathead.

The Exhibit Center was a great place for a swap meet. It was cavernous, filled end to end with cafeteria tables covered in parts, leathers, and anything else to do with riding. By the time we walked in, it was packed with people. There was a faint, biting smell of grease and solvent in the air, mixed with a thick layer of cigarette smoke.

Halfway in, it was no longer just a patch here and there; we were wading through a sea of Mongols. Law enforcement sources later put the number at anywhere from forty to one hundred. There were nine of us Angels. At a glance, it looked to me like we were outnumbered at least four or five to one. I don't care who you are, those are ugly odds.

I was walking next to Kid Glenn, a six-foot-two, 230-pound Berdoo Hells Angel. Like the rest of us, he was wondering what we had walked into. Kid had a linebacker's frame, muscular with no belly. He was quick with a bright smile and was smart for a biker, but had a reputation for toughness. It was the first time we had met. Like everyone else, he knew a bad scene when he was in one.

"What the fuck is going on with all these Mongols? Do we have a problem with them? Why are all these assholes here?"

"I don't know, Kid."

He turned to the other Angels. "We got to stay together, man. If the shit happens, we just hold our ground back-to-back."

Everyone nodded and closed ranks. "Yeah, man." Except for the one person who wasn't hearing him, the Los Angeles Hells Angel.

A clot of Mongols walked toward us, the crowd parting as they came through. But we were Hells Angels. We gave way to nobody. Bud Green was right in the middle of the Mongols. He and the LACO Hells Angel locked eyes. No words, just a look. Then without so much as a "How do you do," the Angel swung on him and connected. It was on. All hell broke loose.

Brawls are faster and messier than anything staged in a movie or on TV. Everyone was immediately pumped with adrenaline and just reacting, not thinking. It was absolute chaos. Fortunately, being outmanned in a close-quarters fight isn't necessarily the worst thing in the world. Only so many guys can get to you at one time. If you can keep your cool, you can maneuver opponents so that they're in one another's way and don't have a clear shot at you. In a place like a swap meet, there is also a lot of stuff lying around that you can use to your advantage. Tables and carts can slow enemies down and create a defensive barrier. Mostly though, there are weapons everywhere. The first thing most of the Angels did was grab something lethal. Prospect Cliff Mowery—a confidential informant, as we would later find out—grabbed a beefy kickstand and started swinging it. Another Angel grabbed a piston-and-rod, which made for a deadly club.

I wasn't a fan of weapons. I was just getting serious in martial arts, and I had come to realize that most street fighters focus more on their weapon than on their own defense. It left them open to counterattack. In the chaos of the first wave, I stopped one Mongol with a punch to the neck followed by a kick to the knee. I grappled another one to the ground and punished him with knees to the head and ribs. Later, Kid Glenn would compliment me on my aggressiveness and talk me up within the club, a great endorsement for the future. He told me I could work with him anytime. I considered it high praise because he was a debt collector.

I was fighting back-to-back with another Angel. Jesse was beside me when he was bull rushed by a Mongol tank. This guy was a barrel-chested monster of a man but not a smart fighter. Rather than grab ahold of Jesse or land a haymaker, he rammed Jesse in the chest and knocked him backward. I watched out of the corner of my eye as Jesse flew and landed across a vendor table. The table collapsed, and Jesse wound up on the floor surrounded by heavy, forged-iron sprockets. It was a lucky break. He grabbed the largest gear within reach, jumped up, and started swinging for all he was worth. I've never seen anything like it, before or since.

The teeth of a machined motorcycle gear have sharp edges. A gear is heavy as hell. The big Mongol was the first to learn how much Jesse loved to fight, as the gear cut open a savage gash in the big man's face, eyebrow to chin. Jesse gave other Mongols more of the same. Chunks of flesh and trails of blood were flying everywhere as he took full swings at attacker after attacker. The Mongols around him were screaming, holding gruesome wounds, divots taken out of their faces.

After a couple minutes, the odds improved. Many Mongols retreated. The fight with the stragglers raged on for what seemed like a long time, but was probably just another couple of minutes. Suddenly, a young cop waded into the middle of everything, his gun drawn. He was a Boy Scout, a skinny guy with a buzz cut and a sharply pressed sheriff's uniform. He looked like he hadn't even started shaving. He was all alone; backup hadn't arrived. It was one of the bravest things I had ever witnessed. This cop wasn't stupid. He knew what we knew. He had a revolver with six bullets, with maybe twenty-five of us surrounding him. He wasn't going to take down more than a couple of us if things went south, and he was going to die in the process. But the ballsy move worked. The air went out of the fight. We were all breathing heavily and the Mongols who hadn't already retreated cut and headed toward a side exit, while the Angels started backing toward the front of the hall, where our bikes were parked.

I collided with a loose Mongol, the two of us going in opposite directions. He was trying to puff up because it was clear the cops were on the scene now. He thought he was safe.

"What's the fucking problem here?"

"You don't know what the problem is?"

"No."

"You're the fucking problem."

I hit him and we went down, grappling for the upper hand. I got on top of him and started throwing punches and elbows trying to get in one last lesson for the Mongols. The other Angels had already made it out the front and didn't realize I was stuck behind. Unfortunately, the backup cops were all over us. Suddenly, I was getting beaten with nightsticks on my head and shoulders.

As luck would have it, several Satan's Slaves were at the meet. Two of them jumped in and covered me up. They were yelling at the cops to stop. The Slaves somehow managed to get me free and hustled me out to join my brothers, who were already on their bikes, getting ready to scoot. I looked back as I headed out the door. The cops were beating the holy hell out of the Mongol I had been fighting. "Poor bastard," I thought.

We headed back toward Los Angeles in the gathering darkness, riding up to the Glendale clubhouse at about ten. News of the fight beat us home. Old Man John was there waiting. We filed inside a little bloody, but nobody seriously hurt. John was chomping his cigar, raging in a fury.

"Those dirty sons of bitches are going to pay." Never mind that we had started the fight. They dared to put hands on biker royalty. They had disrespected the Death Head. It was simple outlaw logic. John got on the phone with someone who knew the Mongols. It was a long conversation, but it became clear that a meeting was in the works. He hung up, grabbed a couple of pump shotguns from the back of the clubhouse, and ordered a prospect to take them out to John's beat-up, rusty, faded red 1965 Mustang.

"Bruno, Ray, you're with me. The rest of you sit tight." Club treasurer

Michael Lee "Bruno" Mason, and Ray Glore followed John out to his car and off they went. Emotions were driving everything. We didn't even know where they were going or what the plan was. Jesse grabbed a beer and we settled in. We looked at each other.

I shook my head. "I think he's making a big mistake."

"What do you mean?"

"We should have let them brew on it for a few days. Let them call us, try to make peace. We need to sweat 'em."

Jesse shrugged and took a hit off his Coors. "Fuck, I don't know. What's he gonna do over there anyway?"

"I don't know, Jesse. I don't think it's a smart move."

It didn't matter what we thought. We were new guys. John was the president. But I was right, and Jesse and I both knew it. Time was going to prove me right.

There was nothing to do but wait. We watched TV until the news came on. The brawl got twenty seconds of airtime. There was no word of arrests. Truth was, 1977 was a different time. Cops weren't as sophisticated or militaristic. They had more common sense and less technology. The Hells Angels had gotten out as a group, everyone accounted for. Maybe some Mongols were busted, but in a messy brawl where only the fighters were hurt and none fatally, it would have been hard to piece together what actually happened. Nobody was going to talk to the cops.

The law was the least of anybody's concern. There was a much bigger, deadlier issue. A rival had fought Hells Angels and lived to tell about it. It didn't matter that we were outnumbered or that an Angel had started the fight or even that we won. It didn't matter that some Mongols ran. In the outlaw world, none of that mattered. What was important was that the Mongols still existed. A defining principle of the Hells Angels is that if you throw down with any Hells Angel, you throw down with all Hells Angels. And if you face off with the entire club, you're headed to one of two places: intensive care or the morgue. It's that simple. At that point in history, especially in California, the Hells Angels were untouchable.

That modest fight started the Hells Angels–Mongol war that continues, in one form or another, to this day. It wasn't the famous Laughlin casino brawl and shoot-out, which came later. Not the bombings or the freeway shootings that writers and journalists would focus on. It was all about a fight that broke out one Friday night in March 1977, a messy old-school rumble at a Southern California swap meet. A stupid fight over a woman, the oldest reason there is.

Sitting around the clubhouse, I chewed on the reality. If your brothers went to war, you went to war. It was a commitment—to your brothers, the club, the patch, and ultimately to the lifestyle—that a lot of people could not understand. If you were in, you were in. So we waited like good foot soldiers. We watched TV until the test pattern came on as the channels went off the air one by one. We were starting to stiffen up and feel sore from the fight. But it was our job to wait. Some guys slept, some drank and smoked, and others sat and thought.

John, Bruno, and Ray came back at about five in the morning. John looked as tired as I had ever seen a man. "All right, we got a peace with the Mongols." That made no sense to me. The Hells Angels outnumbered the Mongols somewhere in the neighborhood of ten to one. They were an afterthought of a club, and we were the world champions. At that moment, they should have been hunkered down in their clubhouse, shaking in their boots, wondering, "Are we going to be crushed under the sheer force of a thousand guys wearing the Death Head?" But, no. Instead, a truce.

"You stupid bastards start all this shit over a woman." John smiled. "She must have been one hell of a skirt."

That was John. Like a father. He'd get mad, rage a little. Then he'd calm down, and then he'd kid you. I believe he thought he was doing what he needed to do to protect his flock, all these young, wild kids that looked up to him. But the decisions he made that night were the beginning of the end of his leadership.

Before cell phones, before the Internet, before pagers, there were phone trees. Networks of connections spread news like wildfire on a hot, windy day. Within twelve hours, every Hells Angel on the West Coast knew about the fight and the "truce." Inside twenty-four, every Hells Angel in the country did. Every single one of them had an opinion, and none boded well for John or LACO.

The truce was never going to hold. Hells Angels don't let sleeping dogs lie. John initially kept it together while a shitstorm rained down from other charters—most pointedly from Oakland. All the phone calls could be broken down into two camps. Some thought we were just plain stupid for getting into such a dangerous situation over a woman. But the bigger heat was coming straight down from the Sonny Barger faction. Sonny was in the last days of a stretch at Folsom. Although he stepped down as the Oakland president when he went in to do his bit, he was still in control. John was getting daily calls from the Bay Area. Guys saying that we'd put Sonny's parole at risk. On our end, Dago—the most gangster charter in the state—was howling for Mongol blood.

Two weeks after the swap meet fight, John bowed to the pressure and stepped down as president. He called a vote, but made it known that the choice to succeed him was Ray Glore, not Bruno. It was a puzzler because Ray was not respected in the charter. What I would understand later was that John's hand had been forced. The guys from up north wanted Ray in place because they knew they could manipulate him. What we needed at the moment was a general, a wise leader. Unfortunately, what we got was Ray Glore.

Ray was sleazy. He was a drug dealer and a meth addict. He was what I would come to call a professional meth user. Cranksters that want to function anything close to normal know that they have to force them-selves to eat and sleep regularly. If they don't, they become empty-shell tweakers. To stay functioning, they have to choke down three meals a day even though they're not hungry, and they take Valium to get a few hours of sleep every night. But eat and sleep like a normal person while using meth like an addict, you wind up with skinny limbs and a weird potbelly.

The meth belly. That was Ray. He had the dark complexion and strong nose of a Native American, with long, straight, greasy hair and shifty black eyes. He had the meth belly and gave off an evil vibe. He used his status as an Angel to build drug and porn businesses. His old lady appeared in the films. Worst of all, Ray was weak.

A week later, Ray and the Mongols' national president set up a phone call. Ray made the mind-blowing mistake of recording that call. On the tape, the Mongol gets right to the point. "Hey, we've been doing a lot of thinking and we're going to go to a *California* rocker." This was a huge deal, a major sign of disrespect. The bottom rocker lists a member's location. Early in Angels' history, the bottom rocker carried the name of each member's charter city. But as the club grew and the number of charters increased, every Angel in the state went to a bottom rocker that said simply *California*. The Angels were the first club to claim an entire state. The change made it hard for law enforcement to pin down at a glance where any individual was from, which was useful. More important, though, it raised the Hells Angels' flag over the second most populous state in the union. For another club to take on a *California* rocker was an insult and a direct threat to Hells Angels' dominance. The Angels took these things deadly serious, as the Mongols would soon learn. But Ray sounded like a complete amateur on the tape, making a bizarre suggestion in response to the news.

"Maybe you could go to a *Golden State* rocker?"

The Mongol president laughed. "No, we're pretty set on a *California* rocker."

There was nothing funny about it as far as the Hells Angels were concerned. In another astounding mistake, Ray headed up to Oakland for the West Coast Officers' Meeting in April 1977, where he played the recording for the top Hells Angels. Hells Angels Officers' Meetings are formal gatherings where serious issues are discussed and debated and often voted on. The East Coast and other countries have their own versions, but the West Coast Officers' Meetings are where the most powerful Hells

Angels in the club gather. Locations rotate now, but in the seventies, the monthly gatherings were held almost exclusively in Oakland. I would first become truly influential in the club at large when I was voted in as the West Coast chairman in 1985 (when I would also push through a vote to rotate the location of the meeting). The chairman controls the meetings and can steer the agenda toward or away from issues, depending on what his aims are. He also adjudicates disputes and holds a lot of sway with all members. The meetings themselves are perfect places to broker relationships and gain power. Or, in Ray's case, to lose it. The other officers sat in stunned silence, exchanging looks across the folding cafeteria tables placed in a square in the main room of the Oakland clubhouse. Ray had been punked by an enemy. He immediately lost any remaining respect or leverage he might have had.

When Ray came home, we set up a meeting. But the grapevine was faster than Ray. By the time he got back, we all knew that Fu Griffin—a longtime Oakland member at the core of power—had called Ray out at the meeting. Fu said what everyone was thinking, that Ray wasn't worthy of leading a Girl Scout troop, much less a Hells Angels charter. They got in a fistfight and Fu cleaned Ray's clock. Ray limped home covered in bruises and dried blood. It was terrible news, but there was worse to come.

Ray wouldn't meet anybody's eyes when he told the charter, "They're talking about shutting us down."

"Who's talking about shutting us down?"

"Oakland. They want to take the charter. They're saying we screwed up with the Mongols." Ray shook his head, like he was talking about someone else's mistake. "You guys never should have fought them."

Suddenly it was "you guys." I was in shock that this asshole was ready to roll over and let someone shut down a charter he was supposed to be leading. Even for Ray, it was spineless. I had never shied away from saying my piece, and now that I was a member, I wasn't about to hesitate.

"Well, what are we going to do about it?"

"What can we do against Oakland?"

"Fuck those guys, they aren't taking my patch. I'm going up there and facing this down."

"You're going up to Oakland?"

"I don't know about you guys, but I'm leaving in the morning. I'm going to the Bay Area, and I'm going to see if anybody's got anything to say to me. Anyone who wants to fight for the charter is welcome to ride up with me."

I left in the morning, the sun barely just up. I rode out alone.

My first stop was the Oakland clubhouse. When I walked in, the members sitting around were obviously shocked to see me. Nobody would talk to me about what went down with Ray and Fu, and nobody seemed to know where the officers were. I took off and rode to Richmond, because I was sure I had a friend in Angelo. When I walked into the Richmond clubhouse, the reception I got was a lot warmer than what I'd received in Oakland. Angelo gave me a hug and a big smile.

He threw together an impromptu meeting, including San Jose, Daly City, Frisco, and Richmond. It was my chance to explain what was happening in Los Angeles. He didn't invite Oakland, and I didn't ask why. I didn't have to. I had already figured out that I had ridden into a hornet's nest. Even though Sonny Barger wasn't yet home from prison, he was clearly controlling Oakland, and trying to control the club. Some charters didn't take kindly to Sonny or Oakland trying to hand out orders.

At the meeting, I laid out what actually happened with the Great Western fight, and what the LACO members were thinking. I got a sympathetic hearing and finished up by saying, "So that's why I rode up here, to say it loud and clear: nobody's taking my patch."

Everyone in the room exchanged glances and went silent. Daly City member Robert Poulin was the first to speak.

"Wait a minute, you rode your bike all the way up here?"

"Yeah. I ride my bike everywhere. You know that."

"But you rode all the way up here, with your cut on, in the middle of a war?" People started shaking their heads.

"I'm not going to hide."

"You might get shot off your bike."

"I'm not worried about that." And I wasn't. As far as I knew, there weren't any Mongols north of Los Angeles. And I figured they were too scared of us to do anything anyway.

The meeting broke up and I got a lot of respect from members for having come up in person. A San Jose Angel, Doug Bontempi, even said, "You're the only person from down south that's shown me anything." He shook his head. "Why isn't anybody here with you?"

"I can't answer that. You'll have to ask them."

Angelo and Robert Poulin took me aside. "So what's your plan now? Where are you going from here?"

"I don't know. I'm thinking of going back to Oakland to straighten things out. They really gave me the fucking cold shoulder over there."

They exchanged a look.

Robert shook his head. "You ain't going back to Oakland by yourself. You're going to come with me."

"Where am I supposed to stay?"

"You can stay at the clubhouse, in Danny Reb's room. You can crash there and relax. Anybody who wants to see you, I'm going to spread the word that they can come to you at the clubhouse. And you won't be alone."

Robert was as good as his word. The Daly City clubhouse had a comfortable bedroom. Robert even introduced me to a girl, and she and I hit it off. It was a change, having a woman treat me like I was something special, like she was interested in me. We ended up dropping acid and spending the night together. I took off her pants and tried to remove her lace panties, but couldn't get them off. She laughed and laughed. As it turned out, it wasn't that I was uncoordinated because I was tripping. She had delicate black lace panties tattooed around her pelvis. We spent three days in bed before Robert politely told me that Danny Reb wanted his room back. It was time to leave.

I headed back to Los Angeles, into a storm of chaos. Oakland vice president Russell Beyea had become a fixture in the Glendale clubhouse. He was a formidable presence. Six feet tall, he was built like a longshoreman, rugged and battle scarred. He had short black hair and a thick goatee, and a nose that had been broken more than once. Russell was known as a dangerous guy even among Hells Angels. He'd done time for killing another bike club member at a famous fight among seven clubs, at the Cleveland Polish Women's Hall in 1971. He was from Oakland, but he gave out orders like he was running LACO. Ray didn't protest. Not even when it became clear to the rest of us that a big part of Russell's interest in Southern California was Kim, Ray's old lady.

We were all on the lookout for Mongols flying a *California* rocker. There were no sightings, but the rumors came in all summer. The first *Star Wars* movie came out. The price of gas jumped to sixty-five cents a gallon. New York City had a blackout that led to riots and citywide looting. Elvis Presley died sitting on the toilet. All the while, Angels watched and waited on the highways of California. The Mongols were still wearing local chapter bottom rockers.

On August 7, in Laurelwood, Oregon, a neighbor found the bodies of Margot Compton, her blond, six-year-old twin daughters, and a nineteen-year-old neighbor. All had been brutally shot, in an execution that made headlines across the country. Compton, a former sex worker, had testified against Frisco Hells Angel Odis "Buck" Garrett and then gone into hiding. The sickening killings (the daughters were executed in their beds, hugging their teddy bears) brought even more heat down on the club. What others weren't doing to us, we were doing to ourselves.

A week before Labor Day, a Mongol was spotted just outside San Diego flying the club's black-and-white colors on top of a *California* bottom rocker. It was our move now. Russell Beyea showed up yet again, and Ray and I were ordered out in a hit team.

The word was that the Mongols were planning a Labor Day run to Lake Isabella, north of Los Angeles and fifty miles east of Bakersfield. Ray got ahold of an inconspicuous late-model, tan, four-door rental. We heard that the Mongols were making camp somewhere west of the lake, so I grabbed a pump shotgun and we started searching. By midday Saturday, we came across three Mongols on their bikes, wearing the *California* rocker. We tailed them back to their campground.

"Drop me off. I'll get up close to their camp and see what I can find out." I had trained in clandestine infiltration in the Marines and was confident that I could find out how many there were, and where they were going.

Ray nixed the idea. "Nah, it's too risky."

"It'll be fine. They don't know me. I'll just make up a story if anyone spots me."

"No, man. You'll get caught and we'll just be in more shit."

That set me on edge. I already had a low opinion of Ray, and backing off an opportunity like that was inexcusable. We found a place just off the road and spent the night in the car. The next morning, we parked near the camp's entrance, under cover of a grove of fir trees. After a few hours, we heard the roar of a pack of Mongols drifting out of the campground. They headed north and we tailed them. Ray was driving and I hopped into the back with the shotgun.

I lay down on the seat and rolled down the window. "Get up alongside them."

Ray gunned it, and when the sound of the bikes filled the car, I popped up ready to take care of business. Ray slammed on the brakes.

"What the hell are you doing?"

"He looked like he was going for something."

"Goddamnit, catch up to them."

From there on he made an empty attempt to catch the pack, oversteering on corners, braking way too hard, until the bikers were just a dot on the horizon. It became clear that the whole trip had been an exercise in futility. I was so frustrated that I had to stop myself from cracking Ray in the head with the butt of the shotgun. After we'd lost the pack, Ray turned the car around and headed for home. But we got one more chance. We passed a Mongol, broken down alongside the road.

"Slam on the brakes, slam on the brakes."

"Why?"

"I'll pretend to help and when he's not paying attention, I'll deal with him."

"No way, too risky. There's too much traffic." Ray just kept on driving and wouldn't even look my way, much less look me in the eye.

I was steaming. This wasn't how Hells Angels act. We drove back to the Glendale clubhouse in silence. I found John and took him outside. I told him everything that had happened. He raised his eyebrows. The first rule of being a Hells Angel is that you take care of business. If you won't, what else are you capable of? Informing? Rolling on the club as soon as the heat comes down?

"This guy's weak. Don't ever make me go out with that motherfucker again."

John didn't even bother trying to defend him. Ray wasn't a stand-up guy and John knew it. "George, I'm not in charge."

"You're in charge as far as I'm concerned. I'm not doing anything with that fucking guy, man. I'm cutting him loose, John."

The next day, Monday, September 5, Jesse and I were sitting around the clubhouse when a call came in from Dago.

John answered, then motioned to Jesse. "Turn on the TV."

A local news team was at a scene of utter carnage on Interstate 15 just north of San Diego. Someone had shot two Mongols off their bikes, causing a pileup that looked like a war zone. Jesse and I looked at each other. We were both thinking the same thing: LACO wasn't the only charter sending out a team. I'd only learn all the facts years later.

Dago president Russell "Gorgeous Guy" Castiglione and members James "Brett" Eaton and Raymond "Fat Ray" Piltz had set up in a gas station just outside Escondido. They had intel that a pack of Mongols were headed their way, riding home from the Lake Isabella run. Sure enough, a column of Mongols rode by, and Brett floored the gas-guzzling boat they had stolen for the hit. He chased and overtook the pack, accelerating until he was alongside the two lead bikers, Mongols' president Emerson "Redbeard" Morris and Raymond "Jingles" Smith. They were riding at the head of the pack, side by side, with their girlfriends on the back of their bikes. They were proudly flying their brand-new *California* bottom rockers. Guy and Fat Ray opened fire with machine guns, leveling the two lead bikes. At seventy miles per hour, the men were literally blown off their bikes, riders and passengers tumbling along the blacktop. The motorcycles in formation behind them didn't have time to stop, and most crashed in a chain-reaction pileup that left bodies and bikes strewn across the highway. The two Mongol girlfriends were shot but survived, one paralyzed from the fall. Redbeard and Jingles were not so lucky. Both men died at the scene, riddled with bullet holes.

A Mongol came on the screen, talking to the reporter and looking utterly dazed and confused. "Why would somebody do this? Who's doing this to us?"

I thought, "Is this guy for real?" Either he was putting on an act, or he was truly clueless. Whichever it was, he was going to figure it all out soon enough. Within hours everyone in the state—from police chiefs to the lowliest hangaround—knew that it was on. The Hells Angels had declared war on the Mongols.

That night, after Cheryl put the kids to bed, I unwound with a workout. I was drawn to martial arts in the first place because it was a world I could control. Every move was simple, clean, and understandable. You throw a kick, then a punch, then a block. Someone does this, you do that. There was an answer for everything. Thinking too much was beside the point. Working out, I quickly forgot about anything else.

Unfortunately, halfway through, Cheryl interrupted to tell me I had a call. It was Jesse.

"Hey, man, I need to see you."

"For what?"

"I don't know. Ray just wants us to get over to Crazy Mike's house pronto. Come in a car." What he meant was don't wear indicia, don't ride a bike, and don't be identifiable.

"Yeah, okay. I'll meet you there."

Crazy Mike was a Satan's Slave. He had a house in the Valley, and I had been there many times for parties. But as I started my car, I knew I wasn't headed to any party. When I got there, the house was dark and Jesse was out front. We waited for half an hour, silent, each of us lost in our own thoughts. Finally, Brett Eaton pulled up in a big, gold, early-seventies Oldsmobile. Guy Castiglione parked right behind him in another car, and Ray drove up in his own car. Brett got out and said something to Ray, and Ray motioned Jesse and me over. As I got near the car, I saw dozens of shell casings scattered across the backseat and back window ledge, glinting in the yellow glow from the streetlight. It was obviously the murder car. We all knew it even though nobody said it. Brett was high as hell on meth, twitching, talking fast, and shifting his weight nonstop from one foot to the other.

He gave Ray instructions a few feet from where Jesse and I were standing. I couldn't make out most of it but heard him say, "The guns are in the trunk. Lose them." I could almost see the wheels spinning in Ray's head. He was a gun nut to begin with, and he wasn't one to miss a potential moneymaking opportunity. Brett hopped in Guy's car and they took off.

Ray nodded at me. "Change of plan. George, you go on home. Jesse and I will take it to the wrecking yard. Jesse, you drive. I'll follow you in my car."

He didn't have to tell me twice. I was glad to ride away from this mess. The club had an arrangement with a wrecking yard in Los Angeles.

Guys used it to chop up stolen bikes and cars and get rid of whatever they needed to get rid of. The idea was to crush that gold Olds beyond recognition, before the cops ever got a chance to look it over. The next day, Jesse told me that before it went into the crusher, Ray pried open the trunk and took out two machine guns. He gave them to Jesse and told him to take them to the garage where the club stored explosives and weapons. Jesse wiped them down before he stored them.

As usual, Ray was all about the money. Machine guns were a popular item on the street. Hot as those guns were, they should have disappeared as quickly as possible. Ray, though, wasn't above jamming up some poor bastard down the line just to turn a buck. He planned to sell the guns, without a second thought that whoever ended up buying them was in possession of a direct link back to a multiple homicide.

The murders got everybody's attention. If the Mongols mistook Ray's poor leadership as a sign that the club wasn't serious, they now knew otherwise. Local and federal law enforcement took notice as well. Those weren't the kind of headlines police chiefs and federal agents liked to read. The killings got big play in the news. The public and every one percenter in the country were aware of them.

Those in the know expected Mongol retaliation, but the Hells Angels were just getting started.

Two days later, the bodies of Redbeard and Jingles were on view at the Lemon Grove Mortuary. A Dago member whose identity remains a point of debate to this day drove up in a white Rambler and parked next to the building. He walked in and dropped a bouquet of red and white carnations on Jingles' casket. The Hells Angels' colors would have been obvious to anyone in the room. I'm guessing that the Mongols in the room either thought it was a peace gesture or were too stunned at the ballsy move to react. The guy simply walked away untouched and unidentified. A couple minutes later, he remotely detonated a bomb concealed in the Rambler. He had parked the car in the wrong place or the damage would have been much worse. Still, the explosion injured three people.

Bombs were a favorite weapon among outlaw bikers. It was easy to get your hands on explosives, it didn't take a genius to wire a crude bomb, they did big damage, and they created real fear. Outlaw clubs also had plenty of military veterans among their members, guys with lots of experience wiring explosives. But I hated bombs. They were messy and cruel. People got maimed as often as they got killed. More than that, I hated the idea of civilian casualties. It seemed stupid to bring that much attention to the club and potentially hurt people who had nothing to do with the beef. Not to mention, you could blow yourself up with a single mistake. Explosives were just way too unpredictable for my tastes.

My opinion wasn't popular. The bomb at the Mongols' memorial had sent a message that everybody wanted sent: "We're not done with you yet." To most of the club, another bomb seemed like a really good idea. I walked into the clubhouse a couple days after the memorial bombing to find Ray meeting with a few other members and some of the guys from Dago. It took me about thirty seconds to realize that they were talking about blowing more Mongols up.

"You guys ever hear of collateral damage? You keep setting up these bombs, this shit's going to go wrong in a big way."

I saw the looks I got. The easiest thing in the club was to make accusations: "Oh, this guy doesn't want a bomb to go off in downtown Los Angeles? He must be an informant. Or a cop. Or he's just fucking weak."

I know that they were thinking all that and calling me a coward behind my back. But it was getting out of hand. I left before I heard any more. Days later, word went around the clubhouse that they had put a bomb down a roof vent in a Highland Park motorcycle shop called the Frame-Up. The shop was owned by two Mongols. Something went wrong with the detonator or the bomb. The bomb didn't go off. John took me aside and told me that I had to retrieve it.

"Are you kidding? Why not just leave it there?"

"George, you have to do this. People need to know that you're going to take care of business no matter what you think about it. The club has to come first. There's guys saying things right now, and you've got to prove them wrong. I already know what you're about. Now you got to convince them."

Belonging to the Hells Angels means doing dangerous things. Your participation becomes your credentials. Waver in any way and you become suspect. A lot of times in the outlaw culture, saying no just isn't an option. This was one of them. "Okay, John, I'll get it done."

"Take Jesse, get that thing out of the roof vent, and take it over to the garage. That's all you got to do. One of the other guys will take it apart."

That's all I had to do.

I knew that, in his own way, John was looking out for me. He wanted to show everyone that I was the stand-up guy he saw, that I would get the job done no matter what. Yet Ray was clearly not the real deal. It was important to make sure everyone understood who could hold their mud and who couldn't. So at ten that night, Jesse and I headed over to the Frame-Up. The shop was in a neighborhood of auto body repair places, metalworking shops, and junkyards. We backed down the alley alongside the building and checked that there were no guard dogs or people around. A pull-down roof ladder was attached to the back wall, and Jesse boosted me up so I could grab it and climb to the roof. I found the vent hood easily enough, and the rope holding the bomb had been tied off to a rooftop vent pipe. I untied it and slowly began pulling the bomb up. It was impossible to do without the bomb's swinging side to side. It was like a game of Operation, and every time the bomb clanged into the sheet-metal vent wall, I thought it would go off.

I got it out and carried it carefully to the roof edge, right above where Jesse was standing. I started to lower it by playing out the rope. When it was inches within his reach, the bomb started swinging, bumping into the wall.

"Jesus, George!"

"I know, I know."

We were both freaked out. But I finally got the bomb down into Jesse's hands. I climbed down and we carried the bomb to the car.

"Where do you want to put it?"

It was a good question. I looked at Jesse and shook my head. I hadn't thought beyond just getting it down off the roof. We still had to take it for a thirty-minute drive.

"Shit, I don't know. The trunk?"

"The trunk's right over the gas tank, man. It goes and we're going to blow like the Fourth of July."

"So where? The backseat?"

"I think it's the best place."

We found a blanket and nestled the bomb on it, as if that would somehow stop the thing from blowing up. We both straightened up and looked at this bundle of dynamite sticks held together with duct tape. It looked cartoonish, like a bad movie prop. We burst out laughing. The absurdity of the situation, along with sheer tension, had built up to the point that laughing was the only way to deal with it. It was hysterical, crazy laughter. We were bent over, tears running down our faces. We calmed down long enough to get settled in the car. I fired it up and moved out and down the street. A block later we went over a set of railroad tracks that was a much bigger double-bump than we expected. It really rattled the car. We looked over at each other and burst out laughing again. It took us the rest of the trip to stop.

We drove the bomb back to the garage and then dropped the car off at the clubhouse, where I picked up my bike. When I finally pulled into my driveway, I took a moment just to breathe. The ride home had put things back in order, in perspective.

Give the club credit for persistence. Just three weeks after the bombing at the Mongols' memorial, Hells Angel prospect Thomas Heath walked a flat motorcycle tire into the Frame-Up. Brett Eaton had rigged a bomb inside the tire, so that it would detonate when the tire valve was unscrewed. After an hour, Heath called the shop and asked if the tire was done. He talked to Mongol Henry Jimenez. They had a heated exchange, Heath pressing for the tire to be fixed so he could get it on his bike before nightfall. Jimenez finally told him he would get it done. Jimenez wasn't alone. Raymond Hernandez, the fifteen-year-old brother of another Mongol, was hanging out in the shop.

You can imagine. A fifteen-year-old kid hasn't even started shaving yet. He was hanging out with this guy he must have looked up to. He was changing oil or helping out as best he could. Learning. Thinking about how, soon, he would have his own bike. This kid knew exactly what type of Harley he was going to have. Maybe a beat-up bobber he could trick out right there. Like every other fifteen-year-old boy with a biker brother or father, he knew exactly how his own bike was going to look, and how cool he was going to look riding it.

But he never got a chance to build or ride a motorcycle. He would never even own a driver's license. Henry Jimenez held the tire steady and began unscrewing the valve. The bomb contacts came together, and Mongol and teenager were instantly killed in a blast that blew the windows out of the buildings on either side of the shop. Heath called again, an hour later. Someone else answered. The sounds of sirens and chaos filled the background.

"Yeah, your tire's ready, motherfucker. Come down and get it."

Heath hung up and laughed. It was a joke to him. For days, he went on about the explosion. "You should have heard that fucking guy. I bet his ears were ringing." He was almost doubled over with laughter as he said it. John finally had to tell him to shut up about it.

Justice would be served decades later when Heath was sentenced to thirty-five to life for a domestic-dispute beef that bought him a "third strike" conviction.

But to most of the club, it didn't matter. War was war and collateral damage was to be expected. Days later, the president of the San Fernando Valley Mongol charter, Luis Gutierrez, went out to his driveway to get in his van. It blew up as he opened the door. He was luckier than the fifteen-year-old; he escaped with his life and his body intact.

The violence drew even more attention. Law enforcement doesn't care when bikers kill bikers, but they don't like innocent kids getting blown up. From that point on, you couldn't wear your colors on a paved road in Southern California without getting pulled over and jacked up. Those of us who rode regularly were not having a lot of fun, and I couldn't get that fifteen-year-old out of my head.

A few nights later, I got home before the kids were in bed. I had been gone for two days and the kids were overjoyed to see me. We had a little ritual. My place in the living room was a big old black easy chair with gigantic, rounded, thickly padded arms. I would sit one kid on each side and wrap my arms around them. Moriya had just taken a bath and she pressed in on me, reading a picture book, humming to herself. Her hair smelled sweetly of kids shampoo. I held Georgie close on the other side as he played with a toy car. The TV was on but I wasn't paying attention. I was just so glad to be home.

The moment was sanctuary. Cheryl wasn't giving me a hard time. Nobody was asking me to juggle dynamite or shoot someone or cover up a felony. There were no psychotic drug dealers here. I had always held a romantic view of the outlaw as hero, but that view was being put to the test. Sooner or later any reasonable person will ask himself what he's gotten into, how it works with everything else in his life. It all started with the idea of having a simple good time. Partying with brothers, hanging out, building and riding bikes, and living our own version of the American dream. The club seemed to have gotten a long way from that in the blink of an eye.

I sat in my little four-foot-by-four-foot square of contentment and wondered how I missed getting shipped out to Vietnam only to wind up at home in the middle of a war. I thought about a fifteen-year-old boy who had probably never enjoyed a stiff drink, a drag race, or sex—and never would. Eventually, I had to ask myself, "How long will I last?" I told myself to cherish the moment. A month and I could be in prison. I could be dead. Cheryl could come to the end of her rope and kick me out. I squeezed the kids closer. Georgie squirmed in my grasp.

There is no halfway in the outlaw world, especially in the big piece of territory owned by the Hells Angels. I always knew that. But questions are natural. They crept in. It didn't mean you weren't committed. I was committed. God knows I would have to be to handle what was waiting right around the corner.

6

In the middle of a war, with the LACO charter in serious trouble, Ray Glore was thinking first and foremost about business. Not charter business, and not Hells Angels business. Drug business.

Cliff Mowery, the prospect who fought so well in the brawl at the Great Western Exhibit Center, had been on the scene for months. He had a reputation as a no-nonsense tough guy. He was big, almost six-four. But unlike a lot of bikers, he didn't carry a paunch. He was a lean, muscular, hard-hitting fighter. I once saw him drop a hangaround with one punch—the hardest I've ever seen thrown or taken. The other guy was out for maybe ten minutes, to the point that people started to get worried that he wasn't ever going to get up.

So nobody had a problem when Ray sponsored Cliff to prospect. What did seem odd was Cliff's girlfriend. They were attached at the hip. Everywhere he showed up, she would be with him. Prospects don't do that. Even married prospects ride alone and usually have something on the side. She was also out of his league and out of place in a clubhouse or bar. Too sophisticated, too well put together. I didn't think much of it at the time. A lot of different types of women are attracted to the bad-boy biker image, and Cliff Mowery was good-looking.

Life goes on, even in a war. California is such a big state that the charters in the north and the south often operated in different worlds. So even though the Mongols were a clubwide concern, Dago was driving the war. In November, Sonny Barger walked out of Folsom a free man, six years short of his full sentence. Key players in Oakland and Frisco were busy protecting their interests in the meth business. Solano County sheriff's inspector Bill Zerby was blown up getting into his car on the way to the courthouse for a prehearing in the meth-possession trial of Oakland Hells Angel vice president Jim Jim Brandes.

Meanwhile, in Southern California, it was common knowledge that Cliff was moving drugs for Ray. Ray had Ventura County locked up and was looking to branch out into the much-bigger meth market in Orange County. I think Ray planned on Cliff being his guy in the OC.

The postholiday lull quieted everything down. But in February, cops collared Robert "Mexican Mike" Johnson and William "Filthy Bill" Peters staking out DA investigator Ray Morgan's house. Ray Morgan had arrested and testified against a lot of Angels, and Johnson and Peters were Dago prospects. Cops searched their homes and found what they called a "hit kit." It included a map to Morgan's house, camo gear, guns, and a parabolic mike. This just proved what every Hells Angel already knew— the Dago guys would take it to any level.

The hammer fell in April 1978, when squads of cops led by the Orange County Sheriff's Department, made drug arrests throughout Southern California. The arrests were the conclusion of an undercover operation using evidence gathered by Cliff Mowery and his girlfriend, who in reality was not only his girlfriend but also an Orange County sheriff's investigator. The cops arrested Bruno, but Ray Glore was the biggest fish cuffed. Russell Beyea rode down from Oakland, picked up Kim, and took her back to Oakland with him. Several years later, Russell would be shot several times for messing around with someone else's woman. Old habits die hard.

It only took Ray a day or so to make bail, which was surprising given the list of charges, and the huge quantity of meth he had sold to the Sheriff's Department. Ray called Jesse and told him to get over to the garage and clear out the explosives and guns before any more search warrants got served. Even though the garage had been rented on the sly and there shouldn't have been a record connecting it to the club, it was a smart move.

John drove Jesse over to the garage. John waited in the car while Jesse went to check out just how much stuff would need to be moved. The minute he slipped the key into the padlock, cops swarmed him. They had been waiting, had already been inside, and knew everything that was in the garage. Jesse was busted, along with John. But John was kicked loose immediately because he was nowhere near the garage when the cops grabbed Jesse. Jesse, though, was looking at serious time. Connecting the dots, it was a reasonable conclusion that Ray had ratted him out.

That theory spread quickly. It made sense to those who knew Ray. He made bail too easily, and as sleazy as he was, nobody had trouble believing that he would flip to save his own ass. I never saw or heard any evidence that Ray had rolled on Jesse, but in hard times it's easy to believe the worst.

Ray rattled around in an empty house because Kim was now Russell's property. Ray didn't get much time to get used to the solitude. I have no idea who he thought was at the door when he heard the knocking, but it had to be someone he knew to have made it past the guard dogs that Ray kept chained up around his property. He must have been some kind of surprised when he opened the door to find Death had come to collect. A hail of bullets greeted him, done before he hit the floor.

Even on a slab, though, he gave the club one more black eye. The cops used the excuse of investigating his murder to toss his house. They uncovered detailed records of every single Hells Angel on the coast, and everyone Ray knew overseas. The cops might have worked decades to piece together this kind of information on their own. But thanks to Ray's stupidity, Christmas came early for the Orange County Sheriff's Department.

Ray's murder had a long tail. There were plenty of suspects. Rumors and detectives pinned the hit, variously, on Jesse, Russell, Tom Heath, or me. Jesse was the prime suspect in the minds of many inside and outside the club. But unlike actors in a movie, real murderers rarely discuss their crimes. I never found out who killed Ray and, truth is, I didn't care. Whoever it was, two things were for certain: it wasn't me, and the killer did the world a favor.

The problem was, law enforcement likes to close cases, especially high-profile murder investigations that smell like professional hits. That means the heat was on in Southern California in 1978 long before summer came around. Some LACO members showed signs of folding under the pressure. Guys were missing meetings, gladly paying fines so they didn't have to have their license numbers jotted down by undercover narcs staking out the clubhouse. Or they'd drive their cars to the clubhouse, park a few blocks away, and walk the rest of the way. I'd be somewhere and see a member riding without his patch. It was against the rules. You're not just a Hells Angel when the patch is getting you women and free drinks at a bar. Tough times are when Angels step up and show they can hold their mud. Something had to be done.

The frustration came to a head for me when we were asked to vote on a member transfer. Michael "Irish" O'Farrell was a tough-as-nails outlaw, ruggedly handsome with long, thick brown hair and sad, soulful eyes that made him a favorite with women. He was fast with his fists and a legendary fighter, which made him a favorite among members. At a time of chaos for LACO, he was the last person we could afford to lose. Especially since he wanted to transfer to Oakland. He was also in prison, and the club had a rule that members couldn't transfer while they were behind bars.

I was the only one to vote against the transfer, but it only takes one. Transfers have to be unanimous. The next day, I got a call from Russell Beyea. He wanted me to come up to Oakland to discuss Irish's situation. The tension between the two charters had eased as soon as Ray was murdered, and I didn't feel like I was taking a chance venturing into the heart of Oakland. So I jumped on my bike and rode up to Russell's house.

We had barely said hello and settled into his living room with a couple cups of coffee when he got down to it.

"Why are you holding up Irish?"

"Because he needs to come down and talk to us like anybody else would. He needs to give us his reasons."

"You know he's locked up. He can't be there to explain it."

"That's why you can't transfer when you're inside. You know that, Russell. Those are your rules, same as mine. He needs to talk to us about it. He needs to explain why one of the strongest members in LA wants to go to Oakland. You guys are complaining about us, but here you are drawing from us, taking all our good people. That doesn't make any sense."

Russell was quiet for a minute. Then he nodded and the slightest hint of a smile played across his face. Russell wasn't stupid, and neither was I. I was right and he knew it.

"Okay, George. I hear you. We'll play it by the rules then."

The Hells Angels is stacked with alpha males. Russell was at the head of the pack. Not many people, inside the club or out, had the balls to tell him no. But I was an alpha male too, even if I was always the most social Hells Angel in the room. I wasn't going to back down when I knew I was right. It's what made me an asset. The Angels operate between the poles of fear and respect. You give and get one or the other. I respected Russell and he knew it. But he also respected me, more so exactly because I didn't fear him. Even as it frustrated his attempt at shortcutting club rules, he respected that I wouldn't let him and the rest of Oakland run roughshod over my charter. As a sign that there were no hard feelings—and that I hadn't ridden five hours for a ten-minute conversation—Russell told me he had someone he wanted me to meet.

I knew who that someone was. Russell Beyea lived in an upscale suburban east-Oakland neighborhood that skirted a golf course, on a street called Golf Links Road. Another Hells Angel lived on that road, down at the end. His name was Sonny Barger.

Russell led the way as we rode down to Sonny's house. It was a sizable piece of property with a small white wood-framed house on it. It had a manicured lawn and well-tended flowering bushes clustered around the foundation. The only thing that set the house apart from the others on the road, the only clue that this wasn't another suburban commuter's tract house, was the tall chain-link security fence around the perimeter.

Sonny met us at the door, keeping his dogs behind him. I played it cool, but there was no getting around the fact that I was starstruck. I'm thinking, "I'm at Sonny Barger's house. I'm meeting Oakland's Sonny Barger." Ralph "Sonny" Barger had founded and built the Oakland charter when he was in his early twenties, and the Hells Angels at large were just Berdoo and Frisco. He had turned his corner of the outlaw world into a base of power almost entirely on the force of his will. Sonny had undeniable charisma. When he wanted to, he could win anybody over. He was an icon, not only of the Hells Angels, but of the entire outlaw motorcycle world. He was also a natural-born leader; even strong, independent men gravitated to him and listened when he spoke. He invited us in and we shook hands. Sonny was smaller than I expected, but built solidly from having lifted a lot of weights in Folsom prison.

He smiled and offered us a drink. "You guys are having a rough time down south."

"It's a little hot."

We all laughed.

"But I hear good things about you from the Slaves."

I found out later that Slave Louie, one of my best friends in the Slaves, had talked me up to Fu Griffin, who passed it on to Sonny. Louie had done time with Fu in Folsom, and all the Oakland members respected him. It was a powerful endorsement.

That meeting was a highlight of my time as a Hells Angel. I understood all that Sonny had accomplished, and I felt like I could learn something from him. Sonny, though, had other things on his mind. Sonny was locked in a power struggle with Sergey "Sir Gay" Walton, who had risen to become the Oakland president. Sergey was a reputed meth cook and drug supplier and was a stone gangster. A lot of people in the Bay Area relied on him for lucrative cash flow. Sonny was battling to reestablish his power in Oakland and, by extension, the entire club. He'd win, but it would take time.

After a quick and cordial talk, we said our good-byes. I headed over to Animal's place to catch up with him, then rode home in the morning. It was a long ride, but worthwhile. I knew I'd made my case. If you're going to be taken seriously in the outlaw world, you have to do the hard things, stand up for what you believe in even when the people you're standing up to are legends. Show fear to anyone in the Hells Angels, and you'll never be respected. So many members didn't understand that basic concept.

Back home, we had a lot of business to take care of inside LACO. A Hells Angels charter needs a strong leader. Without one, it's chaos, and the charter will be seen as a liability by the club at large. The sheriff's operation and Cliff Mowery's infiltration had far-reaching consequences, causing the club problems up and down California. LACO was at the center of all that, and we needed to right the ship fast. That started with leadership. The easy choice was Old Man John. Everybody knew him, he didn't have an agenda, and despite the Mongol war, he was still respected. He had been beat down by everything that had happened, but he agreed when I asked him.

"Everyone will vote for you, John. It will be good for the charter."

"I'll do it if you come along as the vice president, George. I need to know there's someone I trust backing me. You're going to have to carry the water."

The vote was quick and easy. And just like that, with a *Vice President* patch sewn to the front of my cut, I was a Hells Angels officer.

Jesse was out on bail, fighting the weapons-possession case. For safety reasons, the cops had removed the explosives from the garage before Jesse showed up. That reduced the charges considerably. It would play out over time, but ultimately the case would come down to a single count of possession of an automatic weapon. No small beef, but manageable. I took Jesse aside and gave him a soft lecture. I told him he had to lie low and keep his temper in check. If he rode it out, he'd get minimal time, and probably probation. His record was clean with no priors to complicate sentencing.

The first order of business as I saw it—with John's blessing—was to clean house. Half the charter had basically gone to ground. I understood they were scared, but that meant they had to go. You have to know what you're signing up for when you wear the patch. I didn't like cops following me night and day either. But I wasn't going to lock up every time someone knocked on the door. That kind of fear makes you a risk. A minor bust for outstanding tickets ends up with a detective's threat and a scared member talking into a tape recorder.

So we made a list of who was in and who was out. Jesse and I got on our bikes and started knocking on doors and collecting patches. House to house, we told guys they were out and took all their Hells Angels indicia—patches, rings, pins, posters, you name it. Some were ordered to black out any Death Head tattoos or we'd cut them off. The look of relief on some of the faces confirmed that we'd made the right decision.

John sent me up to my first West Coast Officers' Meeting to announce the changes. Jesse rode up with me to the Oakland clubhouse. When the order of business came around to LACO, I stood up and said, "We've made changes. We trimmed a little fat." I read from a handwritten list. So-and-so is gone, this guy is gone, that guy is gone.

The looks around the table could have been translated to "Who the fuck is this guy?" But a charter handles its own business. That's the way it is. I wasn't looking to make a statement. I just wanted to show that we were firmly in control. I didn't want to hear any more buzz about shutting down LACO or bitching about how we had fucked things up. It was also a way to establish myself as someone in the structure who wasn't afraid to take care of business. That day served many purposes.

Most of the Oakland members appreciated how I handled things, even when they disagreed with me—which was often. From that point on, I always got a warm welcome in Oakland. Although the charter's roots were blue-collar, by the late seventies Oakland had become stylish. A lot of money—legal and otherwise—was floating around in the Bay Area, and members weren't shy about spending it. A lot of guys wore boots made from exotic skins and drove brand-new Corvettes or Cadillacs with all the accessories. Their bikes were custom-painted and a world away from the thrown-together rides in the Hells Angels *Life* magazine spread from 1965. Oakland Hells Angels liked their jewelry. They rolled with gold, silver, and diamonds. Southern California style was different—more about trimming your facial hair a certain way, or wearing a trendy pair of shoes or really cool Ray-Bans—but Oakland knew style when they saw it. I liked to stand out and spent time making my bike look just as sweet as it ran.

Jesse never fit in with the Oakland crew, and it bothered me. I always brought Jesse with me and knew that he had my back no matter what. He was a true, honorable one percenter. But he was also a simple mechanic, a workingman through and through. He wore shit-kicking, worn-out black work boots and whatever shirt fell off the laundry pile that day. He was honest, loyal, and tough as they come. His bike always ran, but it looked like a workhorse. It would have ridden just as well off road. It stood out like a poor cousin parked alongside the bikes out in front of the Oakland clubhouse.

The more I interacted with the West Coast officers, and charters such as Oakland and Richmond, the more I found my legs as a leader. There were a lot of examples around of how I wanted to lead, and some of how

I didn't. I started to have a clear vision for LACO. I knew what type of guys I wanted to run with, and I knew I had what it took to ride at the front of the pack.

I was also cutting my teeth in business. All the way back to when I was an independent, I had hung out at a motorcycle shop in Ventura owned by a crusty old mechanic named Lee Stanley. A stoop-shouldered hard case, he had eyebrows like foxtails and hands stained dark from decades of grease that even Lava soap couldn't remove. I had met Lee because I had latched onto an old Indian and taken it to a shop in LA when I had a problem I couldn't figure out. They had only made it worse. Lee was an expert with Indian motorcycles, though he could fix any old scooter. He helped me out and got the bike running perfectly. We had become friends, even though he disliked outlaw bikers. As I hung out, he'd say, "Do you want to try to put these flywheels back together with me?" or "Do me a favor and mike those bearings if you're just going to sit here."

With his help, I learned how to strip down a bike and put it back together much tighter. Lee let me work on my bikes in his shop, and after I learned everything I could, I moved on. I eventually started building a parts business in Oxnard. I'd buy old Harley parts at swap meets, refurbish them, and then sell them through direct-mail ads in magazines and newspapers. The business was called Recycled Harley-Davidson, and it provided a healthy supplement to my DOD paycheck, and was a good way to indulge my love of old bikes.

Things were working out for me, but not for everyone. Four months into his second stint as president, John was done. He'd been diagnosed with cancer but kept it quiet. He couldn't handle the duties of a club officer and probably wasn't going to be able to be an active member much longer. He had never looked young, but now he looked like he had aged ten years in a matter of months. I knew what was coming when he asked me to take a walk.

"Georgie, I'm done. I can't do it no more."

"Jesus, John, it's that bad?"

"Nah, it's not the cancer. I'm too old for this shit anyway. The club's changing and it needs guys like you to lead it. I'm a dinosaur."

"Not to me you're not."

He patted my shoulder. "Next meeting, I'm telling them I want you to take over. It's a good time for it. Those guys up north like you."

"Okay, John. But I'm always going to think of you as the leader." That was a white lie. I already knew I had taken over as the leader of the charter.

The smaller group that we'd become made the vote easy. I switched my *Vice President* patch for one that said *President*.

Everything was changing fast. It felt like I had just made member, and suddenly I was president. Moriya was becoming a strong-willed ten-year-old, a short, cute, smart, tough, spunky kid who was reading two levels above her grade. I could clearly remember her bumping around the living room, barely big enough to walk three steps in a row. Georgie had begun to look like me and was growing into a rambunctious little boy who rarely smiled but had a sweetness about him that just made you want to protect him from the world. Cheryl was always distant and more so anytime I took off for a few days, but the *President* patch on the front of my vest caught her attention. She saw how members deferred to me and heard my side of a lot of phone calls. I could tell that she looked at my power as hers. The gears were turning as she tried to figure how she could use it to her advantage.

For all that, the biggest change was yet to come. I knew how the DOD felt about outlaw bikers. It was a prim and proper work environment. They tolerated my long hair, beard, and tattoos and regularly kidded me about being an "outlaw." But I didn't talk about the life, and I had no problems at work. Then the friend I rode to work with was hanging out with a few of our coworkers one day and let slip that I was a Hells Angel. He apologized to me before I even got called into the office, but it didn't matter. It would have been just a matter of time before they found out anyway.

The foreman sat behind a big tanker desk that took up most of his office. He liked me and I think he hoped what he'd heard wasn't true.

"What's going on, George? I understand you're a member of the Hells Angels?"

"That's right, I am."

"We kind of always thought that was a joke, that you were an outlaw. We didn't think it was real."

"It's real. I'm a member and an officer."

He shook his head. It simply didn't register that someone he got along with, someone friendly and social, was this terrible thing he had read about in the papers or seen reports about on the six o-clock news.

"You know you're going to get pushed out of here, right? You need to make a choice, George. The DOD won't stand for it."

I didn't have to think about it. I quit on the spot. There was no turning back. Now I was only what I was always meant to be—an outlaw, nothing more.

7

Hells Angels are independent people, and it shows in how they choose to make a living. Some drive trucks. Some build bikes. Some hire themselves out as muscle. Others start their own businesses. A fair number of Angels turn to crime. But the most common jobs among members are just about anything having to do with motorcycles—especially Harleys.

Without a DOD paycheck coming in every week, I needed to create income. The parts exchange business wasn't growing. I knew it was time for a change. So I moved my business to a shop in my garage, renaming it California Motor Works.

In the early eighties, Southern California had few high-end motorcycle speed shops. I changed my focus to engines rather than parts because the profit margin was better and custom engines were easy to sell. I became one of the early high-performance-motor builders, long before big builders such as S&S would become household names thanks to reality TV shows. I fabricated whatever I needed, experimenting constantly to get more power out of the engines. When I got it right, the motors were hot-rod power plants and I couldn't build them fast enough.

Around the same time, another business opportunity popped up in Ventura. A friend named George "Scurvy George" Aden owned Ventura

Tattoo. Scurvy George was a biker, but not affiliated. He was so short that at a stop he had to hold his bike up on his tiptoes. He was a funny guy who always rode with a handlebar bedroll even though he never went farther than from one end of Ventura to the other. He had bulky black horn-rimmed glasses and a mane of black hair greased straight back. A real character and a talented tattoo artist, he was well liked by everyone. But we called him Scurvy George because he drank a pint or more of Old Crow every day and didn't take care of himself. He ended up dying from cirrhosis, still a young man. At the funeral, his wife told me I could have the tattoo business if I wanted it. She had no desire to keep it running.

The shop had an established reputation. I took over the lease and inherited a centrifuge and a few black swivel chairs. Tom Heath was a tattoo artist by trade, and it seemed natural to partner with him. Although he wasn't the most trustworthy member in the world, he did know the business. I put up the money for equipment and ads, and Tom handled the ink.

I also sold T-shirts through a free ad in *Easyriders*. Joe Teresi owned the magazine and was a friend of the club's. Having Hells Angels ads in the magazine gave *Easyriders* authenticity in the outlaw world. I started with a shirt that had *Fuck Off* written across the chest in 100-point letters, and it became wildly popular. Sonny Barger sold *Free Sonny Barger* T-shirts the same way, to help fund his defense against criminal charges. My martial arts practice grew as I became more accomplished, and I turned that into a business as well, eventually opening a small martial arts studio and an affiliated equipment and supplies operation.

My businesses suited outlaw life. I could work day or night, leaving me free to handle club business whenever I had to. That was good, because in the summer of 1978, I had a lot of Hells Angels business to handle. Law enforcement was still putting the pressure on in the months following Ray's murder. Several agencies were monitoring Southern California charters. I came up with an idea to counteract that pressure.

The Satan's Slaves were about to patch over and become the San

Fernando Valley Hells Angels. I saw it as a golden opportunity. Cops can't tell one Hells Angel from another unless they know the rider. Police at the time used Field Interrogation Cards for traffic stops. They'd write down your name, nickname, license plate, club affiliation, and identifying features—such as distinctive patches on your cut or tattoos. The notes were kept on three-by-five index cards in pen. They would be copied and used as mini-files all street cops could carry and reference. It gave local law enforcement a way to tell at a glance who was riding where. If I moved the charter from Glendale to Ventura, I'd screw up the system. Cops who stopped SFV members that they thought were LACO Hells Angels would be talking to somebody who had nothing to do with Ray Glore or the Mongols. LACO would get a fresh start far away from those Field Interrogation Cards.

After I made the decision, I set up a meeting with the remaining Question Marks. Jesse and I rode down to Ventura in a sign of respect to old friends. When a new Hells Angels charter opens, the standard protocol is to clear out any other clubs in the area. One way or another. I wasn't about to do that to the Question Marks. But they had done it themselves. There were only four members in the Question Marks' sad little clubhouse when I stood up to speak.

"Look, here's what's going on. You probably heard that the Slaves are becoming Hells Angels. I want you guys to become Angels too. We're moving LACO to Ventura. We want you to join. If not, we're not going to shut you down. Stay like you are, that's fine."

David Ortega would be the only one who could get it together enough to prospect for Ventura. It was a bittersweet pill for David, one that he would never entirely swallow. David had been a core member of an established and respected one-percenter club when I was just an independent. Now, not only was he starting all over as a Hells Angels prospect, even when he patched in, he'd always answer to me in the chain of command. David was one of my closest friends and a true brother, but because of the way things worked out, it would always be a love-hate relationship.

We had already rented Lee Stanley's old shop on Fix Way in Ventura when I rode up to announce the move at the monthly officers' meeting. It nearly came to blows. Old-guard veterans were beside themselves.

"You can't change your fucking name."

"We already have. There were too many negatives associated with LACO. It's a done deal. We're Ventura now."

In hindsight, it was a ballsy move. We were struggling to maintain the six-member minimum necessary to qualify as a charter. The rule regarding the charter size has been around for a long time and is important to the club. In the outlaw world, numbers equal strength. The more members a charter has, the more powerful it is inside and outside the club. Charters are also recruiting centers. Members bring in hangarounds and prospects. With too few members, the charter has no profile and starts to look less than legitimate. It shines badly on the Hells Angels at large. Outlaw territory being what it is, there is usually another charter in the region that can absorb an undersize charter's members. So the club would have been within their rights to shut us down. Even with Richmond and Daly City on our side, there was no predicting how Frisco, San Jose, Dago, and Berdoo might vote. But I survived the meeting. Now I was president of a brand-new charter that I could build the way I envisioned.

As the head of a small charter, you have hands-on responsibility for everything. Presidents of big heritage charters like Oakland and Frisco are political players who coordinate—they tell people what to do. I was a working president. I knew I had to be ready to take care of business, to get my hands dirty. It didn't take long to be put to the test.

There's no way to accurately describe how important a Hells Angel Death Head patch is to a member. It's everything. Your whole identity is wrapped up in this little bit of dyed cotton stitched to leather or denim. The patch trumps your motorcycle, your house, and your possessions. In many ways and circumstances, it comes before your family. It is a bright red-and-white mark of what you stand for, the good and the bad. A Hells Angels patch is carte blanche, a ticket to privilege, women, money, and status. It opens doors. It commands respect. But you're an idiot if you don't understand it's also a bright target for law enforcement and other clubs. Because of all that, there is no bigger sin than to disrespect the patch. You don't touch another man's patch. You don't misplace your own. But even more of a crime, potentially a capital offense, is to wear a false patch.

Just as the Ventura charter was settling in, we got word of a bogus Death Head. A woman from San Francisco had been visiting friends and partying in San Fernando Valley. She met a guy who said he was a Hells Angel, but wasn't wearing his cut. Instead, he had it draped over his arm, something she knew no Angel would do. He was moving coke and pills at the party, and the girl got the sense that he was more drug dealer than outlaw. Unfortunately for him, she knew a lot of Angels in the Bay Area and knew how they carried themselves. When she got home, she headed to a local bar and clued in several members who were there. She told him this guy just smelled wrong, too showy and full of shit. We got a call from the Bay Area, asking us to check into it.

We put out feelers in the Valley and had people ask around at bars and parties. It wasn't long before we found out who this guy was. We quickly put together solid intel including his name, address, and the license numbers of his car and motorcycles. We knew everything except where the bogus patch was.

Two Angels from the Bay Area came down as backup. Although Jesse still had a pending case and should have kept his head down, there was no one that I trusted more. So he and I went out in two cars with the Bay Area members and prowled the Valley bars the drug dealer frequented. At around six in the evening, we drove by a bar and made his license plate. I used a slim jim to break into the dumpy brown Ford four-door. I lay down across the backseat footwell and put a blanket over me. I had brought a .22, with the serial numbers filed down and a homemade silencer screwed to the barrel. I waited for about an hour, but what seemed like ten days sweating under the wool blanket. Then boots crunched across the gravel parking lot coming toward the car. The drug dealer opened the door and slid into the driver's seat. Someone else plunked down into the passenger seat. As soon as the doors slammed shut, I pulled myself up and shoved the business end of the silencer up against the back of the driver's head.

The passenger turned, saw the gun, and stiffened in shock. "Oh my God." He recognized me. He was a member of the Devil's Disciples, a small second-tier one-percenter club. He said, "Hey, man, I'm just going to get out."

I shook my head. "You know I can't let you out."

"I swear I won't say anything."

"You know better than that. Put your hands on the dash where I can see them."

The passenger did what I told him to do, and I pushed on the gun.

"Now you, asshole. Put your hands on the wheel, at two and ten." I reached around and frisked the dealer for a weapon. "I came here to get the patch. Just take me to the patch and that's all I want."

But the driver wanted to play. "I don't know what you're talking about, man."

The outlaw world has a lot of lowlifes, and it always amazed me that they couldn't do simple math. Trying to bullshit a Hells Angel who's found his way to your backseat and is holding a silenced semiauto behind your ear is a whole new level of stupid.

"You don't know what I'm talking about? Okay, motherfucker, let's go. Start the car."

He fired up the engine. "Where are we going?"

"I'll tell you where." I guided him to a quiet side street a couple blocks away. The guys in the two cars followed us. We transferred our two prisoners to the car Jesse was driving, handcuffing them and putting the drug dealer in the front passenger seat, and his friend in the backseat behind Jesse. One of the Bay Area Angels took my gun and slid into the backseat, right behind the drug dealer. The other Angel and I got into the follow car.

We headed onto I-5 and started climbing the grapevine, the stretch of freeway that rises into the mountains right past Fort Tejon. We took a minor exit and started driving east, out into the desert, on a lonely two-lane road. I was following Jesse at a discreet distance when a Highway Patrol cruiser pulled in behind him and lit him up. I wasn't sure what we were going to do. I found out later that the Angel in the backseat told the two prisoners, "If you say one word, I'm going to shoot that cop right in the face, and I'm going to shoot you both in the head. Then we're going to torch the car and leave it here."

It was the late seventies and cop cruisers weren't computerized. This cop pulled over four dangerous-looking guys on a dark, deserted road. It wouldn't have taken a genius to see that something was going down. If the cop had any sense, he understood that he was the one risking the most.

"Where you guys headed?"

"Just going to see some friends."

Jesse didn't offer his license. The other three didn't even look in the cop's direction, and they all had jackets over their laps, covering their hands. It couldn't have looked any worse to this cop. He hesitated for half a minute, then told Jesse he was free to go. Jesse later told me, "That cop knew something was going on, but he didn't want no part of it."

We kept driving, out almost thirty miles. We didn't even know where we were, just deep in the desert. The sun was going down when we drove off the road about a half mile out into the sand. Everyone got out. The air smelled fresher and cleaner than it did in the Valley. It was still a little warm from the day. It was quiet enough to hear the click as one of the Bay Area guys uncuffed the drug dealer. Jesse got a shovel out of the trunk and threw it at the dealer's feet.

"Start digging."

I expected the guy to crumble and spill his guts. Instead, the moron picked up the shovel and started digging his own grave.

The ringing slice of a shovel edge cutting into desert sand has got be one of the loneliest sounds on earth. All of us were lost in our thoughts. I was facing up to what I was going to have to do. Hells Angels don't bluff. This was the ugly part to being committed—you carried things as far as they needed to go. But killing somebody in the middle of the desert is a clear line, and it's a line that you don't step back over. In a way, I felt as trapped as that idiot with the shovel.

He kept at it until he had carved out a crude depression roughly big enough for his body, and about a foot and a half deep.

"Okay, that's enough. Now dig the second one."

The Devil's Disciple snapped to attention. "Wait a minute. You said I was coming back with you."

"Sorry, man. I can't bring you back. You know that. But if it's any consolation, he's going to dig the hole for you. Just relax and enjoy the sunset. It's the last one either of you is going to see."

The drug dealer drove the shovel into the sand next to the first hole, paused, then finally broke down. He started shaking and sobbing. "What would you do if I told you I had the patch?"

Jesse and I exchanged looks.

"Well, what we'd do is we'd head back and get the patch. Then you'd have to pay a tax. But you goddamn well better stop wasting our time. Do you have the patch or not?"

The dealer looked down into the hole he had just dug. "I've got it at my house."

We put the two back in the car and drove back to the Valley. The drug dealer directed Jesse to his house and I followed. We stopped at an unlit corner about a block away. I told the Devil's Disciple to get out. As soon as he opened the door, I grabbed his arm.

"You know I'll come for you if I ever hear anything about this, right? I wouldn't run my mouth."

"You'll never hear a word, I swear." He looked as happy as I've ever seen someone look.

We parked both cars and followed the drug dealer in through the front door of a crappy little ranch house. I made sure I was close enough that he couldn't grab a stashed gun. I held the .22 on him as he rummaged around in his closet and pulled out the fake patch. He presented it to me like a gift. Like that was going to make it all right.

That's not how the Angels do things. One of the Bay Area guys was packing a Taser. He was so pissed off when he saw how much effort had gone into this fake patch, how detailed and convincing it was, that he tased the dealer. The guy let out a high-pitched squeal, dropped to the floor, and started flopping around like a fish out of water. We pulled out the Taser probes none too gently. The guy with the Taser was right back in the dealer's face, threatening him with another zap.

"What else you got here?"

This is the outlaw way. When the situation warrants taking anything, you take everything. We didn't just tax him, we cleaned this guy out. He had $30,000 in cash hidden around the house, and we found two kilos of high-quality coke in a false compartment under his sink. We took all his jewelry—rings, watches, bracelets, and chains. We even found a couple of handguns. It was a memorable haul. Two hours later, the four of us sat at a table in the back of the best restaurant in Ventura, enjoying steak and lobster. We cut lines of coke with a steak knife on the bottom of an upside-down saucer.

Ultimately, we sent half the drugs and money back up to the Bay Area and threw all the jewelry on the bar in the Ventura clubhouse. Members could take whatever they wanted. I wasn't a jewelry guy, so I didn't take any of it. Unexpected bounty is great, but for me, the real reward was that I wasn't forced to shoot two men on a cold desert night. I had felt cornered with no options. I was relieved, but it also made clear to me that I wasn't cool with casual killing. I didn't mind if it stood for something, but killing for stupidity didn't sit well with me. It was the first time I realized that I was meant to be a peacemaker, not an assassin. That set me apart from many Hells Angels. It was an identity I would come to embrace, at no small cost.

8

Hosting runs and parties is a way for a new charter to establish credibility and for the charter's leadership to develop power and influence. The bigger and better the party, the more locked down you are in the eyes of the club. For charters such as Oakland and Frisco, putting together a wild New Year's Eve party or a run to Colorado is business as usual. But I knew that a successful large run could be Ventura's coming-out party, as long as it was a party to remember.

In the summer of 1978, Ventura organized a run to McGrath State Beach in Oxnard. McGrath is a lush strip of watershed along the Pacific Ocean just ten miles south of Ventura. The park has spectacular campgrounds and water wherever you look. The Santa Clara River feeds into one end, and there's not a bad seat in the house.

McGrath was ideal because it was secluded enough to ensure privacy, but located near enough to Highway 1 for easy access from everywhere. Hundreds of bikers rode in, including members from every Hells Angels charter in California and several from out of state. Along with the drinking, drugs, sex, music, friendly fistfights, and exhibitions of bike-riding skills, there was a lot of talk around the bonfire. Most of the buzz was about the Mongols war. But there was also a lot of discussion about the older war with the Outlaws.

In 1969, Sandy Alexander was a New York City outlaw, president of the Aliens motorcycle club. He rode to Oakland to make his case for the Aliens patching over into a new Hells Angels charter. Alexander told me that while he was away, fellow Alien Peter "Greased Lightning" Rogers had taken liberties with Alexander's wife. Rogers took off to Florida before Sandy got back, and Sandy understandably swore revenge. His chance came in 1974, when Rogers—now wearing an Outlaws patch—returned to New York City to visit friends. Sandy heard through the grapevine that Rogers was in town and tracked him down. He beat the Outlaw to the doorstep of death.

Rogers slunk home and told the Outlaws that he had gotten rat-packed by the entire New York charter. His injuries were severe enough to make the lie credible. The Outlaws took their revenge when two Lowell, Massachusetts, Hells Angels—Edwin "Riverboat" Riley and George "Whiskey George" Hartman—visited an ex–Hells Angel in Florida to check that the former member had blacked out his club tattoos. The three were lured into an Outlaw bar under the pretense of a friendly drink between respected clubs. The Angels were beaten, tied up, driven to a quarry, and executed. Within a year, Outlaw Jim "Big Jim" Nolan was on the run with several other club officers, being chased by law enforcement and angry Hells Angels.

The talk at McGrath focused on how both wars started over women, two wars that didn't look like they would ever end. In the outlaw world then, there was no such thing as a peacemaker. One killing led inevitably to another. Truces were painfully rare and amazingly fragile. The conversations around the bonfire put a lot of ideas into my head as the run wrapped up.

The run was exactly what the charter needed. The only black mark had been, as usual, the cops. Several agencies joined forces to harass anyone on a motorcycle within twenty miles. You couldn't find a patch-wearer who hadn't been pulled over at least once on the long two-lane highway that led to the park. The cops took their time, detaining club members on the side of the road for an hour or more, under the pretense of license plates mounted incorrectly and other nonsense. I lost count of how many different badges were staking out the park. It was absurd and annoying.

On his way back to Oakland, Sonny Barger got pulled over. Sonny had a temper and never backed down. Because it was yet another bullshit stop in a weekend of them, and a completely trumped-up charge, he refused to sign the ticket. The cop arrested him and took him to Ventura's jail. Oakland legend Cisco Valderrama and I headed back to Ventura to arrange for Sonny's bond. We met with the bondsman, arranged bail, and waited for Sonny to be processed out. We drank coffee in a diner across from the jail and made small talk. Out of the blue, Cisco dropped a bomb on me.

"You ever thought about coming up to the Bay Area?"

I took a minute because what he was saying was a huge compliment. They only wanted the best of the best in Oakland.

"Look, Cisco, I want to be a Hells Angel like you. Like Sonny and Angelo. I think we need Angels like that down here. I think I can be that Hells Angel for Ventura."

It was exactly what I felt. Southern California needed to assert itself. We needed to carve out our own identity. After all, we were the home of Berdoo, the charter that started it all. We needed to remember that. Cisco nodded his big head, wearing his signature shades over his Fu Manchu mustache.

"Well, you know you got a home if you ever want to come up there."

"Thanks, Cisco. I appreciate it, man."

The run and that talk left me with a lot to consider. Everything was made a little more complicated by a fascinating bit of information that came to me through a back channel a week after the run. I had contacts in the Dirty Dozen, a one-percenter club in Arizona that would eventually patch over to become Hells Angels. They gave me the address where

Big Jim Nolan was hiding out in Arizona. It was an easy opportunity to up Ventura's profile and serve the club in a big way. I could make a difference and possibly end a long war. There was no telling how long the address would be valid. I had to jump at the chance or let it go.

Two days later, I packed my car with a black nylon travel bag and a scope-equipped M14, an all-purpose sniper rifle. I drove to Phoenix, Arizona. It took me forever to find the neighborhood. When I got there, I discovered a sad little corner of the suburban world, a failed subdivision in the middle of nowhere. Half the houses were empty, with sun-faded FOR SALE signs stuck in the middle of overgrown, weed-infested front lawns. Most of the houses needed paint, with a few broken windows and fewer signs of life. Except at the address I'd been given.

It was so clearly a biker hangout that I almost had to laugh. Biker houses often look just like biker clubhouses. This one was no different. The plain, single-level tract house had a split-rail fence around a scabby front yard. The lawn was just patches of baked dirt and weeds. The house was a faded lime green with dirty white trim, and the garage stuck out in front like a chin waiting to be hit. The driveway was cracked, and an old, dust-encrusted black Cadillac limousine was parked at an angle across the sidewalk. Harleys clustered in the street and the driveway, stuck in wherever there was space, leaning on their kickstands at weird angles to one another. Beer cans littered the gutter.

It was about eight in the morning. The sun was already up and blazing, but it wasn't uncomfortably hot yet. I cruised slowly away from the lime-green house, down a street perpendicular to it. I found an empty house about a hundred yards down, with a clear line of sight to the biker house. I parked and got out, looked around, and grabbed the rifle from the trunk. I wrapped it in a blanket and took it with me around behind the empty house. I found an old garbage can and used it to climb up on the roof.

From the roof ridge, I had a clear view to the front door on the biker house. I unwrapped the M14 carefully and spread the blanket over the asphalt shingles. I laid the rifle on the blanket. The metal of the barrel and magazine, and the stock's wood, were all still cool to the touch. I lay on my belly and settled in for the wait.

I'd quit smoking right after I got out of the Marines, so I had nothing to do but think and keep an eye on the house. As I watched, a skinny kid with tattoos on his forearms came out through the garage, shirtless and barefoot. His pants were unbuckled. He had a cigarette in his mouth, which he lit with a silver Zippo. He unzipped his pants and took a piss right alongside the driveway. He zipped up, stretched, and went back in through the garage.

Something was bothering me. Something about all this was incredibly familiar. The house, the kid, the car, the bikes. Then it dawned on me. These guys, they were us. This was a one-percenter house, and it looked like every other one-percenter house. Like Animal's house, and Slave Louie's house. Like Jesse's house. Everybody in that house was proud of the patch on his cut. Every one of them loved the bike he had parked outside. This could just as easily have been a house full of Angels or Mongols or Vagos or Pagans. I had an epiphany. These guys weren't the enemy. Why would I kill them? If I had grown up in the Midwest, I'd be wearing their patch. If the guys in that house had been born in Encino or Los Angeles, there was a good chance they'd be flying the Death Head. We were the same.

I realized we had a common enemy. An enemy that couldn't stand the idea of a bunch of bikers gathering for a run, to do their own thing, bothering nobody else. An enemy that had no problem perverting the law they were sworn to uphold, anytime it came to jacking up a rider with a patch. Law enforcement was the enemy of every one percenter. And always will be. And I was there doing the enemy's work. Hell, if law enforcement had known what I was up to, they wouldn't even have arrested me until I was done.

I understood all this. I slowly realized that I was not going to put a 7.62x51 round in Big Jim. It made no sense. I wasn't going to do law enforcement's job. I just wasn't.

The decision I made on the roof of a dilapidated tract house in some Arizona backwater was the starting point for diplomacy rare in club life. It would be my mark on the Angels and on the one-percenter world. I didn't realize it right then as I bundled up the M14, climbed down from the roof, and quietly drove away. But that decision set the tone for my leadership and my role in the Hells Angels going forward. Sonny was the figurehead. Irish was the brawler. Animal was the crazy one. I would be the peacemaker. And it would cause me no end to grief and trouble.

The word *diplomacy* wasn't in Jesse's dictionary. On a cold night in November 1980, Jesse did what Jesse was built to do. He fought. He got into it with some drunk in a bar in Oak View. He beat the guy to a pulp and bit his ear off for good measure. Jesse was arrested for mayhem, which is assault with great bodily injury. It may sound like an odd charge, but mayhem is taken seriously by the legal system. It can buy you eight years.

After his weapons possession case wound its way through the system, it proved a weak rap to prosecute. It would have smelled a lot like entrapment to any reasonable judge. Jesse agreed to a single-charge guilty plea and probation. Now, with the mayhem charge, he could be violated on the earlier beef and would end up doing time for both.

We tapped the club's defense fund for Jesse's bail, and I called a bondsman to arrange Jesse's release. Tom Heath volunteered to pick Jesse up at the jail. Tom would be one of the last people to see Jesse alive. I never asked Tom where he took Jesse or what he knew about Jesse's death. Those are questions you don't ask in the outlaw world.

December 5, 1980, was a beautiful Friday in Southern California. A retired superior court judge took his grandson out for a horseback ride in the Santa Barbara foothills. The ride wound past precise rows of strung-up grape canes that would fill out with wine grapes in a few months. The pair guided their horses slowly across the rolling, chaparral-covered slopes at the base of the Santa Ynez Mountains, into a shallow canyon. They came to a dry arroyo, and the judge's horse, in the lead, nearly stumbled on a body that looked like a rag doll that had been tossed aside.

Jesse.

He had been beaten and strangled. Two Santa Barbara homicide detectives showed up at the clubhouse to tell me that Jesse was dead. It was the starting point of their investigation. They'd already decided the killer or killers was someone from the charter. That's basic math. These guys were not happy because their captain was not happy. The captain was not happy because a retired judge was downright furious that his grandson has been subjected to the horrible sight of a dead biker polluting their pristine riding trail. Shit rolls downhill. Before Jesse's body made it from the morgue to the funeral home, everybody in the charter had been questioned. We didn't give the detectives a full sentence to write in their spiral flip notebooks. They could go fuck themselves.

But the lead detective was a clever guy. He did an end around and called Sonny, under the assumption that Sonny would know anything going on in the club anywhere. He was wrong. Sonny didn't know shit about Jesse. They had met maybe once. The detective hit pay dirt just the same.

Smart outlaws learn to answer law enforcement investigators with one of two replies: "Fuck you, I don't talk to cops" or "Call my lawyer." Sonny though, he hated cops with a passion. He couldn't stop himself from giving them shit. The detective asks him, "Did Craig Kuhn have any enemies in the Hells Angels?"

"Why is every time we get rid of some shitbag out of the club, and he winds up dead, you motherfuckers start knocking on our doors? Go fuck yourself."

The detective hung up hearing slot-machine bells. He beelined for a judge and got a warrant based on the fact that any member expelled from the club would be considered a liability and a target. Meanwhile, I answered the clubhouse phone, surprised to hear the man I call Ralph on the other end of the line. Sonny didn't call people. People called Sonny.

"I think I fucked up."

"What do you mean?"

He told me what he had said to the detective. Sonny was smart enough to know that he had given the detective the basis for a warrant. But what could I say to him? This was Sonny Barger. If he screwed up, you didn't give him shit about it. We both knew what was coming, though.

Two days later, I was at the clubhouse with Cheryl, Moriya, and Georgie. David Ortega was there too, with his latest hangaround honey. The clubhouse had a workshop in the back where an entire bike could be taken apart and put back together. I was tinkering with the rocker arms on an old panhead, talking to Moriya. She was perched on a steel work stool while Georgie played with a cluster of valve springs on the floor. My morning tea was just getting cool enough to drink. I took a sip and looked out the window. A caravan of cops was hauling ass down Fix Way. I sprinted into the front room, where the locked security door was buzzer-activated. The cops were already pounding on the door. The girl who had been hanging out with David was headed for the buzzer.

"Don't let them in."

She ignored me and buzzed the door lock open. Santa Barbara sheriffs poured into the clubhouse. Ventura cops stayed outside as observers because it was technically their jurisdiction. The sheriffs wore flak jackets and riot gear. They carried automatic weapons and waved them around like it was a war zone. They were way too amped. They hustled us outside into the bright morning sunlight, heat waves shimmering off the blacktop of the clubhouse parking lot. The crackle of police radios filled the air. The sheriffs ordered us to spread-eagle against the clubhouse wall, kids included. This was a violation of two unwritten codes—the Angels' and the cops'. I prided myself on keeping my head in tense situations, but I was about to boil over and do something stupid. Two of these assholes had automatic weapons trained on my children. Fortunately, one of the sheriffs still had an ounce of humanity. I heard him tell the others, "This is too much." He took the kids by the hands and led them out to the Ventura cops, where Sergeant Carl Handy collected them and comforted them. He knew Moriya and Georgie and, more important, they knew him.

The lead detective took me inside to execute the actual search. The warrant listed all kinds of documents that might be linked to Jesse's murder: meeting notes, disciplinary reports, written orders, even photos that had been marked up or scratched out. The Ventura cops had made clear to the Santa Barbara guys to be respectful. Ventura police had to deal with us daily, and they didn't want blowback. The search turned up nothing, except for four Valiums I had in a toolbox. The lead detective ignored them. He wasn't there for a misdemeanor drug bust that probably wouldn't have been supported under the terms of the warrant anyway.

The harassment didn't stop there. I came out of my house in the morning two days later to find two sheriffs with my trash spread out on a blue painter's tarp, in the middle of my driveway. Trash was a plain-view exception to the Fourth Amendment, so they had the right to search it without a warrant. It made me glad that we threw the dog's shit in the trash can. In the end, after months of no-cause traffic stops, blatant and intrusive surveillance, and general harassment, the sheriffs had plenty of suspects, but not one bit of evidence. The last I heard of the investigation was a call from the lead detective.

"Look, I don't know what you got going on down there, and I don't know how you got this much influence around Ventura, but nobody's talking to us. So hats off to you, George. But I got something to tell you, and I want you to listen real close. Don't dump your trash in Santa Barbara. You tell all those assholes in your gang, they find somewhere else to do their littering. Do we understand each other?"

"Yeah, I think I understand what you're saying."

"Now you can go pop a couple of those Valiums, and we'll go our separate ways. As far as I'm concerned, the investigation is closed."

Jesse's murder had all the signs of an internal hit. There was a lot of suspicion to go around. Whenever someone didn't do the time he should be doing for a crime or was staring down the barrel of a long jail term, members got concerned that he might roll to go free. It was a legitimate fear; a lot of rats had done just that. George Wethern, an Oakland member in the sixties and seventies, had done just that and tried to pin multiple murders on Sonny before George and his wife disappeared into the Witness Protection Program. I knew beyond a shadow of a doubt that Jesse would never have cooperated. But other members didn't know him as well as I did. He never fit in up in Oakland. I believe the mayhem charge caused somebody to worry that eight years behind bars was enough to make Jesse talk. He knew a lot about what had gone on in the Mongol war and could have told a lot of interesting tales. I think somebody took steps to head off that possibility.

Craig "Jesse" Kuhn left behind a widow and a young son. He also left behind friends like me who understood that Jesse was a true, stand-up guy. He embraced the best of what outlaws represent—rebelling against an overbearing conformist culture and overreaching government, choosing your own path regardless of where it takes you or how hard that path might be, and living your life true to your own values and definition of honor. I was proud to call Jesse "friend," and I can think of no man I'd rather have had backing me up in a pinch.

His murder was a blow. No charter likes to lose members, especially in such a gruesome fashion. But it's a special kind of pain when it's a close friend. He was the first Hells Angels brother I lost to a violent end, but far from the last. I'd be reminded of his unsolved murder many times as law enforcement continued its dogged persecution of outlaw bikers in general, and the Hells Angels in particular.

9

Law enforcement can be like a dog with a bone. They obsess on a target and can make things very personal. If somebody in power gets it into his head that the Hells Angels or George Christie is a criminal menace, he's not necessarily interested in whether he is right or wrong. These type A personalities make up their minds and don't look back. Indictment and prosecution are the endgame. Cops and prosecutors often ignore inconvenient facts that don't line up with a case. Career advancement hinges on high-profile investigations and busts, even if those arrests don't result in convictions. I'm biased, but I don't believe the word *justice* gets mentioned much, if at all, inside the offices of the DEA, ATF, FBI, or any other alphabet agency. In my experience, decency and fairness are much rarer qualities within law enforcement than they are in "outlaw" motorcycle clubs. Law enforcement gets away with things outlaws would not tolerate other outlaws doing.

When I first started riding motorcycles, we had relationships with local cops. There were lines. Cops didn't plant evidence. Club members didn't assault cops. If they chased you and you got away, you won that round. But when the feds decided the Hells Angels, Vagos, Bandidos, Mongols, and Outlaws were the next big threat to society, all that changed.

Starting in the late seventies, the new rules of engagement were clear. By the early eighties they were standard operating procedure.

Local cops might harass you, but they had regular calls to handle. No local force could focus all its time and attention on stalking outlaws. The feds, though, had bigger budgets and more time on their hands. Ambitious feds could make what they called OMGs (outlaw motorcycle gangs) their specialty. Federal agencies formed task forces. The more turmoil they churned up, the more arrests they made, the more money they got. Funding relied on finding wrongdoing whether it was there to find or not. In the two years prior to the 1984 Olympics in Los Angeles, the Bureau of Alcohol, Tobacco, and Firearms (ATF) decided that the Hells Angels were a threat to public safety in general and the Olympics in particular—a threat that needed to be neutralized.

Ventura is a city, but a lot like a small town. It's what I've always loved about the place. There's a charming downtown with a main drag, and beautiful beach where anyone can fish from the grayed deck of the longest wooden pier in the country. The neighborhoods are real neighborhoods, where people watch out for one another and gossip makes the rounds at the speed of sound. News travels fast in Ventura.

That's how I found out that federal agents were visiting local merchants, spreading propaganda and soliciting information on the Ventura charter. They were painting the club as an imminent terrorist threat to the Olympics, and a menace to local citizens. Ironically, those same merchants knew what clubhouse neighbors know around the country—a Hells Angels charter keeps crime away. Somebody starts robbing local businesses, stealing cars, or vandalizing buildings, any local charter will deal with the problem even before the cops do. And pity that criminal. Every Hells Angel wants his home turf to be calm, quiet, and law-abiding.

So not only was the federal heat misguided and irritating, it was insulting. I decided to do some checking of my own. Outlaw motorcycle clubs often use private detectives. Most big charters and club officers have relationships with PIs, and a good one can be incredibly useful. They

are usually ex–law enforcement themselves and can quickly check out
prospective members, unearth law enforcement motives and investigations,
and uncover supporting evidence for criminal trials. I had my private
detective look into who these guys were, and why they were in Ventura.
My guy was an ex-FBI agent who had worked organized crime. He came
back with some bad news.

"They're ATF, George, be careful. They're dangerous. They're the
Greensboro boys."

I knew what he was saying. In 1979, an ATF agent named Bernard
Butkovich had infiltrated the Greensboro, North Carolina, chapter of
the American Nazi Party. The Ku Klux Klan had joined forces with the
Nazis to confront anti-Klan demonstrators at a Communist Party rally.
As the situation exploded, the heavily armed Klan members and Nazis
overpowered the demonstrators with handgun and rifle fire. Five demonstrators were killed. Mysteriously, no police were present at the rally.
A member of the Nazi Party would later testify that Butkovich had urged
the members to arm themselves and be aggressive in confronting the
demonstrators. It seemed to me that the ATF unit that ran that operation played by their own rules and were reckless about the consequences
of their actions.

That made the ATF topic number one at a bar in the Valley, where a
small group of Angels from Ventura, Berdoo, and the Valley gathered to
have a few drinks. All the Southern California charters were being harassed by the ATF. There was also a lot of talk about the documentary
called *Hells Angels Forever,* which was just about to be released. Sonny
Barger and Sandy Alexander had worked with a couple of Hollywood
producers on the film and had producing credits. Angels coast-to-coast
had appeared in the film. I was tapped to do press for the film, and the
prerelease buzz was fantastic. I was learning how to frame the club as a
bunch of good guys who held freedom dear and just wanted to live life
their way. I was figuring out how to craft an appealing message for the
media and the public. I thought we could use those lessons to push back

against the feds. The Hells Angels normally kept a low profile in the face of law-enforcement pressure. Doing the opposite would surprise everyone and could be incredibly effective if done right. We needed to go with the "Hells Angels love America more than anybody" angle. That idea ran throughout *Hells Angels Forever*. We had always been patriots. Many of us were veterans. But most citizens didn't know that. It would be a great peg to hang our hats on.

Harlan "Tiny" Brower had been a Satan's Slave before becoming a San Fernando Valley Hells Angel. We were friends, and he and I thought a lot alike. Sitting there in that bar, we came up with the idea that someone from the club could run a leg of the Olympic torch relay. I had read that you could buy a one-kilometer section of the torch run and sponsor a runner for $3,000.

"Tiny, I think that's it. They want to make us the bad guys of the Olympics, we'll be the heroes. Let's see how they like that."

We took the idea to the next West Coast Officers' Meeting. There was more resistance than I'd anticipated. Sonny had been diagnosed with advanced throat cancer in 1982. Doctors had removed his voice box, and he hadn't yet got comfortable talking with the handheld device they'd given him (he'd eventually be fitted with a patch over the hole in his throat, which he would press on to talk). Irish had taken over as Oakland's president. In Sonny's absence, a lot of factions pushed and pulled on any issue. The Hells Angels is made up of a lot of strong personalities with many different points of view. It makes putting even simple proposals up for a vote an adventure. As soon as I had finished explaining what we wanted to do and why, guys were blurting out objections.

"Fuck the feds and fuck the Olympics."

"Who cares what citizens think?"

"We're not a fucking charity."

It seemed so straightforward to me. But some guys would oppose anything on the table.

"No, look, this is going to be a problem for us. We got to get out in front of this."

I managed to get the proposal passed. Then we were faced with the question of who was going to do the actual running. There were a lot of big guys and big bellies around the table. Most Hells Angels are built for fighting and riding: long legs, big chests, thick bodies that are heavy and solid. They all looked at me. I was lean. Everybody knew I was a runner and a martial artist.

Robert Poulin said what they were all thinking. "You're going to do it, George. You're the only one in shape enough to get out of his own way."

We agreed that the $3,000 application fee would be divided among the members countrywide. Everyone would kick in, but it was such a small amount per man that nobody could complain.

The next step was getting the application by the Olympics Torch Foundation. The line on the form for the sponsor's name was short. *Hells Angels Motorcycle Club, United States* wouldn't fit. So I wrote our common abbreviation for legal documents: *H.A.M.C.U.S.* The same thing happened when I went to the bank to get a cashier's check for the application. We weren't trying to deceive anybody, but it wound up creating a funny scene in the Torch Foundation's committee meeting.

Claire Spiegel was a reporter for the *LA Times*. She was always balanced in her reporting on the club, but she knew a good story when she had one. The torch run applications weren't prescreened, so Claire went to Torch Foundation official Steve Montiel and asked him if he knew what H.A.M.C.U.S. stood for. I'm sure he thought it was just another corporate acronym. She spelled it out for him and put him in a no-win position. If he rejected the application, there would be a firestorm about why. If he approved it, he was green-lighting the Hells Angels' participation in maybe the highest-profile Olympic ritual. After an hour of deliberation, he gave Claire a statement: "Anyone contributing $3,000 to a youth organization and agreeing to conform to our regulations can participate in the torch relay." The Angels were in.

I knew we'd get some press, but I had no idea of the frenzy the application would touch off. Within days, Claire Spiegel's articles got picked up on the newswires, and reporters started ringing my home phone off the hook. Cheryl wasn't happy about it. She didn't like the attention I was getting and wasn't about to act like my press secretary.

"I'm not answering that phone one more time. If you're not here to answer it, I'm not picking it up."

We didn't have an answering machine. So we distributed the Ventura clubhouse phone number as the main press contact. Reporters started calling from as far away as Australia. I had prospects man the clubhouse phone twenty-four hours a day, fielding interview requests.

Irish was spending a lot of time in Ventura and enjoying the chaos. After I had voted against his transfer, Irish had been forced to come down when he got out of prison and explain why he wanted to transfer to Oakland. He respected that I stuck to the code. I ended up voting for the transfer and we became tighter than ever. He would always be held in high esteem in Southern California, and he was a close brother. So, by the time the torch run rolled around, Irish was the obvious choice as wingman.

I put on my white running shorts and T-shirt underneath my street clothes. Cheryl perched on the back fender of my bike and we rode to the clubhouse. It was pandemonium. Fix Way is a short street. The cops had both ends blocked off. Only patch-wearing members and reporters with press credentials got through. Hells Angels from all over the world were going to ride with me to the torch run site. The inside of the clubhouse was off-limits to anyone but members, so that we could have a little sanctuary from the crowd. Cheryl headed inside and stayed there, holding court among the other members' women.

The torch run was originally planned for Main Street in downtown Ventura, but officials decided that the crowds would be too much for the town. At the last minute, they moved the site to the two-lane Las Posas

Road, a desolate stretch that cuts through the bean fields between Camarillo and Point Mugu Naval Air Station. As we closed in on the start time, the crowd and noise grew. The thrum of police and news helicopters added to the racket and the crazy atmosphere.

Motorcycles were everywhere up and down Fix Way when I finally fired up the shovelhead I had finished building a year before. Irish rode right beside me. Cheryl wrapped her arms around me as Irish and I throttled down the street. The collective explosion of a hundred Harleys roaring to life pushed us forward. Bike after bike followed in two-by-two formation as I took a left onto Main Street. Smiling people packed the streets along the route, waving miniature American flags and shouting their support. You get so used to scowls and fear in people's eyes when you wear a patch that it's easy to forget people can root for you too. They can be on your side. I felt an overwhelming camaraderie, not only with my brothers, but with all these everyday people, people who we separate from outlaws with the word *citizen*. But in that brief moment, we were all on the same side. The sound washed over the scene. The raw-emotion rumble of a hundred Harleys is something you feel as much as hear. My heart was in my throat.

An empty freeway in Southern California is a magical thing. The Highway Patrol had blocked off freeway entrances and we had a clear shot to the run site. Irish and I sped forward and an army of outlaws followed. When we turned off for Las Posas Road, I glanced in my rearview mirror. It was one of the most powerful moments I've ever experienced as a Hells Angel. I rode at the front of my charter often. The formation reflected the pecking order. But leading a column of riders so long that you can't see the end of it reminds you that you are part of this incredibly powerful force. The Hells Angels were strong individuals, but we were strongest in our numbers. The club has been about that from the start: fight one Hells Angel and you fight all Hells Angels. We would only get in trouble when we forgot that.

We rode by a huge white sign with great big letters spelling out CITI-

ZENS SUPPORT THE HELLS ANGELS. At the entrance to the run site was a tunnel of full-size flags, formed by people holding them at intersecting forty-five-degree angles over the road. We stopped to admire the view.

Irish yelled to me what we were both feeling. "Goddamn, George, I've got goose bumps."

"I can't believe it, Irish."

He flashed a bright grin, a smile that broke the hearts of a thousand women from Tijuana to the Oregon border. "Let's do it, man."

We led the pack through the tunnel and off to the shoulder. The crowd was thick and sprawling, and the media pressed in. I stripped down to my running clothes, and Ventura sergeant Carl Handy walked me to the starting line. He was my Ventura liaison to other law enforcement agencies.

"You've got three FBI agents who'll run with you, George. When you pass the flame, they're going to stay with you instead of running on. Don't get confused. They'll be stuck to you."

He introduced me to the two male and one female agents, all dressed like torch runners. In the lead-up to the run, I'd gotten a lot of death threats. The irony wasn't lost on me that the feds would give a Hells Angel a protection detail. Anybody who attacked a Hells Angels president with hundreds of members surrounding him should pray that the feds got to him first.

Behind me, Sonny—who my kids called Uncle Sonny—grabbed Georgie, lifted him up, and put the boy on his shoulders so that Georgie could have a clear view of his father running with the Olympic torch.

A kilometer is .62 miles. Just over a thousand yards. That day, running as best I could holding up the torch, trying to process everything that was going on—the noise, the flags, the feelings, the adrenaline—it might as well have been ten feet. It seemed like just a few seconds had gone by when I was handing the torch off to the next runner. The crowd collapsed around me as the FBI agents tried to maintain some semblance of a protective bubble. I looked over my shoulder at the man who had taken the torch from me. I didn't know his name. He ran off to do his leg, with no crowds, no flags, no cheering. What he was doing was no less important. It struck me as odd, the strange circumstances that put one man in the middle of a historical storm while another jogs off the stage. So much of life, so much of mine, was a matter of being in a certain place at a certain time.

The run was over, but the pandemonium continued. I signed autographs, shook hands, and was photographed. I thought, "This is going to be great for the club. Let's see the feds make us the enemy now." I could picture some fed sitting down to his breakfast, unfolding his morning newspaper, and staring down at my picture, torch in hand, crowds cheering and flags waving. Eat them Wheaties, ATF. Sonny and I walked to a bank of microphones, and I stopped short and let him take the lead. He was the figurehead of the club, the icon. But in a magnanimous gesture, he put his hand on my back and pushed me forward. This was my moment and he was giving it to me. During our conflicts in the years to come, I'd come back to that moment many times.

In all the confusion, I was separated from Cheryl. By the time I said a few words into the microphones, waded through the crush of people, and put my street clothes back on, she was nowhere to be seen. Most of the Angels headed back to the clubhouse. There were plenty of rides for her, so I rode back solo.

It was an epic party, limited to members and family. I could hear it even before I shut down my bike. Members were having a good time the Hells Angels' way. Booze was flowing, music was blasting, and my brothers were all hugs and smiles. It seemed like nothing could mar the occasion, until I came face-to-face with one very pissed-off tiny redhead. In the midst of this wild, happy celebration, Cheryl looked as mad as I'd ever seen her. I had to shout to make myself heard.

"What the hell's wrong?"

"You fucking left me."

"Cheryl, I didn't leave you, we got separated."

"You fucking left me out there alone, you asshole. I had to find my own way back."

It wasn't about me leaving her. It was about not having control, not being at the center of power or attention. It was about Cheryl standing in my shadow. I had upstaged her, and now she was determined to be the cloud over the party. I got the silent treatment until we left, and then two more days of silence at home. But I had found my voice. I realized that I was at home with the media, that I was good at it. On some level, Cheryl understood that. That gave me power that she didn't have and couldn't tap.

The torch run was a huge victory. Irish and I became the voices of the club. Even hard-liners, guys who had been against the torch run and all the media attention, give me credit for a win. And I learned. The media was another way to rebel against the authorities and conformists. It was a weapon that I could use to fight back against the overwhelming odds law enforcement had on their side. It was a tool to fight the bullies.

As good as I felt after the torch run, I had to face that Cheryl was never going to be happy, never going to support me, never be satisfied. She could see the dark side to a pot of gold. The Olympic torch run, and the press buzz around it, would be one of the final bricks in a wall between us.

It wasn't the only conflict to come out of the run. You could specify on the torch-run form where you wanted your donation to go. I had designated the $3,000 to go to the Special Olympics. The organization struck a chord with me. The people who competed in the Special Olympics were, in my view, a lot like outlaws. Society didn't want to deal with them and didn't appreciate them. Society wanted the disabled to be invisible, the same way it wanted patch-wearing outlaws to disappear.

You could specify exactly where you wanted the money directed—the Washington Special Olympics headquarters or to a specific local branch. When the first wave of press coverage had broken, the mother of a mentally disabled boy from Pottstown, Pennsylvania, had sent me a handwritten letter. Pottstown was dirt-poor. The money would make a huge difference. These kids wanted blue blazers so they could look spiffy when they went to competitions. Simple blue polyester blazers. The money could buy a lot of blazers. So I wrote in the Pottstown Special Olympics chapter as the intended recipient.

Eunice Kennedy Shriver, President John F. Kennedy's sister, had founded the Special Olympics and ruled it with an iron hand. She was a member of the closest thing America had to a royal family and acted every bit the part. Despite what I specified, she directed that the club's $3,000 be kept in Washington, so that she could decide how it would be used. That sparked a three-year legal battle. I filed motions myself, to the amusement of more than one judge. At one point, I answered a call from Eunice's husband, Sargent Shriver, the former ambassador to France. He tried to get me to give up and then asked me if I'd like to "speak to President Kennedy's sister." Like that was going to impress a Hells Angel.

"Sure, but it's not going to change anything."

She got on the line. More of the same. "We have the money, and we'll decide where it goes."

"No, you won't. It's on the form. It's in writing where it's supposed to go."

"Is that so? Well, do you really want to come back here to Washington and file a legal claim?" She thought she was talking to some brain-dead biker, and I was getting more pissed off by the minute. I'd dealt with more than my share of lawyers and had seen how the club was going after people on trademark infringement. The Hells Angels knew their way around a courtroom, criminal or civil.

"No. The contract originated in Ventura where I signed it. You'll be coming to court in Ventura. And the media loves a Hells Angels story. You really want to buy all that bad publicity?"

She paused, wrestling with the shock of this member of the lower classes standing up to her. Then I got an icicle voice that I'm sure was reserved for the poor servant who broke an expensive vase.

"Do you know who you're dealing with?"

"Lady, do you know who *you're* dealing with? I'll see you in court."

Those were the last words I ever spoke to Eunice Kennedy Shriver. It took some time and doing, but that three grand finally made it to Pottstown. In the meantime, when the club heard what was going on, we took a vote for another collection. The vote was unanimous. The Pottstown kids got their jackets courtesy of the Hells Angels, and an extra $3,000 when all was said and done.

That was a true feel-good win, for the club, for me, and for those kids. But some people in high places saw it differently. The authorities simply don't like the Hells Angels getting good press. They consider it an offense and an injustice that needs to be fixed. That's why every win in the outlaw world comes at a price. As I was about to learn, the feds were the ones sent to extract payment.

10

The Hells Angels and the feds. It's like the Hatfields and McCoys. The feds have an irrational hatred for the Angels. This isn't just law enforcement doing their job. It's an ongoing vendetta for some. Bullies with badges are one thing, but the ATF is far more dangerous. They have a scary stop-at-nothing mentality. In my experience some truly despicable, soulless people work for the ATF. After the Olympics and what many saw as my intentionally showing up the authorities, feds were gunning for Ventura—most figuratively, but some literally.

The FBI had just wrapped up a three-year nationwide drug buy dubbed Operation Rough Rider. Scores of Hells Angels were arrested from the Bay Area to New York City, including Sandy Alexander. He had become as powerful as Sonny Barger, and it was a big score for the feds. Almost everyone arrested would take a plea or be convicted. Sandy would eventually plead guilty to selling coke and would do just short of six years in prison. The feds would even unsuccessfully try to take the New York City clubhouse in forfeiture, as an asset used in furtherance of the crimes Rough Rider alleged.

I did a lot of press trying to push back against the federal propaganda machine behind Rough Rider. The FBI was once again asserting that the club was an overarching criminal enterprise, in an effort to turn Rough Rider into a full-blown RICO act (Racketeer Influenced and Corrupt Organizations) prosecution. Rudy Giuliani had used RICO to gut the Mafia's five families in New York in the early eighties. Now the FBI wanted to use it wherever outlaw bikers were arrested. I made the point in interview after interview that regardless of what individual members might do, the club was organized around shared values, not crime. Ultimately, the RICO case fell flat.

Then events took a darker turn.

We had a cardinal rule in Ventura. Never leave the clubhouse front door open. Violating it meant a $100 fine. David Ortega was fixing an engine in the clubhouse workshop one Sunday and breaking that rule. He walked through the arched passageway that led to the front great room when he heard a strange "pinging," made by what appeared to be a trailer hitch bouncing across the floor. He told me later, "I'm thinking, 'Why the hell would someone throw a trailer hitch in here?'"

They wouldn't.

What looked like a ball trailer hitch was actually a military-issue frag grenade. It bounced along the concrete floor, coming to rest under a steel workshop chair. The concussion from the blast blew out the windows and flattened the tires on motorcycles parked alongside the clubhouse. Tom Heath called me. He was out of breath. "Get down to the clubhouse. Someone just threw a grenade in here and David's all fucked-up."

It was a fifteen-minute ride from my house in Oak View to Fix Way in Ventura. I made it in five. The Ventura police and bomb squad were crawling all over the place. Someone else had beaten me there as well. A group of ATF agents stood across the street, watching. What they were doing in Ventura's desolate warehouse district on a Sunday night was anybody's guess.

David wasn't the only one hurt. Ventura member Rocky Robinson was asleep upstairs when the blast tore through the first-floor ceiling, launching him off his mattress. His arm was a mess of shrapnel wounds, and he headed to the hospital while the EMTs worked on David in the back of an ambulance. The aftermath was shocking. A grenade is small, but the explosive force is unbelievable. It left a jagged crater in the concrete floor. I could see through the ceiling to the second floor. Small pieces of drywall, metal, and other debris crunched underfoot. An acrid burning smell filled the air. It was pure luck that David had survived. The steel chair redirected the blast force. What was left of the chair was twisted into a piece of modern art. If you didn't know it had once been a chair, it would have been unrecognizable.

Little evidence was left behind, but the Ventura cops found a spoon, the grenade's safety lever. Once the pin is pulled, the grenade is thrown and the spoon pops off. When the spoon releases, the fuse assembly triggers and detonation begins. The spoon had survived the blast relatively intact.

The next day, I met with my private investigator. I asked him to get the police report and check out the spoon. Grenade spoons are stamped with serial numbers that can be traced back to a specific lot and location. I told him to track it down. Then I called every reporter I knew and threw together a press conference in front of the wrecked clubhouse. A small group of reporters showed up—from local papers, the *Los Angeles Times,* and a local TV news affiliate. I made a statement, hoping the articles would go out on the wire. One reporter asked, "Who do you think did this?" It was the big question. Whoever did it wanted the Hells Angels and the public to think it had been a rival. But if the Mongols or the Outlaws threw a grenade into a Hells Angels clubhouse, it wouldn't be a secret for long. When a club sends a message, they make damn sure the target knows who's sending it. I told the reporters, "I have a long list of people I suspect. And law enforcement's right at the top of that list." They all seemed skeptical, but they reported the quote.

The ATF's being on the scene along with everyone else felt suspicious to me, especially when they used the grenade attack as the basis for a search warrant. Years before, Tom Heath had legally purchased two High Standard pump shotguns from Big 5 Sporting Goods. We had mounted them in a rack, a type of wall decoration common to Hells Angels' clubhouses. The Ventura cops had taken the guns down and inspected them. I had been curious why they would show so much interest. Now I knew. The two guns were listed by serial number on the ATF's search warrant. I could not shake my suspicion that someone connected to the ATF may have tossed the grenade through the clubhouse door and that had created a case for a search warrant. It was too incredible to be true but that suspicion made me sick and angry in equal amounts.

The feds built a "felon in possession" case. The dubious foundation was that if the clubhouse contained weapons, anyone with a key was in "constructive possession" of those weapons. Any member who was a felon was therefore a felon in possession. It was a tortured use of the statute.

ATF agents arrested Rocky and Tom. Fortunately for other members who were felons, the agents bragged about how they were taking us down by using the keys. Word spread and everyone threw away their keys. The charter hired a Los Angeles criminal attorney, Louis Bernstein. He told me, "George, this is a really complicated trial. There really is no defense to the underlying charge. Why don't we go with a court trial and make it clear we're not interested in wasting the judge's time? We throw ourselves on the mercy of the court and use the opportunity to provide an explanation of the circumstances. It's really the best we can do."

A "court" trial means the defendant forgoes a jury and agrees to let the judge decide the case. We took Bernstein's advice. It was clear from the start that it was a smart strategy. The judge was openly appreciative that we streamlined the trial. He was also aware of the ATF's stretching of a law meant to stop dangerous felons from walking around with firearms on their person. In the end, Rocky got four months, and Tom got six. It was as close to a pure win as we could hope for.

In the meantime, my investigator got back to me after tracing the grenade's serial number. It had been reported stolen from an armory in Akron, Ohio—home base of the ATF crew. The more I thought about it, the more I felt that maybe this wasn't just about a warrant or a fishing expedition for bullshit convictions as I had suspected in some dark moments. Maybe this was about attacking a way of life, about payback for a Hells Angel who dared run with the Olympic torch and stand up to Eunice Shriver Kennedy. I truly felt that someone connected to the ATF may have been involved—however rogue or unauthorized.

With the evidence I had compiled, I got David to file a civil suit against the federal government. We figured that at the very least they would settle out of court and he would be set for life. We didn't have to go at them head-on. We could take the angle that the government was responsible because it had lost control of a highly dangerous grenade that resulted in David's injuries. But David didn't take the case seriously and wasn't committed. He missed court dates, and the case died of inertia. David bought a new piece of jewelry, a plain silver-chain necklace with a tiny glass vial hanging off it. For years after, he would pick little pieces of metal and glass out of his leg as they surfaced. He'd unscrew the vial's tiny cap and drop the wound debris inside. It was his way of dealing with the attack.

That was the last we'd hear of the ATF in Ventura. But where one law enforcement agency goes, others follow. The press around the grenade attack hadn't gone unnoticed in the bland FBI offices on Wilshire Boulevard. It would take them until mid-1986 to get around to me. When they did, they'd pull out a whole new bag of dirty tricks that would make the ATF seem like rank amateurs.

The Bureau had arrested a high-ranking member of the Mexican Mafia (known on the street as La Eme) in the late seventies. Staring at decades in prison for multiple offenses, heroin addict Mike Mulhern became a paid informant. He had been the number three guy in the Mexican Mafia, so there was no end to the people he could set up. Mulhern not only turned on his own guys, he went out of his way to help the FBI entrap outlaws. It is just one of many examples of the feds trading the devil for a sinner. When Mulhern eventually stepped out of the shadows as an informant, he would admit in court to being directly or indirectly connected to almost twenty murders. A serious heroin addict, he both used and committed crimes while under FBI protection. But he brought cases to the FBI, and careers were made.

I met Mulhern for the first time on the sidewalk in front of the Ventura clubhouse. The members were packing their bikes for a trip to Oakland, to bury Doug "Doug the Thug" Orr. Doug was an Oakland Hells Angel and club legend. He had been violent on a level that was astounding even for Hells Angels. Most of his life was spent in San Quentin, where he was a fearsome presence in the population. Doug had spent some time in a mental hospital, but he was beloved in the club. The problem was, he liked heroin. He died in his cell after shooting one fix too many. As iconic a Hells Angel as he might have been, the club had a long-standing hard-and-fast rule against heroin use. Heroin led to addiction. Addiction inevitably led to informing. Nobody would have suggested Doug might have rolled on his club brothers, but he had broken one of the most serious Hells Angels rules.

The debate about whether Doug should be buried with full honors as a Hells Angel had been long and heated. Oakland members who died in good standing got an impressive club burial. The hearse rode with a motorcycle escort of hundreds of members from around the country. The member would be laid to rest among other club notables in a section of Evergreen Cemetery reserved just for Hells Angels. The gravesite would be marked with a huge gleaming black granite Hells Angels tombstone, complete with a sandblasted patch and a picture of the deceased. A Hells Angels' funeral was a sight to behold, and every Angel wanted one when his time came.

In the end, Doug was too much of a Hells Angel to be buried as a citizen. The circumstances of his death would be kept quiet, at least until

Sonny wrote about it in his memoir. So I was surprised when some random, skinny, half-Mexican/half-white kid sauntered up out of nowhere and seemed to know far too much about club business.

"Hey, man. You don't know me. I'm Mike Mulhern. I was in the joint with some of your brothers. Everybody calls me Slim."

"That so?"

"Yeah. I was in with Doug the Thug. Too bad about him."

Now my radar went up. Few people outside the Angels even knew that Doug was dead. I instinctively didn't like this guy. Mulhern was obviously a drug user. He was jittery with dilated pupils. His eyes darted all around even when he was talking right at you. He ended each sentence in a nervous little laugh.

"Look, man, you got any work for me?"

"No, I don't have any work."

"Okay, okay. Something comes along though, I'm your guy." He licked his lips and looked up and down the street. Then he leaned in. "You heading north for the funeral?"

Hells Angels' business is Hells Angels' business. In the old days, people knew there was an Angel funeral when they saw a hearse trailing three hundred bikes. Not before.

"Might be."

"Doug did have a little problem, didn't he?"

"Excuse me?"

"Ah, we all got an itch we got to scratch once in a while. Ask your friends in the Bay Area about me. They'll tell you all about me. You just ask them about Slim."

He nodded and shuffled off down the street. I felt a tingling in the back of my head. I didn't know Mike Mulhern, but I knew I didn't like him.

At the funeral, I pulled Sonny aside. "You know a guy named Mike Mulhern? Did time in San Quentin?"

"Slim? Hell, yeah, I know him. He's a dangerous son of a bitch. Better take what he says seriously. His word's gold." It was a solid reference, and it meant I had to consider Mike Mulhern a stand-up guy. A week after I got back from the funeral, he showed up at the Ventura clubhouse. I walked outside to talk to him, unaware that an FBI surveillance team had me in their binoculars.

"Hey, man, how was the funeral?"

"We buried him. What's up?"

"Look, man, I got to tell you the real reason I came around. You know Tom Chaney?"

I did know Tom Chaney, a Ventura hangaround who turned out to be an untrustworthy, drug-dealing son of a bitch. He was a lowlife who wanted a patch on his back to help his business. I had personally run him off, and he had been arrested for possession with intent to distribute.

"Yeah, I know him."

"He owes us ten grand." By "us" Mulhern meant the Mexican Mafia.

"And?"

"If you guys don't pay the money, he's going in the hat. You know, we got a good relationship with you guys, I don't want to ruin it."

"What does that have to do with me? That guy's not in the club."

"That's not what he's saying. I'm just letting you know because we don't want any misunderstanding. We don't want you guys coming at us, saying, 'Hey, he was one of us.'"

"He's not a member. Do whatever you have to."

He walked away, and I figured that was the end of it. I was wrong. Mulhern came by almost twenty times in the weeks that followed. It was always the same discussion. Because he was the leader in a noted gang, I had to show him respect. The Mexican Mafia owns California prisons. A lot of Hells Angels behind bars benefited from the relationship with the gang. You never had too many friends inside prison. But I just couldn't seem to make this guy understand that I wasn't going to pony up $10,000 for some club reject. Like a bad penny, Mulhern came back all through the summer of 1986. Finally, after about the last visit from the greasy character, I'd had all I could take. He said the same thing he always said.

"Yeah, as long as it's a for-sure, they'll whack him. I don't want you guys saying what the Italians always say. 'We didn't okay that. . . .'"

I was so tired of this guy. Chaney was a nobody. I was beyond frustrated at having to deal with this scum Mulhern. My frustration led me to say the wrong thing.

"Look, I'd do it myself if he were here. He's a fucking troublemaker."

Mulhern nodded his head as if I had finally gotten through to him. "Okay." A week later, I heard that Tom Chaney had been killed in prison. It was actually all part of the FBI's sting. Chaney was perfectly fine, hidden in an FBI safe house.

In August, Ventura hangaround Danny Fabricant was arrested for possession of meth. Danny agreed to a deal with the court—a reduced sentence for delivering illegal machine guns, to get them off the street. At the other end of the gun deal? Mike Mulhern.

Danny gave me $1,000 that I was supposed to pass on to Mulhern. Mulhern told me to meet him at a Motel 6 on Harbor Boulevard in Ventura. It was a typical two-story motor lodge, with all the doors opening onto the parking lot. Inside his second-floor room, Mulhern was even jumpier than usual. I handed him the envelope from Danny. He pulled out $500 and pocketed it. He asked me to go into the bathroom to talk. I figured it for junkie paranoia. He talked a little more about Chaney, feeling me out if everything was cool, then made small talk. I wasn't going to stick around to chat with the likes of Mike Mulhern.

The FBI had the bathroom wired. When I stepped out of the motel room's front door, I was swarmed by agents in blue windbreakers. They arrested me and brought Mulhern out in cuffs. After I was booked, I called Alan Caplan. Alan was a tough criminal attorney who had successfully represented the Cleveland Hells Angels, as well as several mob guys. But even before I was arraigned, Alan had a motorcycle accident and had to have his foot amputated. I replaced him with Barry Tarlow. It was a happy accident, if not for Alan, for me. Barry Tarlow was a courtroom legend, a superstar Los Angeles defense attorney.

Barry had charisma to spare. He dominated trials in a way that made prosecutors unhappy as hell. He knew the games feds played and was fearless in calling them out. Although he wasn't tall, he had real presence. He had a great smile and eyes that always sparkled as if he were about to tell a funny joke. And Barry was the smartest guy in the room. Quick on his feet, he was a talented legal strategist at the top of his game. He inspired confidence. I needed that in a big way. When the bailiff called out, *"The United States versus George Gus Christie, Jr.,"* it hit me in the knees. The most powerful country in the world had a problem with me. I was facing twenty years on one count of conspiracy, and life on a count of murder for hire.

Most federal criminal cases end in a plea deal for a reason. The defendant takes the sure thing of a few years behind bars rather than risk growing old in prison. It's just playing the odds. The prosecutor gets his win and both parties chalk it up to the "game." Even innocent defendants will plea rather than face a system stacked against them, especially if they can't afford a good attorney. The federal government spares no expense when it goes to trial, and the conventional wisdom in 1986 was that you could not beat a federal rap. Few attempted it, and even fewer succeeded. But most defendants didn't have my case, and they didn't have Barry Tarlow.

Barry was adamant from the start that the case was garbage and entirely beatable. It was bungled entrapment, and the prosecution's argument stood or fell on the words of a heroin-addicted murderer who had gamed the system again and again. They had taped two meetings, mysteriously failing to tape more than fifteen others. My fingerprints weren't on the bills Mulhern produced. And only the $500 he left in the envelope made it into evidence. Along the way, he said I passed him the pink slip to a used car I'd never seen. My fingerprints weren't on the pink slip either.

Despite all that, the fight wouldn't be easy. That became clear in our first interaction with presiding Judge Dickran M. Tevrizian. He might as well have sat at the prosecutor's table. The judge denied bail because I was "one of the most callous characters" he had ever encountered. Never mind that I had businesses, a family, and a home in the community and had never been arrested. That didn't matter. Judge Tevrizian ruled that I would spend the duration in a holding block at the Federal Correctional Institution, Terminal Island, in San Pedro. During the bail hearing, Judge Tevrizian gave Barry a lecture while shaking a pencil toward the defense table. "I'm well aware of you and your courtroom shenanigans, Mr. Tarlow. I want you to understand something. I run my courtroom like a train schedule."

Barry was never at a loss for a comeback. "Well, let's hope my client and I don't get caught under your wheels, Your Honor."

We had a lot of ground to cover before we ever got to the courtroom. Just presenting the complex case would take almost nine weeks. While we worked on the pretrial preparation, I settled into custody. Hells Angels don't fear prison. We were either feared or respected behind bars. I also had friends waiting for me. Guy Castiglione, the Dago president, was doing time for the murder of the two Mongols in 1977. He was there to welcome me as I walked through the receiving center's sally port. He took me aside for a Prison 101 chat.

"Listen, George, don't talk about your case. Don't fucking trust anybody. Don't borrow any money, and don't loan any. Anything you need, you come to me. I got it all under control."

"Good to know, Guy, thanks."

"We got a cell all set up for you. All the stuff you need's already in the cell. But, George? One thing."

"What's that, Guy?"

"Saturdays I sleep in. Don't wake me up until after twelve."

Terminal Island mixes convicted felons with defendants awaiting trial. There are plenty of dangerous people inside. A lot of them are La Eme members and associates, guys who have the run of the place unless they're classified Level 6, which means they spend all day in lockdown. I spent a lot of time with the gang's associates. One day in chow line, one of the guys told me he was in for a bank robbery that he pulled with a guy named Mike Mulhern.

"Are you kidding, man? That's the rat that put me in here."

His buddies went silent. One of them, a large Mexican named Jorge, got in my face. "Hey, man, you shouldn't be talking shit about someone like him unless you got something to back it up."

"I've got the paperwork in my cell." The pretrial discovery documents listed Mulhern as the key prosecution witness on the case. You didn't have to read far to see that Mulhern was an informant.

"Let me check it out."

We left the chow line and headed to my cell. I pulled out the papers and handed them to him.

He slowly read through them. "I got to make a call." He ran to the closest pay phone in the cell block.

I caught up with him just as he identified himself to the person on the other end of the line.

"It's Jorge. Hey, listen, fucking Slim's no good. . . . No, man, he's a *rata*. I got the paperwork right here. I'm looking at it right now. Pass it on."

Terminal Island pay phones are monitored. I have no doubt that within an hour the FBI had Mike Mulhern scurrying into the pitch-black darkness of Witness Protection.

You fall into a routine in prison, broken up only by court appearances and lawyer or family visits. I had one four-hour visit each week with Cheryl. Sometimes she would bring the kids, and a couple of times my parents came. But mostly, it was just us.

In a way, the visits were as disruptive as they were necessary. They reminded me that a normal life was still going on without me, beyond those gray, two-foot-thick concrete walls, imposing guard towers, and menacing barbed wire. Time stops inside. For everyone else, it goes on. Reference points, things that happened right before I was arrested, were

Dressed as an outlaw for the first time.

A high school freshman.

A new Marine.

Platoon buddies. I'm the one smoking.

My mother, father, Cheryl, and me on boot camp visiting day.

Relaxing in Slave Louie's garage. I was always close with the Satan's Slaves.

As a Hells Angels prospect. Not my happiest time in the club.

Working on my first bike in my own garage.

With Moriya and Georgie.

A new full-patch Hells Angel.

A tough crowd. Paul "Animal" Hibbits stands on my right and Craig "Jesse" Kuhn on my left.

The Satan's Slaves, one of the earliest Southern California outlaw motorcycle clubs.

The young Ventura charter in front of the clubhouse.

A cleaner look in the early years of my presidency.

With friend and fellow rider Mickey Rourke.

Enjoying a beautiful sunny Southern California day with my son Georgie on the back.

Two hallowed symbols— the Olympic torch and my patch.

The actual Olympic torch run was a crowded affair. I'm flanked by FBI agents.

Proudly holding the Olympic torch with Michael "Irish" O'Farrell on my right and Sonny Barger on my left. Georgie managed to get the top of his head in the frame.

With Liza Minnelli in Paris. She threw me a party on my first visit to the City of Lights.

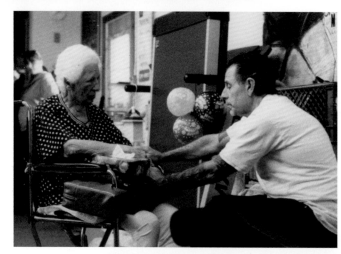

Meeting with my terminally ill mother. She'd live only a few days more.

I tried to get Ventura Police Department sergeant Carl Handy in a little hot water by grabbing him for this photo. In reality, he was a stand-up guy who was always respectful and decent.

In the yard at Terminal Island prison.

Meeting with Harry "Taco" Bowman, the international president of the Outlaws Motorcycle Club at the time. He would put a contract out on my life shortly after this photo was taken. He's now doing life without parole.

The core of the "new" breed of Ventura Hells Angels. From left to right: Vince DeAlba, my oldest son, Georgie, Mike Kapp, and Sabian Reynoso.

Georgie and Moriya during our 2001 trial. He would get probation and subsequently quit the club.

The Ventura charter at its largest and at my most powerful point as president.

Nikki and me at a club party in the yard of the Ventura clubhouse. She could always handle her own in a room full of outlaws.

Mike Mulhern, the government informant in my first case and an admitted heroin addict, a leader of the Mexican Mafia, and a multiple felon and murderer.

Moriya and I share a happy moment at the conclusion of my 2001 trial. The government's case fell apart, as almost everyone got probation.

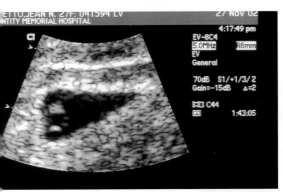

The sonogram of my son Finn: I saw the Hells Angels Death Head in the image and was sure Finn would succeed me as Ventura president.

With my third child, Aubree.

On the set of the History Channel's six-part series *Outlaw Chronicles: Hells Angels*.

Nikki, Finn, Aubree, and myself. A family I cherish.

An outtake from a family photo session. Finn was none too happy about taking the picture.

Marrying the love of my life, the stunning Nikki Nicoletto.

Two guys napping. Finn after he came out "the other side" of autism.

old news and irrelevant to anyone visiting me. So the conversations Cheryl and I had all came back to our relationship. We talked about what I had done wrong, and what she had done wrong. How it could be different, what we would change when I got home. The more we talked, the more candid we became. The more honest we were, the more we started committing to change. Always, it was "When you get home . . ." "When I'm home . . ." We were making a game plan for a new life, the life after I got my freedom back.

Inside, you have a lot of spare time. Some inmates read. Some stew on their situation. I reflected on things. Naturally, the first question was "How did I get myself here?" But more important, I started to look at all my decisions. I had lots of time to consider and do all the what-ifs.

I had cheated on Cheryl. Many times. I hated the idea of cheating, and although it didn't make perfect sense, I hated Cheryl for making me cheat. My infidelities were about sex, plain and simple. I wasn't looking to leave Cheryl. I didn't want another partner. She was the mother of my children. I loved her. But I had a sex drive and she didn't. Plain and simple. I wasn't going to be celibate. Sure, she didn't want to share me that way, or any other way. But I think she was just as conflicted. When I was getting sex somewhere else, the burden was off her. The more I thought about it, the more I wanted to set things right. The more I wanted a marriage like my parents had. I wanted to be a better parent to my kids.

Our visits were the only time I discussed life after the trial. Most people—my parents, other Hells Angels, and certainly law enforcement—thought I was done before I started. I saw it in their eyes, and the way my family didn't like talking about the trial, especially what it would be like *after* the trial. They didn't think I was coming home, and they didn't want to get my hopes up.

Some outside law enforcement were going to be happy with me behind bars for a good long time. Jim Clark was a Ventura member who decided my arrest was a gift-wrapped opportunity. He went on a smear campaign from the moment I was arrested, hoping to oust me as president. It pissed David Ortega off, and David made sure that word got back to me.

I called Jim at the clubhouse, and he disrespected me as soon as he picked up the phone. He was sarcastic and condescending, as if I weren't even a member, much less president.

"Hey, Jim, I found out something today."

"Yeah? What's that?"

"There's a front door on this prison. They let people out of it sometimes. So if I were you, I'd keep that in mind."

Jim Clark and the other doubters didn't understand who Barry Tarlow was. Seeing him handle himself in the courtroom was like watching a master craftsman create a sculpture out of rock. Every time we met, I came away more certain that I would beat the case. He always had a plan, and a reason for doing something. He was on top of every detail. As the trial date approached, Barry and cocounsel Mark Haney had me try on a suit. When they saw me in it, Mark said, "Oh my God, take that thing off." I looked like a gangster.

So we agreed that I would play it straight up. The gallery was going to be filled with Hells Angels wearing colors. In a suit, I'd set myself apart. But I was one of them. I wasn't ashamed of that. So we decided I would wear my street clothes and my cut for the entire trial. Barry had me write a letter to Judge Tevrizian explaining why I would be dressed as I would, and telling him that I meant no disrespect. Part of Barry's unique way of doing things was to leave no room for complaint.

He was shrewd. For his opening statement, he blew up a photo of me running with the Olympic torch, in my bright white shorts and official white tank top, smiling ear to ear. On the same easel, he displayed a blown-up photo of Mike Mulhern. In the photo, Mulhern held a submachine gun, wearing a suede blazer and sporting a menacing smirk on his lean, ferretlike face. Barry introduced the government's key witness long before the government did, painting him as the personification of evil. It was courtroom artistry.

The government was in trouble from the start. Before long, they were desperate. A few days into the trial, Judge Tevrizian announced in open court that a marshal had been approached by a Hells Angel. The marshal said that the Angel asked where the judge ate lunch and where he lived. From that point on, the judge was escorted to his car by armed marshals. It was a ham-fisted attempt at helping the prosecution. Hells Angels can be reckless, but none of them would have been so stupid. And no Angel would ever approach law enforcement for information.

It was the start of what my defense team came to call the "dirty-tricks campaign." Within days, the prosecutors claimed my mother had discussed the trial with a juror because a security tape showed her and a juror entering the same elevator after lunch recess. Both said under oath that they hadn't exchanged so much as a "Hello." It didn't matter. Judge Tevrizian dismissed the juror and sat an alternate. It seemed clear to me that the government was willing to falsely arrest my mother just to put pressure on me to cut a deal.

Knowing what the other side was capable of, I smelled a rat when an inmate who went by Spanky sidled up to me in chow line. He started making small talk, asking about what it was like being a Hells Angel. He told me he had always wanted to get a bike. He became an unwanted shadow, asking question after question. Inside a week, he tried to sell me on escaping with him.

"You and I can get out of here. It's an easy escape. You're looking at life, man. I can get us out of here. Your connections with the club, you can go anywhere in the world. They'll never find you."

I made it clear that I had no interest. Spanky was trouble. The one thing I didn't need was more trouble.

"You go ahead. I'm taking my chances with my trial."

A few days later, I was in the yard when the speakers blasted an urgent message on a loop: "Return to your housing. The yard is now closed. You have ten minutes to return to your housing. Anyone outside after ten minutes will be out of bounds."

We headed back to our cells. By lights-out, the rumor mill was running full speed: Spanky had escaped. The next day, he showed up at my house in Oak View. I'm a paranoid guy. I had fortified the property line against any potential attack. The house was fronted by an imposing brick archway flanked by a steel fence and secured with a heavy steel gate. It could only be opened by buzzer.

Cheryl heard the intercom buzz, and then a voice.

"Hey, it's me, Spanky."

"Spanky who?"

"Come on. Open up, come out here so I can talk to you."

"Who are you?"

"It's me Spanky. I came for the car."

"What are you talking about?"

"You know, the car. You're supposed to hook me up with some money, a gun, and a car. I have to get the hell out of here. I just escaped from Terminal Island."

"I don't know what you're talking about, but you better get out of here."

Cheryl called Barry Tarlow, who put it all together in a heartbeat. It was a transparent play to jam her up on an aiding-and-abetting charge and then use her as leverage to get me to plea. Spanky "escaped" in the back of a marshal's car. I have no doubt his run lasted all the way to a motel, where he got to enjoy his freedom and junk food until the feds figured out neither Cheryl nor I was going to bite. Barry raised holy hell in court, but the prosecutors claimed ignorance and the trial proceeded.

Each passing day, it became more obvious that the prosecution's case was falling apart. People around me started to understand what was happening. They were shocked. I expected it from outsiders, from guys in Terminal Island who knew "you never beat a federal rap." I didn't expect it from Cheryl. In the rare gesture of kindness, the courtroom marshals eased up on a courtroom rule. They allowed Cheryl to sit behind me, so that we could exchange a few words when I was in court. One Monday, midway through the trial, Barry systematically dismantled the government's case. You could see the looks on the jurors' faces as they came to doubt anything the federal prosecutors said. During a break right before lunch, Cheryl leaned forward, onto the wooden rail separating the defense table from the gallery.

"George, you could really win this thing."

She meant it as a positive. But it hit me like a baseball bat. What had we been talking about for months in the Terminal Island visiting room? How many times, sitting there in those crappy orange plastic chairs under those harsh fluorescent lights, had she said, "When you get home . . ."? How many times had we committed to all the things we were going to change? I saw in a flash, sitting there next to Barry, that everything Cheryl had said had been lip service. Up to that moment in the courtroom, she had thought I wasn't coming home. As happy as I was to be winning the case, I felt like a complete fool.

By the time the case went to the jury, everyone in the courtroom knew what the outcome would be. Barry convinced me to take the stand. I held my own, carefully crafting long answers to any question, making the points I wanted to make. Assistant U.S. Attorney Stephen Czuleger was so frustrated that he appealed to the bench. "Your Honor, can you control the witness . . . ?"

When the jury came back with not-guilty verdicts on both charges, I thought the judge was going to pop a blood vessel. In an unusual move, he demanded the jury be polled. Polling juries is normally a last-ditch defense strategy. If you can find one juror that admits to being bullied into changing his or her vote, you have grounds for a mistrial or the foundation for an appeal. Barry had never seen a judge poll a jury. One by one, they got up and announced their not-guilty votes.

The system loves nothing more than to screw with you, even after you've been found innocent. Rather than release me, they kept me in a court holding cell for almost five hours, until most of the press had left. Barry complained to the marshals, and they explained that the FBI was doing an NCIC check. National Crime Information Center checks are also called wants and warrants searches and are usually done when a suspicious person is pulled over during a traffic stop, or a career criminal is booked into jail. They had nearly a year to do an NCIC check, so it was one last petty jab before the FBI reluctantly released their claws and let me walk.

David Ortega and three other members had ridden to the courthouse and brought my bike. As soon as I walked out a free man, I rode back to the clubhouse, where I was treated like a conquering hero. Cheryl and the kids were there, along with my defense team. It felt incredible to be free after so long.

Barry came up with the idea to throw a party for the jurors. I was all for it because I wanted to rub the government's face in the acquittal as much as possible. A week later, my dad took charge of a huge charcoal barbecue grill in the clubhouse yard. We set out tubs of soft drinks and beer, and stereo speakers broadcast the Grateful Dead. Five of the twelve jurors showed up, along with one of the Utah state troopers who had testified to arresting Mulhern for multiple felonies, only to see him walk thanks to the FBI's protection. Mickey Rourke, who I had become friends with through New York member Chuck Zito, showed up. So did about thirty Hells Angels and a few reporters. It was the best I had felt in a very rough year.

As the buzz died down, Cheryl and I were faced with putting actions to all those words we'd spoken over almost a year of prison visits. That truth hit us both hard. She didn't suddenly like sex, and I knew that club business would sooner or later take me away from the family for long nights and lost weekends. In the short term, we walked on eggshells around the house, and I tried to be the best father I could be.

The attention I got in the trial's aftermath didn't help. Reporters kept calling. The David-versus-Goliath angle to the trial made for good copy. The reporters were not the only ones. An executive from Paramount

Studios reached out to me. The studio wanted to do a film about me and the trial. Cheryl's need for control killed the deal. She demanded approval over all depictions of her and me, and Paramount wasn't having it. I watched $250,000 walk away because of Cheryl's overbearing insistence on getting involved and getting her way. It created yet another rift between us.

I had plenty to deal with at the clubhouse as well. The first thing I did once I was back was to straighten out Jim Clark. David and I took Jim for a walk five blocks down to the Ventura River, on the other side of the Ojai Freeway. It was a desolate location. We didn't say a word until we got to the edge of the river.

"You know, Jim, I don't think this charter is big enough for both of us. I don't want you here anymore."

"I'm not going nowhere."

"Well, let me tell you something. See the river? At the bottom of that river is an eternity. And if you don't leave Ventura, that's where you're going to be."

David and I turned around and walked back to the clubhouse. Three days later, Jim Clark packed up and transferred to Berdoo. Within a year, he was out of the club entirely.

The bigger challenge was money. When outlaws don't think you'll be coming home, they put their hands in your pockets. My businesses were unraveling. The tattoo shop was in shambles. The books were a mess and there was no money in the business account. It looked like Tom had been skimming. I offered to buy him out for $3,000 and he refused. So I opened my own shop, calling it the Ink House. Tom was arrested on an assault charge shortly after. I got a call from the jail.

"Hey, George, I've been thinking. I'll take your offer. Put the three thousand dollars on my books."

"What offer?"

"For the shop, for my half of the business."

"Tom, I left. I have my own shop."

It would become a long-standing beef between us. I decided to keep things square anyway. I had prospects tear down his shop and put everything into storage so that it would be there when he got out. But he never resurrected the shop because he wasn't a businessman to start with.

My martial arts equipment business had done well in my absence, but I had nothing to show for it. I'd left a Ventura member and his girlfriend in charge of the business, and they'd emptied out about $30,000 worth of inventory. Within a day of my coming home, the two had packed up and slunk off, never to be heard from again.

Thankfully, the club's defense fund had paid for Barry Tarlow and my defense team. So I had some cash from my own savings to carry me. But it would take a lot of hard work to get my businesses back in shape.

The feds would be working just as hard. I hadn't been the only one the FBI had targeted among the Hells Angels. They had a rat on their payroll. Tony Tait was a biker who became a paid FBI informant after joining the Hells Angels Anchorage, Alaska, charter. Tony was a disgusting excuse for a human being who wanted to have it both ways. He liked to play the big tough outlaw, while pretending he was the noble good guy serving justice. In truth, he wasn't either one. He was a weak blowhard with a Prince Valiant pageboy, beady eyes, and no spine.

For a time, I couldn't show up anywhere without Tony Tait being there. I finally asked him outright how he could afford to fly everywhere. He froze like a deer in the headlights because the FBI was bankrolling his travels. He stumbled through a bullshit story about dating a stewardess who let him use her miles. It didn't track. I made a mental note that something was off about the guy.

I ran across him again at a Rough Rider defense-benefit concert at the Limelight in New York City. Joan Jett had agreed to perform in support of the defense fund. Every Hells Angel there wanted to get as close as possible to Joan, who was sexy, tough, cool, and famous. She was also incredibly nice. Her manager asked that we clear her dressing room so she could get ready to perform. Tony Tait threatened to knock him out for "disrespecting" the Angels. Joan Jett was doing a major favor for the club, and her manager was just doing his job. Tony and I almost came to blows as I straightened him out on that account.

While I'd been in Terminal Island, the Anchorage charter president, John Cleve Webb, was shot to death by two Outlaws outside a biker bar in Louisville, Kentucky, in August 1986. It brought the embers of the Outlaws–Hells Angels war back to life. Tait had already set up several Hells Angels for drug busts. On the heels of the murder, he was aiming for bigger fish.

I heard that Sonny and Irish had photos of the two shooters and had shown them at a meeting in Oakland. Tait aggressively pushed for revenge. He had been made West Coast sergeant at arms and sat right next to me at a West Coast Officers' Meeting in the fall of 1987. He wore a bright white cast on his arm. Any biker who breaks his arm gets his cast filthy inside a day. At the meeting, Tait lobbied hard for the club to bomb the Outlaws' clubhouse in Kentucky. He tried to enlist my support. But that type of thing isn't discussed at an officers' meeting. The more he pushed, the more suspicious I got. We were already at war with the Outlaws. If he was so set on taking care of business with the Outlaws, he could have driven to Kentucky and done what he said needed to be done. And I kept coming back to that pristine cast.

"What happened to your arm, Tony?"

"Broke it. Dumped my bike."

"Wow, you must be the luckiest guy I know."

"What do you mean?"

"You get in a bike accident bad enough to break your arm and you have no road rash? No other injuries? That's pretty lucky."

I was onto something. I'd later learn that the cast was fake and contained a bug. The FBI was waiting for someone in that clubhouse to conspire with Tony Tait. They struck out at the meeting, but they'd have better luck in a smaller setting. Tait met Sonny at the Golf Links Road house. He showed Sonny photos of the Outlaws' clubhouse and discussed how the clubhouse could be blown up. Tait finally told Sonny that he thought the bomb could potentially kill five or six people. Sonny was recorded saying, "That'll be really nice after that Joliet thing." A month earlier, Cleveland charter president Kenny Yates had been shot and wounded in Joliet, Illinois. Rumor had it that the Outlaws who had shot him took his patch.

Tait set up both Sonny and Irish as he went through the motions of arranging and executing the bombing. The two Oakland legends were arrested for conspiracy. They were convicted, but were free awaiting sentencing when they rode down to attend a funeral for Berdoo Hells Angel Aristeo "Art" Carbajal. Art had been stabbed to death in a wild fight with the Mongols at the *Queen Mary* Tattoo and Bike Show in Long Beach, in February 1989.

Andy Shission was at the funeral, having transferred from the Cleveland charter to Ventura six months before. Andy was a financial wizard who always had a legitimate moneymaking scheme in the works. He had put together a video project, a tape of the annual run to Sturgis, South Dakota, with interviews of club members and images of how wild the place could be. Andy wanted to sell the tape to club supporters and the public. There was a decent market for it, but Sonny was against it because the tape prominently featured the patch. I believe the real reason was because Sonny wasn't offered a piece. Andy didn't think he needed Sonny's permission, and they squared off at the funeral service.

Nobody would swing first on Sonny. It just wouldn't happen because the repercussions could be severe. On the other hand, Sonny wasn't known as a fighter. I had never seen him fight, and nobody I knew considered him a physical threat. So unless he punched Andy, it would stay a shouting match. But Andy wouldn't back down.

As the two argued, Irish quietly moved up behind Sonny's shoulder. This was a statement. If Andy decided to get physical, Irish would step in and clean Andy's clock. Andy was a Ventura member, so I stepped up behind him. Irish and I locked eyes. We had been friends for so long, but situations like this test friendship. Loyal to an old charter or your current one? Loyal to the club leader, or someone else? Irish smiled ever so slightly, then nodded. He was Sonny's guy. Push came to shove, he was going to back Sonny's play, even against me. I nodded back. I wasn't about to let Sonny jack up a Ventura member. Like it or not, I had Andy's back.

It was the first time Irish and I had ever squared off. I didn't like it. It felt like something was very, very wrong. It wasn't old-school push-and-shove around a bonfire, or even a fair-and-square fistfight you left behind after it was done. Sonny and Andy separated. Irish and I didn't speak for the rest of the funeral. Most of the members in attendance were in one camp or the other. It turned into an even sadder gathering than it needed to be.

I didn't see Irish leave, and I would never see him again. On June 5, 1989, just before he was supposed to be sentenced for the bombing-conspiracy conviction, Irish went to a bar. He was drinking with Aryan Brotherhood members. The AB is a white supremacist group that is a force inside Folsom and San Quentin prisons. They have a good relationship with the Hells Angels. But Irish got into an argument with an Aryan Brotherhood member. Rumor had it they were doing meth off the point of a knife when the argument exploded. The Aryan Brother stabbed Irish in the neck, chest, and back. According to rumor, Irish told his attacker, "Is that all you got?" At which point, the Aryan Brother pulled a gun and shot Irish four times, killing him on the spot.

Every Hells Angels funeral is a somber affair. But Irish's was the saddest I ever attended. He was universally respected and loved. There was an air of confusion, because everyone at the funeral knew the Aryan Brotherhood was responsible. Why were they not being killed in the streets? Why were they not being killed behind bars? Why was Sonny not screaming for blood? He was about to go inside on his conspiracy conviction, and the AB would be there, but that's not a reason to stop a war.

I don't know if Sonny wanted to keep things calm so that he'd have a few less worries in prison, or if something else was behind his silence.

As Sonny went to prison for conspiracy, drugs were the big news nationwide. Meth was everywhere, replacing cocaine in the media's headlights. That focus was shining brightest on outlaws. A producer from *60 Minutes* called me at the Ventura clubhouse in January 1990. Mike Wallace was going to do a *60 Minutes* segment on meth, and they wanted me to come on the show and defend the club against law enforcement's claim that the Hells Angels were serving as a nationwide distribution chain. I called Barry Tarlow and asked him what he thought.

"Mike Wallace is the bear trap of interviewers, George. Just keep that in mind."

At the next West Coast Officers' Meeting I brought up the topic and explained that if I didn't agree to go on camera, they would say in the segment, "We contacted Mr. Christie and he declined to be interviewed for this show." Everyone in the room had seen *60 Minutes*. They knew how it worked. Absence was as good as an admission of guilt.

Cisco was the Oakland president in Sonny's absence. He told me that he wanted to go on the show with me. I knew it would be a mistake and tried to diplomatically back him off the idea.

"You know, Cisco, it looks a lot easier than it is. Especially after they edit it. They're going to talk to us for twenty minutes, thirty minutes. And then they'll cut it down to two or three minutes and try to make us look bad. It's a short amount of time but it's grueling."

I'd done a lot of press by then. It was easy to see how Wallace and the show's producers could manipulate the interview. I knew Mike Wallace wasn't in awe or afraid of anyone, and he was no friend of the club's.

Cisco didn't care. "It looks pretty easy to me, man."

"It's not, Cisco. Mike Wallace is considered the best in the business. He'll hit us with trick questions."

"Shit. I've been up against a lot tougher dudes than Wallace. Fuck Mike Wallace."

Then everyone laughed, but I wasn't laughing. I knew this was going to be a problem.

On a sunny, early-spring day in April 1990, Cisco and I rode to the hotel in Los Angeles where CBS wanted to film the segment. Although any hope Cheryl and I might have had about turning our relationship around after I got home from Terminal Island was long dead, she came along for the ride. She said it was for support, but I knew that she just wanted to be in on the action.

Mike Wallace was charming and smart. I could see he was going to be trouble on camera. Even so, we hit it off. He had just come back from Cuba, and as the camera crew set up for the interview, I asked him if he had visited Che's hands (after the revolutionary Che Guevara was executed in Bolivia, his hands were amputated for identification. The hands were believed to be in Cuba). Wallace was startled. Like a lot of people who met me when I was wearing my patch, he assumed I was a knuckle-dragger. We discussed Fidel's rule, Raul Castro's relationship with the Russian military, and the Cuban revolution. He was surprised that I was a history buff, but I could see it didn't change his mind about attacking the club in the piece.

He didn't waste time once the cameras rolled. In the intro to the segment, he called the Hells Angels the "principal distributors of methamphetamine in the United States." And he was just getting warmed up. Wallace paraded Tony Tait out in fake beard, nose, and hairpiece.

Sitting next to Cisco, I made the point that Tait, like a lot of rats, traded information for money. The more information he gave the FBI, the more money he got. I described how Tait had shown up in early 1984 whining about being broke and asking me to set him up in the drug business. I told him no because I wasn't in the drug business and didn't like meth to start with.

Cisco got into trouble when Wallace asked him about the Oakland members who had gone down on meth convictions. Cisco fumbled when Mike asked him a relatively easy question—did he know how many members had been convicted nationwide? Mike moved on to a bit of theater. He read from a typed set of old bylaws seized from Oakland Hells Angel Kenny Owen's house during a police raid. One of the rules listed was "No Drug Burns." This was a holdover from the sixties, when some Angels sold oregano to hippies in place of pot. It gave the Hells Angels a bad reputation in the emerging drug scene and Haight-Ashbury culture. The club put a stop to it with a rule that, to any outsider, sounded much more sinister than it was. Mike asked Cisco about the rule, and Cisco stared at the paper for what seemed like a year. Cisco was sweating and having a hard time looking Wallace in the eye. Wallace prompted him to say something.

"It's hard to answer."

"It is hard to answer."

I realized we weren't going to get the time or chance to fully explain the rule. I asked to see the paper and then told Wallace that there was no way to know if it was authentic because none of us had been at Kenny Owen's house during the bust. We survived the interview, but I knew Cisco's "deer in the headlights" performance was going to be a problem.

After the interview, Wallace showed a lot of interest in Cheryl. It might have been no more than a gentlemanly gesture, but it looked a lot like a pretty, petite redhead had caught his eye. I found it amusing because after trying to savage us in an interview, he was openly lavishing attention on a Hells Angels president's wife. That attention might have earned most men a beating, but Cheryl and I were having such a tough time of it that I thought, "Great, take her off my hands." Mike complimented her on her figure, and the conversation took off from there. Mike and Cheryl were openly flirting when she jokingly mentioned that she'd like to be on *60 Minutes*.

Mike couldn't have been more accommodating. "You would? Would you like me to interview you?"

Cheryl lit up like a Christmas tree. The attention was on her and her alone. Mike talked with his crew and then sat Cheryl down across from him, in the same room where he had interviewed Cisco and me. The makeup woman fussed with Cheryl's face, the klieg lights came on, and the camera rolled. Mike Wallace interviewed my wife for about fifteen minutes. What was it like to be a Hells Angel's wife? Did she worry about other women? On and on it went. Cheryl was beaming.

The show, featuring the segment on meth, aired on Sunday, April 22, 1990. I watched it in the Ventura clubhouse. Even before Andy Rooney came on to close the show, I started getting calls from charters around the country. Everyone was clowning Cisco. "Wow, George, you should have given him the stage hook." I realized that it was just the front edge of the storm. Hells Angels love nothing better than to rib a brother. There would be no mercy. I was sure Cisco heard about it endlessly, the obvious sweating and how he couldn't look Mike Wallace in the eye. It would be six months before Cisco would talk to me again. He blamed me for the whole thing.

In the meantime, a huge opportunity for peace between the Hells Angels and the Outlaws presented itself. Behind bars, outlaw bike club members tend to suspend hostilities for the sake of peaceful coexistence in a confined space. The Outlaws and Hells Angels locked up in the high-security prison in Terre Haute, Indiana, had actually come together to petition the warden to allow a bike show on the prison grounds. Prison bike shows had been allowed a couple of times before and made for good press.

The Outlaws invited me to the show, and I got to meet many of their key players. I found a lot of goodwill at the show. Afterward, I thought I could make progress on a truce by talking with the Outlaws' international president, Harry "Taco" Bowman. He hadn't attended the show, but I heard he was staying at a motel a few miles away. I was alone, and there's a protocol to setting up a meeting between clubs. Each side usually brings enough members to ensure security. But this was a rare chance. I thought it would be weak and foolish to let it slip away. I drove my rental car over to the motel, where about a dozen patch-wearing Outlaws were milling about in the parking lot in front of one of the rooms. As I walked up to them, most recognized me. Those that didn't sure as hell recognized my patch. They puffed up, but I could tell they weren't sure what to do.

"What do you want?"

"I'm here to see Taco."

"Does he know you're coming?"

"Nope."

The Outlaw looked at me like he thought it was a trick I was pulling. "Wait here."

He knocked on the door of the motel room and went inside. A minute later, Taco walked out, looking amused. Taco always wore black head to toe. His trademark look included a headband, dark glasses, and a Pancho Villa mustache. He always looked angry. But he was having a hard time not smiling as he met me in front of his troops.

"What the fuck are you doing, George?"

"I came to talk to you."

"Talk about what?"

"Peace. We need a truce, Taco. I know the beef goes way back, but the only thing separating us is geography."

"What do you mean?"

"If I had been born in Chicago, I'd probably be an Outlaw. If you had been born in California, you'd probably be an Angel."

Taco nodded and we talked for fifteen minutes. At the end of it, we agreed to meet in Sturgis at the famous rally's fiftieth anniversary. There was a lot of concern in the outlaw world that there was going to be trouble, given all the major outlaw clubs would be there and old animosities were sure to flare up.

The Sturgis rally in August 1990 drew the most people in its history, over a half million motorcyclists, outlaws, and gawking citizens. A day after the Angels rode in, I led a small contingent of members over to meet Taco and the Outlaws at the Molly Bee, a nondescript truck stop and motor lodge at the edge of town. We got off our bikes and waited. A few minutes later, a rumble filled the air and Taco rode up at the head of a group of Outlaws, who broke formation to form a skirmish line facing us across the parking lot. They were all wearing trench coats with their patches on the outside, and most had on bulletproof vests. It didn't surprise me. The Outlaws were known as a paranoid club, and I was pretty sure they had come heavy, with plenty of firepower. I wasn't armed. I didn't believe you could get a diplomatic solution out of a firefight.

Taco and I met in the middle, and he asked me to walk and talk, to avoid parabolic mikes. We started walking across the span of the parking lot, a few chosen members from each club trailing us. Taco reached into his coat to grab a pack of smokes. As he pulled his hand out, it caught the butt of his matte-black Smith & Wesson .45. The gun popped out and dropped to the ground with a heavy clunk. Everyone froze.

I smiled at him. "I didn't know we were bringing guns, Taco."

"That's not for you."

"Then put it away."

He picked it up, holding the grip with his thumb and forefinger, and slipped it back into his coat.

Flashes of weaponry aside, it was a good meeting. We tentatively agreed to a cease-fire. As the international president, Taco had complete decision-making power. That's how must outlaw clubs worked. But the Angels were different, more democratic. I had to bring the proposal back to the club and have all the charters vote on it. The cumbersome process dogged me more than once. Still, we got the cease-fire through, and it held for years.

A couple months later, Cheryl got a package in the mail, wrapped in crisp brown paper with a prominent CBS logo on the front. She opened it to find a VHS tape of her *60 Minutes* "interview," along with a note from Mike Wallace. Even though the interview never aired and was just a vanity piece, Cheryl made copies to send to family and friends. It was her fifteen minutes of fame. It was the first time in a long time I had

seen Cheryl truly happy. It would also be the last time. Our fraying relationship had become a cold war. As hard as I tried to put family before
club business, so much was going on that I had to deal with. When you're
inside a bad relationship, it's hard to see things clearly. But this much I
could see: Cheryl and I were headed to a showdown, and it wouldn't be
pretty.

11

You can't lead a Hells Angels charter nine to five. That's not how it works. So as hard as I worked to create a normal home life in the aftermath of my trial, I still had club obligations. Cheryl had her own issues and still had no interest in a physical relationship. In the months after I got home, it became clear that we weren't on the same page in any other part of the marriage, either.

I was frustrated. I had given up a lot of opportunities for Cheryl. Even before the trial, I had turned down Diane Keaton, who wanted to put me in her documentary *Heaven*. Cheryl was irrationally jealous that something might happen between Keaton and me. I'd said no to director Michael Mann when he approached me about doing a movie based on the trial because Cheryl worried about how she would be depicted. Those opportunities weren't going to come around again. I resented her and blamed her for holding me back. Despite what we'd pledged in the Terminal Island visitors' center, we were still letting each other down. The marriage didn't need much to go up in flames. The spark came late one Friday night.

I was determined to build the charter. Prison had given me the opportunity to reflect on the kind of leader I wanted to be. I had always been leery of anyone who came around the club. I was naturally a little paranoid. But if you're going to grow, you have to take chances. You have to cultivate new members.

The Hells Angels require individual charters to maintain at least six full-patch members. We'd worked around that rule for years by bringing in transfers—sometimes on paper alone (Animal had technically transferred from Oakland for a short time, to keep us at the minimum). But it had gone on long enough. I needed new blood. That meant being more accessible, opening up, and showing prospects and hangarounds why the life was so great.

From the day I'd gotten back from Terminal Island, I had been home every night before the kids went to bed. But one Friday, I stayed late at a clubhouse party. Walking through the door a little past midnight, I found an angry redhead waiting to pounce. Cheryl had a full head of steam, and the argument started before I could take off my patch.

"You met somebody down there. That's why you're so late. Don't pretend you didn't."

It pissed me off. This was always how it went. As far as she was concerned, I was always cheating on her. Or planning on cheating on her. Or thinking about cheating on her. But I'd kept my part of the bargain, the fidelity we had discussed in Terminal Island. I'd done what I had promised. That didn't matter. Our sex life wasn't any better. That part of our life obviously wasn't going to change. The bitter irony wasn't lost on me. I had been so discreet about the affairs I'd had that Cheryl never had any real evidence. I could have gone on lying forever. Now, here I was being faithful and getting blasted with both barrels.

We argued until we went to bed. A few hours of rough sleep was just an intermission. The fight started again as soon as we woke up. It got more heated as the morning went by. By noon, Cheryl was nearly hysterical. She finally said the words I think I had been waiting a long time to hear.

"Just get out. Get out. I don't want you here anymore."

"Are you sure that's what you want? Because I'm telling you, Cheryl, a king leaves his castle, he doesn't come back. He goes and builds a new castle."

It was a clumsy way of making sure I could say I'd tried. I wanted to put the failure on her. I wasn't going to be the "one who left." I gave her one last chance, almost holding my breath that she wouldn't take it, because I wanted more than anything else in the world to just walk out the door.

She screamed, "I told you, get out."

The kids had picked up on the fight and made themselves scarce. I didn't see them as I went into our bedroom, threw some clothes in a small black flight bag, and walked out to the front door.

"You sure this is what you want?"

"Just go. Leave. I can't stand you."

I tossed the bag onto the passenger seat of my van. I started the van and drove up the driveway as fast as I could. As I rolled out onto the main road, I fought the urge to stomp the gas pedal. I was excited, like the kid who has stolen cookies out of the cookie jar and is getting away with it. It was like a small miracle. I was unreasonably happy as I drove along Highway 33, following the winding two-lane road back to the clubhouse. I felt absolutely free for the first time in as long as I could remember. I knew I wouldn't be going back. No matter what happened, no matter what she said.

I bunked at the clubhouse for a couple of weeks. Away from Cheryl, things were so much easier. If I met someone, I wouldn't have to feel guilty. If I took off for a weekend in the Bay Area, I didn't have to wonder what I'd be facing when I rode home. The Hells Angels could be my primary concern. I was going to be the best leader possible, for my charter and the club.

I bought a large, metal shipping container that had been converted into a studio apartment with just enough room for a bed and a table. It wasn't much bigger than my cell in Terminal Island, but it was enough. I had inherited my grandparents' house in Ventura. I had the container apartment delivered on the back of a flatbed truck with a crane that hoisted it into the backyard. I used the house as a martial arts studio, and having the apartment in the backyard was the ideal setup.

I had been married at eighteen. The last date I had been on was in 1965. Dating in the nineties was a whole new experience. When I wasn't working on club business or working out, I was having fun. I discovered that sex isn't a chore for most women. In fact, every woman I dated enjoyed it just as much as I did. And unlike Cheryl, a lot of women liked me.

Cheryl sprinted to a divorce lawyer. We worked out an informal visitation schedule, and I continued to pay the bills and give her spending money. But she had a friend whispering in her ear about taking me to the cleaners. Even though she had lived the reality—she did the books for the Ink House and my martial arts supply company—she wanted to believe that I was the millionaire mastermind criminal that law enforcement made me out to be. Once the papers were drafted, though, she didn't move forward with them. I think it hit her. She wasn't social and she had a lot of serious baggage. Cheryl was smart. I think she knew that if it wasn't going to be me, it probably wasn't going to be anybody. It would be almost a decade before she finally signed off on the divorce. She'd never have another romantic relationship.

In the meantime, I tried to be a good dad. Moriya was as steady and strong as ever, in college and excelling. She had always been smart and grounded, with great instincts. She didn't take sides in the separation and remained the voice of reason. I wasn't surprised when she got accepted into law school. Her analytical mind and self-discipline were perfect for law. Given what she'd seen of the authorities in action, she naturally decided to focus on criminal defense.

Georgie was more of a challenge. He was fifteen and as moody as any teen boy. But he was also his mother's son. Cheryl manipulated him, and he clearly took her side in the breakup. It put a big crack into what had been an incredibly tight father-son bond. I had always been his hero. Suddenly, he saw me as the man who hurt his mother. He had grown up the prince of Ventura. Being the son of a local Hells Angels leader gave him a lot of power, and that he didn't leverage that power made people like him even more. A good-looking kid, with soulful brown eyes and a big smile, he was social too and traveled easily among the many different cliques in high school and in Ventura.

Cheryl and I had always made an effort not to argue in front of the kids, so although Moriya had long ago figured out that serious problems lay under the surface, Georgie was blindsided by the split. Fortunately, he still loved the Hells Angels. That love would be the common ground that would bring him and me back together.

If I had thought my leaving was going to get Cheryl out of my life, I was wrong. Even after I moved out, she never missed a chance to tear me down. If she found out I was dating someone, she'd make sure it got back to me that the woman was "too tall" or "too young" or "just dating George because of the patch." She told mutual friends that I left her broke. She played Georgie against me every chance she got. Cheryl was still all about power, but the only power she had over me now was the ability to cause me stress.

I didn't make the obvious connection when I got sick. Stress is invisible, but my fatigue wasn't. I was dragging myself through club events, fighting to stay up past ten at night. In the morning, it was a battle just to get out of bed. I was losing five pounds every two weeks, and I had been thin to start with. I finally went to the doctor when I noticed the lymph nodes in my groin and underarms were swollen. The doctor was visibly alarmed. She wanted me to have a biopsy on the lymph nodes. But a Richmond Hells Angel had gotten sick several years before. He'd undergone a biopsy and died a few months later of cancer. The rumor that ran through the club was that the biopsy itself had spread the cancer. It was foolish. But bone tired and fearful, I bought into the rumor. I told the doctor I wasn't going to have a biopsy. Luckily, she was young, dedicated, and caring. She started researching and trying to figure out what was going on without the benefit of tests. She sent me home after telling me I had to make a concerted effort to gain weight. At our next appointment, I had gotten worse.

"Look, I know who you are. I read the paper. You seem to me to be really unhappy. Is there anything specific in your life right now that's causing you stress?"

I had to laugh. "What, you mean other than every cop in the world trying to put me behind bars?"

"You know what I mean. Seriously, George, is there something stressful going on in your life?"

"Nothing really." I shrugged. "Well, I just broke up with my wife. We were together since 1965. High school sweethearts."

The doctor stared at me. "Oh my God. Why didn't you tell me before? How do you feel about it?"

I had to think about it. "I guess I'm conflicted. I'm glad that it's over, but I feel guilty that I'm glad."

She sat down and wrote out the name and number of a local psychiatrist. She handed me the slip of paper. "You need to deal with that if you're ever going to get better."

It went against everything I was. Greeks don't go to shrinks. Hells Angels don't go to shrinks. Men of my generation don't go to shrinks. But it seemed like the only alternative to a cancer diagnosis, so I called the number and made an appointment. On the day of the first session, I dressed for an undercover mission. I wore all gray—no insignia, jewelry, or other club indicia. I drove my white van because my bike would have been too easy to identify. I drove around in a big circle until I was sure no one was following me and then parked in an alley behind the psychiatrist's building.

Her office was a clean, boring, simply furnished room with a big wood desk and a couple of comfortable brown easy chairs set at an angle to each other. It was like sitting in someone's living room. I was careful about what I told the psychiatrist, but I felt better immediately. I'd end up going to her for almost a year.

It was a relief to have a completely objective viewpoint about what I'd gone through growing up, and in my relationship with Cheryl. We covered a lot of ground. I never discussed club business, and I went to great lengths to make sure nobody discovered I was seeing her. I had it in my head that if the club found out, they'd kick me out, kill me, or both. In reality, I don't think the club would have cared. Some members might have thought I was weak, and maybe I would have lost some of my influence. I would probably have been voted out as West Coast chairman, a powerful position I had been elected to a year before. But paranoia doesn't have boundaries. When the psychiatrist asked me to draw a picture of myself, I took it seriously. I went to an art store in Ventura and bought a full set of art supplies. I gave this interesting, revealing exercise my best shot. But I kept the drawing hidden, rolled up and stashed behind boxes in a closet.

The therapy helped. Within a month, I stopped losing weight, had more energy, and felt happier. I kept busy. I spent time with the kids. But my focus was the club. I worked hard to build membership. One early addition came out of the blue.

Leonardo Martinis was Brazilian, a member of the Rio de Janeiro Hells Angels. His mentor, the charter president, had gone to prison on a drug conviction. An opposing faction had taken control of the charter. When the president came back from prison, an argument led to a gun battle. Martinis's mentor was killed, and Martinis fled Brazil. There was, no doubt, more to the story. But one thing was for certain. The Rio Hells Angels were looking to kill Martinis. Making his way to the States, he showed up at the Oakland clubhouse and asked Sonny Barger for help. Sonny—wisely as it turned out—told the kid that he could do nothing for him. Sonny was always careful about extending himself for someone who looked like trouble and had nothing to offer him.

I was the next stop. Martinis convinced me that sending him away would be condemning him to death. I let him hide out in Ventura and reached out to the Brazilian charter. I eventually brokered an agreement. I told them Martinis wanted to transfer to Ventura. I had enough juice within the club that Rio had to agree, as long as Martinis came down and requested the transfer in a charter meeting. It was the same rule I'd used years earlier with Irish. I made clear to Brazil that I was sending him back, but that he was under my protection.

"You guys harm this guy, or if he disappears, you won't see me, but I'll be there. Do you understand me?"

"Yeah, we hear you."

They were not happy about it, but Martinis returned from Rio safe and sound, with a transfer letter in hand. He was also a talented tattoo artist, so I put him to work in the Ink House. He became the first in a new generation of Ventura Hells Angels.

Georgie would be the face of that generation. He had wanted to be a member since he was a boy. He had always come along on runs when he didn't have school (and often when he did). Hanging around the club is the best training for becoming a member. Sometimes, you even get hands-on experience. In 1992, when Georgie was just sixteen, he got his first taste of what it was like to ride as a Hells Angel.

The charter was headed to the biggest motorcycle rally in the country, held once a year in the first full week of August, in Sturgis, South Dakota. Sturgis is motorcycle mecca, and the Hells Angels are always there. The pack pulled out of Ventura around midnight, trying to make it through the Nevada desert early enough to avoid the brutal, unforgiving sun. The second stop in the trip was Grand Junction, Colorado. The town was a pretty, quaint Old West town with a welcoming feel. It was always a friendly place for Hells Angels. We stayed at the same motel every time, a clean and cheap motor lodge with an attached restaurant that served good diner food. I washed the road dirt off with a quick shower and then found most of the members drinking beer and finishing dinner in the diner. Aaron Lauer had patched in a month before. He took me aside, and I sensed I wasn't going to like what was coming.

"Hey, George, do you know where the airport is around here?"

You don't expect or want to hear this type of question on a run. "Why?"

"I've got a court appearance tomorrow and I've got to get back for it."

"Jesus, Aaron, why didn't you let me know sooner? What are we supposed to do with your bike?"

"George, it's not a problem. Just put it in the van."

One of the things I loved—and sometimes hated—about the new guys who were coming up in Ventura was the live-for-today outlook. They were free spirits, fun, and spontaneous. It was a true outlaw attitude. But they had absolutely zero sense when it came to planning. They just assumed everything would work out.

Like most clubs and charters, we had a support vehicle following the pack on runs. For Sturgis that year, Cheryl was driving my Dodge van, with Moriya and Georgie. It was the last trip we would take as a family. Having Cheryl along was just too awkward for both of us. But it was handy to have a driver who knew the drill. The van was full of extra parts, gear, and supplies. There wasn't room for another motorcycle tire, much less an entire 1994 Harley FXR Super Glide. We didn't have a tow bar set up, so towing the bike was out of the question.

"Your bike's not going to fit in the van."

"Have Georgie ride it back. I got no problem with him riding my sled."

Short of leaving an $8,000 motorcycle at some motor lodge in the middle of nowhere, we were out of options. If Aaron missed his court date, they'd issue a warrant on him. Still, I was leery of throwing my sixteen-year-old on a member's bike for days of fast riding to Sturgis and back home again.

I talked it over with Cheryl. She gave me some grief because that was our routine, but I could see she wasn't digging her heels in. She knew, like

I did, that Georgie was eventually going to join the club. Sooner or later, he was going to ride with a pack. It might as well be sooner. But even after Cheryl agreed, it was still up to Georgie. He was nervous and backed into a corner. If he said no, he knew as well as anybody else that he would lose members' respect. He also had a lot of Angels urging him on. Hells Angels love anything that bucks the status quo, and having a teenager ride in a pack seemed like the best idea in the world. I knew Georgie was mature enough, but I was concerned about the physical demands. He was a surfer, a martial artist, and a strong kid all in all. But he was also just shy of five feet five and probably 130 pounds soaking wet. A road-ready FXR weighs in north of six hundred pounds. Riding in formation doesn't leave a lot of room for error when you have to swerve to miss a deer or a pothole. The pack moves faster than seventy miles per hour. Riding in tight formation can be a challenge for even seasoned motorcyclists, and Georgie had never ridden anything bigger than a dirt bike. Things can happen in a blink.

"Do you think I can do it?"

"Of course you can do it." I was talking to myself as much as to him.

Everyone shouted their riding tips as Georgie practiced figure eights and low-speed maneuvers in the motel parking lot. It was easy to see he had a feel for it.

Hells Angels ride in a strict two-by-two formation. Most charters arrange it from front to back in order of chain of command. I always rode front left, with the vice president on the front right. Ventura did things a little differently because our sergeant at arms was also our road captain. He rode at the back to keep the pack tight. I told David Ortega, the vice president at the time, that I wanted to break protocol and have Georgie ride on my right at the front of the pack. That way, I could make sure he was riding tight and I'd have some chance to intervene if he got into trouble. David, like all the Ventura members, loved Georgie. He had no problem giving up his position to my son.

So the next morning, we pulled out of Grand Junction right on schedule. Within a couple miles my nerves settled down as Georgie fell into the rhythm of the ride. He handled the bike like he owned it. I was always proud of my son, but never more so than riding alongside him at the head of a pack of Hells Angels, seeing him grinning ear to ear. When we finally pulled up in front of Gunner's Lounge on Main Street in Sturgis, Georgie was the man of the hour. Hells Angels from all over the world swarmed him, and I realized that this was a watershed moment, a rite of passage.

The ride back was even better. Georgie was completely comfortable in the saddle. The wind was at our back as the pack made its way past the Custer Battlefield Memorial, over the beautiful Big Horn Mountains to Cody, up into Yellowstone, and back across the desert home. Two short years later, Georgie would make that trip on his own bike, wearing a patch on his back. In the meantime, he spent more and more time around the clubhouse. He was the youngest hangaround we had, but far from the only guy in his generation showing interest. The others came from an unlikely source.

For a small town, Ventura had more than its share of street gangs. The Avenue Gangsters had been around the longest, but ran up against Pierpont, Midtown, and the Haoles, as well as a couple of skinhead gangs. Most of the gang members were high school kids or recent graduates. They were rough around the edges but basically decent kids who were rowdy and lacked direction. They were focused on having fun and being a little wild. They didn't like authority, and they made their own rules. In short, they were natural outlaws.

There had been street gangs in town for as long as I could remember, but the level of violence was getting worse. After a couple drive-by shootings, citizens were up in arms. Carl Handy had been made the head of the Ventura police gang unit. He asked me to take a shot at reining in the key players. I put the word out that I wanted to meet with the gang leaders at the clubhouse. They showed up with attitude to spare. Once they settled in, I laid down the law.

"If you guys don't get your shit together, we're going to get it together for you."

"What does that mean?"

"What do you think it means? You think the Hells Angels are going to take the time to bring you guys to our clubhouse and then have you tell us to go fuck ourselves?"

These were just kids. They weren't thinking past their little corners of the gang world. Most didn't have a clue about the history, traditions, or power of the Hells Angels. But they could sure as shit see I was serious. The shotguns in the rack and the autopsy photos we had pinned on the memorial wall—of the two Angels killed in Florida by the Outlaws—told them that.

"You guys need to start communicating. If you want to fight, I understand. But you're taking it to a different level right now. You're doing things that are going to get you in some deep shit, and I don't mean just with the cops. This is a Hells Angels town."

I think nobody had talked to them so directly before. I was showing them respect, addressing them as equals. But I was also more to the point than the cops. They could play games with the cops, mouth off and commit petty crimes without much blowback. For most of them, it was the first time they were faced with a strong, no-bullshit father figure. I wasn't a feel-good social worker, but I also wasn't law enforcement. I wasn't telling them they were bad boys. I was telling them they were being stupid boys.

Things calmed down after the meeting. Then something unexpected happened. First, an Avenue Gangster named Jay Adams bought a bike and became a hangaround. Then a Midtown member did the same. Then a Pierpont guy. Gang members started buying Harleys. These kids saw something in the red and white that they weren't seeing in gang life. Future and potential. They brought fresh air into the charter. They came with different perspectives and a new attitude. They were fun. It was the start of a new era. Sadly, it was also the end of an era for me.

My father had been having health problems for years. I didn't think it was anything serious when he went in the hospital for some tests. Riding through Ventura, I had the urge to go to the hospital and see him. He was due to get out the next day, but I just felt like talking to him. We were together in his room, shooting the breeze about Georgie and the club, when he started having trouble breathing and grimaced in pain. One of the monitors he was connected to broke into a high-pitched alarm. Suddenly the room filled with nurses. They told me to leave. As I stepped out into the hallway, I could see a look of panic in my father's eyes. Neither of us knew what the hell was going on. The nurses wheeled him out of the room. He called out to me as I stood helpless in the wide, brightly lit hospital hallway.

"Son, don't let me die in here, help me."

An hour later, he was dead from a massive heart attack. Only as we planned the funeral did I realize how many questions I still had for him. I'd always loved my father, but it had only been in the last few years that he had started opening up to me. He had revealed that he had owned a bunch of old motorcycles at one time, including a Henderson, an Indian, and a Harley. Out of the blue one day, he had let slip that he had done time at juvenile offender's camp because he'd taken a car for a joyride. There was a lot about him I didn't know. Now, I never would. My mom was devastated. So I offered to put together a gathering after the funeral.

"What do you think? You want to do it at the clubhouse?"

"Yeah, let's do it there. Your dad always liked coming down there and visiting you."

She was right. The members treated my dad like royalty, with sincere respect and fondness. He was always warmly welcomed at the clubhouse.

"What about the relatives? What if they don't want to come?"

"To hell with them. If they don't want to come, they don't have to come."

Hers was the last word on the subject. We put together a nice party and had it catered. Everyone attended, and it was a great memorial. My dad's sister Lulu even told me, "Your dad would have really liked this. I like the family feeling you've got here."

When a man loses his father, especially such a good father, he looks for something to grab ahold of. You need an anchor to divert your attention from the grief. For me, that was Georgie and the club. The deeper he got into the Hells Angels, the more I felt like he was coming back to me. He was the first of the new guys to get voted in as a prospect. I didn't realize until much later that it also served Cheryl's purposes. Georgie was a conduit to power and knowledge. As her son worked his way toward membership, Cheryl used him for invites to clubhouse parties and events. She showed up much more regularly than she ever had as my wife. She'd pick a corner and hold court, like the once and future queen. She always had a dig or two for me or my latest girlfriend, or a piece of "advice" about a prospect or member she had decided might be a problem. I avoided her as much as possible, which was difficult in the confines of the Ventura clubhouse.

A year later, Georgie got his patch and became the youngest Hells Angel in the world. It was a violation of club rules. Prospects have to prove they are at least twenty-one to become a member. Georgie had grown up around the club. Everyone knew he was seventeen. At the first officers' meeting after Georgie was voted in, more than one old-timer let me know that several members weren't at all pleased about the move. The majority, though, were like uncles to Georgie and had no problem with his membership. The most powerful advocate was "Uncle Sonny."

"Does he have an ID that proves he's twenty-one?"

"He sure does." Georgie had been using a fake driver's license for years.

"Then that's all he needs. That's what the rules say."

Leading a young and growing charter was exciting, but I continued to have a larger role in the club as a national officer and unofficial spokesperson, both of which took up a lot of time in the nineties. Those roles meant being high profile, which literally put me in the crosshairs. Because Taco Bowman was a key law enforcement target, it came as no surprise when he was indicted on a slew of racketeering charges. What did surprise me was that one of the charges in the indictment—one that he would ultimately be convicted for—was ordering a hit on me. He had assigned a hit team to go to Ventura, and an Outlaw had made the trip. Law enforcement discovered that the would-be assassin had maps of Ventura and a map to my house, along with a silenced pistol and other gear. I never found out why the shooter didn't take a shot, but I was certainly glad he didn't.

I didn't have long to mull over the reality of Taco's case because I remained the lone peacemaker in the Hells Angels, and there was a war overseas. Old vendettas between outlaw motorcycle clubs extended even to foreign charters. The Scandinavian Hells Angels were in the midst of an incredibly bloody conflict with their counterpart Bandidos charters. The clubhouse in Malmö, Sweden, had been bombed, and an antitank rocket had been fired into the Copenhagen clubhouse. The outlaw community was calling it the Nordic Wars, and if it continued, it was going to destroy all outlaw clubs in Scandinavia.

In the winter of 1994, the officers in the Scandinavian charters asked me to come over and meet with them to discuss how to end the war. I flew to Amsterdam to attend a two-day summit, where we discussed how to quietly approach the Bandidos charters to establish a dialog and lower the heat on the boiling pot. I also agreed to work with the Bandidos' international president, George Wegers, to get him working toward a resolution from the Bandidos' side. I had a good relationship with George, one that we've maintained to this day. We both saw the benefit to the clubs' coexisting in peace, and in a unified front against law enforcement.

George and I would eventually meet with the two highest-ranking opposing officers in the conflict—in Spokane, Washington, and in the basement of Gunner's Lounge in Sturgis. It would take a long time, and a lot of effort, but the clubs would eventually reach a truce in 1997.

In the meantime, I continued to grow the Ventura charter as other "new generation" Angels followed in Georgie's footsteps. Within two years, the charter more than tripled in size. These young guys brought a whole new style to the charter. Not everyone was on board with the transition.

Shortly after Jay Adams was voted in, he was surrounded by his former friends in the Avenue Gangsters. They trapped him in a dark parking lot off Ventura's main drag and rat-packed him, beating him senseless. One of the Gangsters broke into his car and took his patch. That's where they crossed the line that the Hells Angels long ago drew in the sand. You don't touch a member's patch, much less steal it. I put the word out that I wanted a sit-down. Three Avenue Gangsters showed up at the clubhouse. I invited the one in charge to sit across from me at the clubhouse bar.

"We've got a problem. I don't care about the fight. One day we'll settle that. But that patch is club property. It has to come back here."

"I don't know anything about a patch."

I pulled out my .45 Sig Sauer and laid it on the bar. "Let me put it this way. Either that patch comes back or I have to answer to the club for it. That means I have to either shoot myself in the head or shoot you in the head." I leaned toward him as if I were going to tell him a secret. "And I'm not going to shoot myself in the head."

I slid off the bar stool, picked up the gun, tucked it into my waistband, and stared at the guy to let him know the meeting was over. The patch was delivered to the clubhouse twenty minutes later. The gangs were learning who the Hells Angels really were.

But even some club members took offense at the changes. The younger Ventura members wore baggy jeans, long T-shirts or basketball jerseys, and skater shoes. They rocked the street fashions of their generation. Decades before, outlaws had moved from denim cutoffs to patches on black leather vests. At that time, old-school members like Old Man John had thought leather vests were bullshit. But fashions are window dressing. Looks change. The patch doesn't. What it means to be outlaw is the same.

Some club members are just bound to get bent out of shape anytime change is in the wind. They'd complain when the young guys threw the Beastie Boys or NWA on the stereo at runs or wore their baseball caps backward. Some hard-liners felt old and outnumbered. As many new members as we brought to runs and events, we trailed double that number of hangarounds and prospects. Most were nineteen or twenty. I got an earful from established Oakland members on a run to Santa Cruz.

"These guys are way too fucking young."

People had short memories. "How old were you when you came around the club? Sonny was seventeen. Are you guys that old that you forgot how to rock and roll? Come on. What the hell? We can't bring wild young guys around the club? What are we, a Rotary Club?"

Clubs, like so much else in the world, evolve and adapt or die. I only wanted the club to move forward. We needed new blood. It didn't mean we were compromising the outlaw spirit or our ideas of freedom and brotherhood. It was just a new cast of characters. It bugged me that these guys were so stuck in their generation that they couldn't see that.

The differences were most glaring at big events like runs. A long party weekend was a different experience with a much larger, younger charter behind me. As fun and wild as these kids could be, things could also go south in a hurry. That's what happened in Steamboat Springs.

The biggest run on the Hells Angels calendar—one that involves every charter in the United States—is the annual USA Run. In 1996, the run was held in Steamboat Springs, Colorado. We brought every Ventura member. We stopped for the night in Grand Junction. That left us a three-hour ride to Steamboat Springs the next day. Before dinner, I was cleaning up my beard with a small trimmer when I noticed my hair was its usual untamed mess. A long day of riding without a helmet, wind blowing across your head at eighty miles an hour, left long hair hopelessly tangled and crazy-looking. You could find bugs in there. It was a frustration on long rides. But looking in that mirror, the small buzzing trimmer in my hand, I had an answer. On a whim, I gave myself a buzz cut. It felt great.

At dinner, everyone was blown away by the look. Outlaws had, since the sixties, been defined by long, unruly hair on their heads and faces. A buzz cut was a shock, an outlaw act. The entire charter instantly dug it. First one guy, then the next, borrowed the trimmer. Some went even further, shaving their heads down to nubs. Only one guy decided not to do it—the one who would, coincidentally, become an informant. It became a spontaneous group-bonding exercise and created an incredible camaraderie.

We rode to Steamboat Springs the next morning, moving tight and fast. We didn't even check into our motel before we rode to the run site, a timeworn hotel called the Iron Horse Inn. The club had taken it over, and there were hundreds of Angels inside and out as Ventura thundered into the parking lot. People were amazed. Other charters couldn't believe what we'd done, and they couldn't stop smiling. I walked up to Sonny and gave him a hug. I could tell he liked the look, a whole charter together in radical unity.

"Jesus, George, that was pretty impressive. It was like the old days."

That was high praise from Sonny and it felt good. I'd seen the Ventura charter through some rough times. I also realized that even though Sonny had stepped away from an active role as the club's main contact with the media because of his throat surgery, he wasn't totally comfortable that I'd picked up the ball and run with it. So the compliment sat well. I had always respected Sonny and, at that point, it still mattered to me what he thought.

It was a great start to the run, but we had a problem. A young Ventura member was on a meth bender. The first day of the ride, we'd had to talk him down because he was sure that a hit team was following the pack in a car. Meth is an incredibly powerful central nervous system stimulant. The speed jitters go right to your brain. Keep doing it and you'll quickly become sleep deprived. Delusions and paranoia are common side effects. It's why I came to hate meth. But by the time we made the run site, I thought the kid had calmed down and got a hold on things. I was wrong.

The run was a typical Hells Angels' party. By the time we rode in, everyone was going full tilt. In Southern California, we called the meth users in the club the Fast Lane Crew or just cranksters. These guys were the crazier members, and things could go off the rails in the blink of an eye. I wasn't thrilled when my member started partying with these guys.

I never got high on runs. I wasn't a big drug user to begin with—I did cocaine recreationally and rarely—and I always wanted to be sharp at club events. I had once thought that meth was the ideal club drug because you could do a little and stay sharp for a long ride, or the entire weekend of a run. But I'd seen firsthand how it was destroying members from the inside out. I stayed sober at club events. Big club gatherings had a lot of politics. You had to be on your toes. I also believed that a good leader always kept a clear head.

I went back to the motel, about a mile down the road from the Iron Horse Inn, at around midnight. I had just gotten into a deep sleep when the phone rang. It was a frantic voice I didn't recognize.

"One of your guys shot someone. You got to get down here and straighten this shit out." The next call came from the cops, telling me to get down to the Iron Horse. They were in a standoff with the Angels. It had started out as normal Hells Angels bullshit. Angels love to party hard. But in typical outlaw fashion, the games are often dangerous. In the early days, members would spike someone's drink with a couple tabs of acid. After a few bad episodes, the club instituted a rule that you couldn't spike someone's drink. It went hand in hand with the "no throwing ammo in the bonfire" rule that was put in place around the same time. Outlaws will be outlaws.

Noticing that the kid was paranoid, two members had started fucking with him. It was juvenile stuff, stoking his delusions with offhand comments. He got more and more worried. He began imagining that the members were working with the guys he thought he'd seen earlier on the trip following us. Everybody was setting him up. It got all mixed up in his head and he couldn't sort it out.

Things went from bad to worse when another member came inside with the plastic sheeting he had used to protect his saddlebags from rain. The guy unwrapped the bags and smoothed out the plastic so he could use it on the ride home. The kid, though, decided the sheet was going to be his body bag. He worked himself up until he went over the edge. The two members toyed with him for three or four hours straight. Finally, an older member talked the kid off the ledge. "There's nothing going on here, brother. You've been up too long. Everything's cool, man."

Unfortunately, the older member turned in a little after I did. The kid started freaking out again, telling one of the guys that he wanted to call George. The guy said, innocently enough, "It's too late for that." Everyone knew I hit the rack by midnight. The kid took it the wrong way. "It's too late" meant they'd come to the point of no return. He panicked. He went into the bathroom, pulled his gun, and came out shooting. The shots sent people running. The two guys who had been working on him all night were hit. One was shot in the hand in what turned out to be a fairly minor wound. But the other was seriously hurt, shot in the chest, neck, arm, and back. The hotel manager called the cops. Overwhelmed by the size of the run, the local department immediately called in support from all surrounding agencies.

I threw on my clothes, jumped on my bike, and raced to the Iron Horse Inn. It was complete chaos. Riding up to the scene, I found well over a hundred cops in a mix of uniforms standing around. The squawk of police radios shattered the early-morning stillness, and the play of dozens of multicolor cruiser lights bouncing off of buildings gave the scene a carnival feel. In the darkness, there seemed to be a lot more confusion than direction. I arrived at the standoff and began to negotiate with the cop who seemed to be in charge of the scene.

"Give me a chance to go in there and calm it down or there's going to be even more of a shoot-out here." Among the hundreds of Hells Angels at the run, most had access to a gun. The situation was a powder keg. The cops knew it too and let me through.

The ambulance had taken the wounded Angels to the hospital. Inside, a group of members were holding the kid at gunpoint, debating their next move. Everyone was pumped on adrenaline, booze, meth, or a combination. I made my case for these guys not to kill him, and not to give the cops a reason to start a massive firefight. The negotiations went on for over an hour. I went in and out between the cops and the angry Hells Angels. The risk that everyone in the room could die or go to jail for life was all that was keeping these guys from murder.

Outside, I convinced the cops to give me time. Some of them had seen too many movies and thought their job was to storm the hotel and end the standoff regardless of the body count. As I was outside negotiating, members dismantled the room, removing bloodstained drywall, slugs, and any other evidence they could find.

I decided it was time to push the issue. The kid was done as a Hells Angel. The question was, would he live beyond losing his patch? I stood between him and the other members, laying down what I hoped would be the final word.

"He's coming with me. We're going to get on my bike and get out of here. We can open the run back up, let the cops do their thing. But you guys need to put your guns away and let us ride out of here."

I told the kid to take off his patch and fold it up, as a sign to everyone that everything would be done by the Hells Angels' code. Outside, we rode slowly through a cordon of pissed-off members who had gathered as word spread throughout the run. He slumped against me as I made a beeline for the street, hoping no one would be reckless enough to take a shot at us.

We made it out of the parking lot to the police line. I told the sergeant they could go in. The cops didn't register who my passenger was. They breached the room in force, only to find it empty, with sections of drywall missing and no evidence of a shooting. Back at the motel, David gathered the Ventura members. We all crowded into my room and quickly and unanimously voted the kid out of the club.

I headed back to the run to let the club officers know what was going on. I was operating on about two hours of sleep, feeling like I'd been kicked in the head with steel-toed boots. I rode up only to be stopped by a group of furious cops. They threatened to dump a load of charges on me. Destruction of property, tampering with evidence, felony this and arrest that. After a night of being the diplomat, I was done.

"Are you fucking kidding me? Would you have rather had a full-blown shoot-out?" I was at the end of my rope. Dressing people down in colorful language is a Hells Angels art form known as motherfucking. I motherfucked those cops up one side and down the other. Knowing that they had no evidence, and that tempers were still running hot, they backed off and let me through.

I met Sonny and a group of senior members for breakfast in the Iron Horse Inn's dining room. We discussed the incident, and I was hoping that the charter's having kicked the kid out would settle things. I told everyone at the table about the vote, and that we would take him home, but that we had his patch. Some of the members still wanted their pound of flesh and made noises that it wasn't enough of a punishment.

"There's no way to make it right. I can't change the fact that those guys got shot. But I'm not handing him over to anyone."

Sonny's raspy artificial voice cut through the conversation. "I wouldn't have kicked him out."

I was stunned. "What? We had to. It's the rules."

"Hey, man, those dudes were bullies and they got what they deserved. They asked for it, and they got it."

Sonny and I had certainly had our disputes. We had different styles, and conflicts among leaders are just a normal part of the life. But we had never disagreed about the rules. I was disappointed. I respected Sonny. But if he was willing to break the rules for some first-year member he didn't know, would he hesitate to break them himself? We weren't just having a difference of opinion, we were disagreeing about the code that kept us all in line. The run divided into two factions: one that supported kicking the kid out or worse, and the other that sided with Sonny.

Hells Angels charters—like individual members—don't bolt in the face of trouble. The run went on and Ventura stayed to the end. I kept a tight leash on my members. I wanted everyone together and accounted for at all times. It wasn't beyond imagination that a drunk or high Hells Angel with the wrong agenda might decide that shooting one Ventura member was just as good as shooting another. Even after we heard from the hospital that both the wounded members were going to recover, I didn't relax. I was happy to see the run end. As we got ready to leave, I gave my guys a lecture.

"We're leaving as a charter. Everybody is leaving together and nobody stays behind. We'll tow the kid's bike and he'll ride in the truck."

I couldn't leave him out in the open where someone could take a shot at him. Others could get caught in the cross fire. He was understandably destroyed, coming down off a meth binge with dozens of guys he'd called "brother" a week ago who would now gladly shoot him in the head. He had lost his patch and his identity. Back home, he would sink further into drug addiction. At that moment, though, I didn't give a good goddamn how the kid felt. I just wanted to get the charter home safe.

Outlaws have short attention spans. It didn't take long for the storm to blow over. It helped that huge news came out of Oakland. Sonny Barger, the man who'd built Oakland into a power base and the center of the outlaw world, was transferring. He had done his time for the bombing-conspiracy conviction at the Federal Bureau of Prisons' medium-security facility in Phoenix, Arizona. He took a liking to the dry, hot climate and wide-open desert landscape he could see beyond the fences of FCI Phoenix. After the Dirty Dozen patched over to become the first Hells Angels charter in Arizona, the stage was set. In August 1997, Sonny requested a transfer to the Cave Creek charter. It was a formality. Nobody was going to debate the issue.

The move was part of Sonny's settling into a different role within the club. He became more of a figurehead than an active leader. He wasn't the guy that the media went to for comments. I was. He wasn't running the West Coast Officers' Meeting. I was. By 1998, I was at the height of my power as a Hells Angels leader.

My vice president at the time went on the run from pending charges. We didn't hear from him (no member on the run is allowed to enter a Hells Angels' clubhouse), and I got a tip that he was arranging to give information in exchange for having the charges dropped. The charter voted him out and, in a high point of my time as an Angel, voted Georgie in as my vice president.

The World Run that year was held in Ventura. World Runs were high-profile events that drew Hells Angels from around the world. They took much more preparation and planning than regular runs because hundreds of members would make the trip, flying in from as far away as Australia. We combined the World Run that year with the club's fiftieth anniversary. The anniversary was held in Berdoo because it marked both Berdoo's anniversary and the founding of the Hells Angels. The Berdoo party lasted a week, and Ventura hosted the run over the weekend. We took over the town. We had help from a group of high school kids who called themselves the Outfit and liked to wear Hells Angels support gear— red-and-white T-shirts, jerseys, and caps with slogans like *Support Your Local 81* (*H* and *A* represented by the numbers 8 and 1, respectively). The kids cleaned up around the clubhouse yard and at run locations, painted the clubhouse, and did other odd jobs in exchange for free support gear, a few bucks, and a chance to be near the center of excitement. Law enforcement eventually fed the local media the nonsensical idea that the charter was recruiting high school kids as a drug-dealing network. In reality, those kids were fans. Some of them eventually became hangarounds, and all of them thought it was cool to show off the support gear at school, until the school district outlawed it.

I was focused on bigger things. As the host, I was responsible for keeping everybody happy. Ken Corney had replaced Carl Handy as the Ventura police liaison. Corney and I would eventually become adversaries, but over that weekend, we worked our respective sides to make sure nobody—cop or outlaw—caused a problem in Ventura. The run came off without a hitch. To cap it off, we gathered the hundreds of members in attendance and took a picture on the stately steps of the historic Ventura City Hall. It was the most impressive building in town, built in a neoclassical, Beaux-Arts style with imposing thirty-foot columns along the façade. The photo pissed off law enforcement and gave rise to a rumor that Corney voiced to me and that would make its way to the media.

"This is your coronation, isn't it?"

"No. It's nothing like that."

Everyone from DAs to local cops told reporters that I was heir to Sonny's throne. It was silly. In the first place, the club didn't operate like that. Each charter had its own personality, and local charters often rebelled against dictates from Oakland or anywhere else. International charters were even more independent.

But Sonny and I *were* going in different directions. He wanted a quieter life in Arizona. I liked the action we were seeing in Southern California, and I felt good about the charter's growth. But I had no desire to replace Sonny. I had my own identity and was comfortable with it. I was also all too aware that guys at the top make the biggest targets. Other clubs want to take you down. Members get jealous and scheme for your position. But most of all, the feds want to bring you down. They'll let murderers go free if it means convicting a Hells Angels leader. I'd already beaten them once, but that was just another reason for vengeance. The cops don't go away. They remember, and they wait. And they wouldn't have to wait long after the fiftieth anniversary party. Within two years, the Ventura district attorney would build a mountain of a case on the molehill of a misdemeanor.

12

A fifty-nine-count indictment looks like a giant, serious problem. Hear fifty-nine counts read aloud after your name, flip page after page of the indictment, and the charges seem insurmountable. It's another law-enforcement trick. Multiple counts are almost always combined and whittled down into the most serious charges. They pile on in hopes that something—anything—sticks. So the most surprising thing about the fifty-nine-count indictment I would be hit with in 2001 was that it could stem from a simple misdemeanor charge and a work furlough requirement.

Zorana Katzakian was an attractive blonde who had bounced around from the Bay Area to Southern California in the late seventies. A bit of an outlaw groupie, she spent a lot of her free time in Hells Angels bars and clubhouses. She wound up as Tom Heath's house mouse. When Tom got tired of her, she was broke and needed work, and I needed an office manager for the Ink House. A tattoo shop can be a circus. Artists show up late or not at all. They often have substance abuse problems and all the baggage that comes with those issues. They make deals for tattoos. You have to make sure nobody is bartering stolen goods, guns with a history, or drugs—or just keeping money from cash transactions. It's a struggle to keep the business clean and profitable. I needed someone reliable, someone who wouldn't rip me off or let the artists run wild. The woman we called Zee turned out to be that person. She called Ventura home for two decades and fit in well.

But she had her own vices. Zee had been busted for some minor offense in the late nineties—I never learned the details. A probation violation later led to the choice between jail or work furlough. Anyone facing jail time jumps at the chance to do work furlough. You need to have a regular, full-time job, which either gets you out of your cell during the workday or gets you out of going to jail at all. A source would later tell me that Zee's work furlough paperwork was the start of a tax investigation against me. The Ventura County work furlough program required you to be a full-time employee and submit pay stubs so that the program could calculate how much they would take out of each check (prisoners were charged for the privilege of work furlough).

Everybody at the Ink House was paid as an independent contractor. They got a lump-sum check and were responsible for their own insurance and taxes. That included Zee. The artists liked the setup because it gave them a lot of leeway in how much income they claimed. By law, I didn't have to file for them, so I didn't. I'm sure many of the artists didn't bother with taxes. I didn't care. It wasn't my responsibility.

But as my source would reveal to me, Zee gave the work furlough officials what she called pay stubs but which were just check receipts for her gross pay. Of course, no taxes were removed. Someone in the district attorney's office got the bright idea to check the tax rolls and discovered I hadn't paid any payroll taxes. What would normally have merited an IRS interview became the DA's point of attack. Zorana Katzakian, the woman who would become Sonny Barger's fourth wife, had just brought a world of heat down on our heads.

It was no secret that Ventura district attorney Michael Bradbury didn't like me. I'd heard through the grapevine that he was furious when the *Ventura County Reporter* ran my profile next to his in their annual

"Movers & Shakers" article. After that, it seemed like Bradbury made it his personal mission to bring me down. He wanted my patch. Bradbury fancied himself a cowboy, and he and his wife had bought a small ranch in Ojai, where he kept horses. He had the round face and white hair of a kindly grandfather, but the athletic build and mentality of a fighter. He was a political climber with his eye on the California attorney general's office, and a take-no-prisoners approach to prosecutions. I think he figured that the Ventura Hells Angels would be a neat little stepping-stone on the path to that office.

With the help of a sympathetic judge, he used the tax investigation to secure broad search warrants. The warrants covered my house in Ventura, the Ink House, and Cheryl's house because she was listed as my business partner in the Ink House. After the split, Cheryl had moved out of our Oak View house, into a smaller, more manageable hillside condo in Ventura, overlooking the ocean.

My accountant kept most of my paperwork, so the DA investigators were never going to find tax documents. But they found better fuel for prosecution. The search of the Ink House turned up a variety of illegal prescription drugs at the artists' workstations. They also found what's known as a "pay-owe" sheet, a ledger of drug fronts and money owed. Wherever it came from, it had nothing to do with me. My name wasn't on the sheet, it wasn't in my handwriting, and my fingerprints weren't on it.

The search of Cheryl's condo turned up something much more potentially damaging. Investigators discovered a neat stack of seventy-five bottles full of Vicodin—thousands of tablets worth tens of thousands of dollars—in a hall closet, covered by Georgie's clothes. Georgie had lived in the Oak View house for a short time, renting rooms to a few Avenue Gangsters who were friends of his from high school. It was the perfect party palace for a bunch of wild young men. But ultimately, he wanted to be closer to the clubhouse and have his own space. He had moved into the container apartment that sat unused in my backyard. I had moved into my grandparents' house after completing a yearlong remodel.

Georgie would regularly go over to Cheryl's to use the shower and visit with her. It was a natural place to store clothes because he had no extra room in the container apartment. But it cemented the link between him and the drugs. The cops also confiscated $100,000 in cash from a safe in Cheryl's bedroom, to go with $30,000 they took from my house. We'd never see that money again.

Juicy as they seemed to the DA's investigators, these discoveries came with a problem, one that would plague the case all the way to the end. Drugs and money weren't listed as targets on the warrants. Existing law defined what investigators could and could not seize during the execution of a search warrant. The whole idea behind search warrants is that for the government officials to violate your Fourth Amendment rights, they have to demonstrate a basis for and description of the criminal evidence they hope to find. Otherwise search warrants would just be fishing expeditions.

I knew about the drugs. Georgie was buying Vicodin from a U.S. Air Force clerk named Joshua Adams. Adams was stealing them from the base pharmacy, and Georgie and other members were selling them to friends and connections throughout Ventura County. The younger Ventura members were regulars at clubs and shows, and they knew everyone on the scene. It was an easy way for them to make money. As long as it wasn't heroin, the Hells Angels didn't care. As long as it wasn't meth, I didn't care.

Drugs had been part of outlaw life since I had become a Hells Angel. Most Angels used drugs at least recreationally, and many sold them. It was never an organized effort. In fact, I had to stop some of the Ventura members from coming to blows over disagreements about who was selling what, to whom, and where. You didn't talk about that type of thing in the clubhouse, and you worked out your problems without creating bad feelings or fighting with your brothers.

I had my hands full running my businesses, so drug dealing was not a temptation. Even if the money had been attractive, I'd seen way too many situations where drugs had brought down heat on the club. They had been the basis of numerous prosecutions and long jail terms up in the Bay Area. As far I was concerned, people always made mistakes with drugs and eventually got busted. And cops were rabid about drug busts.

As soon as the drugs were discovered, Bradbury started making his case in the media. The narrative was that the Ventura charter was dealing to high school kids (although the words *high school* were left out of many stories, to drive home the "evil bikers" angle). Law enforcement tried to connect the charter to the Outfit, the kids that had helped spruce up the clubhouse during the fiftieth anniversary party. Even after all was said and done, the media would never point out that the DA didn't have a single example of a hand-to-hand drug deal between a Hells Angel and juvenile.

That didn't change the fact that the Vicodin found at Cheryl's condo was a big problem, one that shouldn't have been a problem at all. When the tax investigation first came to light, I knew that they would search the Ink House. I told Cheryl she should take her name off the business to avoid her getting caught up in the hunt. She thought I was trying to get over on her and refused. I also told Georgie that he should get rid of the drugs, but like many kids, he knew better than his old man.

Cheryl and I were arrested. But because of the flaws in the search, they couldn't hold us. Bradbury regrouped. Meanwhile, Cheryl and Georgie called me up and asked me to come over to the condo. They showed me a big surprise. While the investigators had been busy patting themselves on the back over the haul in the closet, they missed an even bigger stash in Cheryl's garage. Georgie had filled a white wicker laundry hamper with even more Vicodin than was in the closet, along with six pounds of hash. Here these two were, with this huge liability sitting in the garage, and their first idea was to call me. George will fix it. Just like he fixes everything. I decided they'd both learn a lesson out of it. I agreed to take care of it. I backed my car into the garage, loaded the hamper into my trunk, and drove it to a contact I had. I sold everything for a bargain-price, lump-sum cash payment. I added it to my defense fund. Georgie came to see me that night.

"Did you get rid of it?"

"It's gone."

"How much did we make?"

"Who's 'we'?"

"That was my stash."

"Look, you want to be a big boy, you need to put your big boy pants on and take care of business. But you wanted me to take care of it, and I did. That means the money's mine."

He was angry, but as far as I was concerned, he'd just learned an expensive lesson. The outlaw world can be brutal, and you need to take care of your own business.

The DA's investigators started handing out search warrants like candy on Halloween. The clubhouse was searched several times. Members' houses and vehicles were searched. Moriya's law office was searched as the DA tried to ruin Moriya's career by personally involving her in the investigation and indictments. Eventually, they even searched my mother's house. Some members were caught with pills in their possession. Everyone in the charter knew that indictments were coming. They didn't know what that meant, what being in the system entailed. I tried to maintain an air of calm. Young guys who have never been arrested or done time let gossip and their imaginations run away with them. I had to continually remind them that we were a long way from a trial. Any quiet time I could find away from the clubhouse became priceless.

I was watching TV at home one Sunday when the phone rang. I tensed up. I answered it expecting a bail bondsman, a cop, or a member in trouble. Instead, It was Mike Ness, the lead singer and guitarist for the punk band Social Distortion. I had been a fan from the band's start in Southern California in 1978. Mike and I had been friends for several years. Social Distortion was playing a show at the Ventura Theater, and it was a big deal in town. Most of the charter would be there.

"Hey, man, are you coming to my show tonight?"

"I hadn't planned on it."

"Why not?"

"You know, it's Sunday night. I've got a big workweek coming up."

"Oh, man, I never thought George Christie would be too old to rock and roll. You really can't come for one set? A couple hours to see old friends?"

"Mike . . ."

"Tell me it isn't true. You're not going soft. Come on, man."

"Okay, I'll be there."

On the other side of Ventura, a pretty young woman named Nikki Nicoletto was getting the same line from a friend who didn't want to go to the Social Distortion concert alone. Nikki too finally gave in and agreed to go.

The Ventura Theater defined downtown Ventura. It had been there forever. Funky 1920s, mission-style architecture showcased one of the hippest music venues in a hundred miles. It had an old, velvet-curtain stage, soaring ceilings, great acoustics, and a nice feel inside—intimate but high energy. I walked in wearing my patch, thinking I would say my hellos, stay for a few songs, and be home in bed before the late news wrapped up. I looked around for other Ventura members and locked eyes with that beautiful young girl who had been coerced into coming. She flashed me a smile that seemed lit from within. I smiled back. She looked so young, but didn't lack for confidence. She walked right over to a Hells Angel president and started a conversation like we were two kids at a school dance. She said her name was Nikki. She looked eighteen, and my usual paranoia went into overdrive. I thought it could be a setup for an underage-solicitation bust.

"How old are you?"

"Twenty-two."

"No, you're not. Show me your ID."

She laughed and passed me her driver's license. She was telling the truth. She was thirty years younger than me, but the more we talked, the less it mattered. We were on the same wavelength. I relaxed and felt happy for the first time in a long time. This brown-haired girl with the sparkling eyes, hip haircut, and trendy clothes was completely comfortable in her own skin, unguarded and fearless. I felt like I could ask her anything and she'd give me the truth. In the middle of our conversation, a guy in a black staff T-shirt tapped me on the shoulder and leaned in toward my ear. He told me Mike Ness wanted me to come backstage and hang out.

I turned to Nikki. "You want to go with me?"

"Where are we going?"

"We're going to go hang out with Mike Ness."

She rolled her eyes and laughed. "Sure we are."

"No, really. We're going backstage. You want to come?"

Her eyes twinkled. "Okay."

As we sat and talked with Ness about the music business and Southern California punk culture, I kept sneaking glances at Nikki. She was special. I realized I was attracted to her in a way I'd never been attracted to any other woman. As the band wrapped up the set, we headed over to the clubhouse, where a party was in full swing. On a whim, I asked Nikki if she wanted to go hang out at my house. The walls were covered with Hells Angels memorabilia, souvenirs of the places I'd been, and pictures of my parents, kids, and club brothers. The house was all me, and I wanted to show her who I really was. She hesitated, then agreed to go. We wound up sitting on my overstuffed black leather couch, talking until almost four in the morning.

After I dropped her off at her house, I rode slowly home. Meeting someone special can change your perspective in a flash. Nikki seemed like this purely good thing that had just dropped into my life. I had never believed in love at first sight. Two people who don't even know each other exchange a glance and, wham, love? But riding home through the quiet streets of Ventura on a moonless night, I realized I was crazy about this girl I had just met.

I called her two days later. She invited me to her house, where I met her five-year-old daughter, Aubree. Nikki was up-front about what mattered to her, and what I needed to know if we were going to go out.

"Me and Aubree, we're a package deal."

"I can see that."

"If that's not cool, we might as well stop now."

"It's cool. I get it."

From that point on, Nikki and I would be separated only when the government locked me up. Bradbury was trying as hard as he could to make that happen. Over the next year and a half, he convened two grand juries. Nobody he subpoenaed would talk, the evidence was sketchy, and both grand juries returned no-bill rulings. *No bill* means that the grand jury can't find sufficient evidence, or the evidence is too flawed for an indictment. But Bradbury wasn't about to give up a high-profile case that he had already tried in the media.

Even when you're waiting for the other shoe to drop, life goes on. I had businesses to run. Searches, arrests, and media attention didn't hurt traffic at the tattoo shop. In fact, it helped. Nikki was a hairstylist, with a loyal clientele, and we hit on the idea to combine our businesses. The mostly male tattoo shop customers often had to sit around waiting for an artist. The same was true of mostly female hair salon customers. Combining a hair salon and a tattoo shop meant that those people would mingle, and customers waiting for their other half could get a tattoo or style while they waited.

We remodeled the space, installing a plush four-chair hair salon in the front, and moving the tattoo operation to the back. The tattoo area had corrugated-metal panels, exposed brick covered in graffiti, and even a few bullet holes. The combination was wildly popular. Nikki worked one of the chairs and kept an eye on the business.

It didn't take long for me to realize that Nikki was the love of my life and that I wanted to marry her. In June 2000, I took her for a ride to our favorite spot at Pismo Beach, right off the road to a lookout where dra-

matic jagged cliffs loomed over whitecapped waves. I showed her a dia-
mond ring I had ordered custom-made and told her that the three of us
needed to be a family. She said yes.

Nikki had spent enough time around the clubhouse to know what the
Hells Angels were about. She knew the written and unwritten rules and
could easily hold her own in a room full of outlaws. But a clubhouse party
is one thing, and Nikki had never been to a big Hells Angels gathering.
The 2000 World Run was being held in Hämeenlinna, Finland. With rumors of a third grand jury floating around, I thought it was the perfect
chance for us to get away, relax, and for her to experience the sheer size
and reach of the club.

We flew into Helsinki-Vantaa Airport and were met there by a contingent of Helsinki Hells Angels. I was, at that point, the voice of the club and
well-known for having beaten the feds in my first trial. The Scandinavian
members treated me like a head of state. The club had rented a castle with
luxury accommodations, and the run was a wild, nonstop party. Nikki and
I couldn't sightsee without someone buying us a drink or dinner. The Swedish members insisted we come back to Sweden with them after the run. It
seemed like a once-in-a-lifetime opportunity to see the land of those original outlaws, the Vikings. So as the run wound down, we took the ferry from
Helsinki to Stockholm with a small group of Stockholm Angels.

In Stockholm, I sat in on a meeting with members from Denmark and
across Sweden. They were in the aftermath of the war with the Bandidos,
and the 1997 truce was showing signs of fracturing. The Swedes asked for
my input on negotiating tactics, and how best to work around the authorities.

They also wanted Nikki and me to visit the local charters. We decided
to drive over to the east coast, to the Gothenburg charter. After that, we'd
make our way down to Malmö, at the southern tip of the country. Half a
dozen Stockholm Angels led the way on their bikes, as Nikki and I followed, chauffeured by a member and his wife in a high-end Mercedes.

We drove through wild, ancient forests with giant trees that seemed to be growing out of low-lying mists. The highway skirted the slag-strewn shores of pristine sapphire-blue lakes. The scenery was right out of a movie. About halfway to Gothenburg, we rolled up to a roadblock across the entire highway. A group of Swedish cops in dark blue paramilitary uniforms and neon-green safety vests pointed Ak 5s at the car. They ordered the members off their bikes and everyone out of the car. These idiots were pointing automatic weapons at Nikki, and it was freaking her out and pissing me off.

"Who in the hell is in charge here?" I asked. A cop came over to me and I told him, "Tell your guys to stop pointing their guns at us."

The cops looked stressed to the point of breaking. The cop told me to stay calm and asked us to pop the trunk of the Mercedes. They pulled out Nikki's suitcase and threw it on the ground. Two of the cops opened it up and started pawing through her clothes, tossing shirts and pants on the highway. Now it was Nikki's turn to get angry.

"Stop throwing my stuff on the ground!"

The cops ignored her. Suddenly, they stopped as if they'd found a bomb. They pulled a giant sponge from underneath a stack of sweaters. The sponge was bright yellow, about the size of a coffee-table book, and three inches thick. One of the cops held it up like a trophy.

"What is this? What is this? Why do you have this sponge here?"

Nikki stared at them. She couldn't believe she had to explain it.

"It's a sponge. I'm making a SpongeBob SquarePants doll for my daughter."

SpongeBob SquarePants had just come out on Nickelodeon, and it was Aubree's favorite cartoon. Nikki was using the long flight to make Aubree a doll. They hadn't heard about SpongeBob SquarePants in Sweden. It took a lot of explaining in two languages to convince these cops that a big yellow sponge wasn't some sort of secret weapon or threat to national security.

As soon as we got back on the road, I realized that Nikki was rattled. It's no fun having automatic weapons pointed at you. Your adrenaline kicks in and you can have the shakes for a long time afterward. It had soured the trip for Nikki.

"I don't think I can do this. I think I'm in over my head, George. I want to take the next plane home."

"Nikki, everything's fine. We're safe, it's okay. This stuff happens."

"We weren't doing anything. They went crazy over a sponge."

"It's the cops, Nikki, it's just cops. We're cool."

We drove in silence until Nikki had a few minutes to process everything.

"Look, I can put up with all this stuff. But you have to take me shopping." We both started laughing.

Luckily, Gothenburg is the second-largest city in Sweden, with an incredible shopping district. We broke the bank, but it was well worth it to see Nikki laughing and smiling again. When we got back to a hotel, I got a phone call from Moriya. She had been trying to track us down for hours. I had been subpoenaed to a third grand jury. We had to get home. We packed up, told the Swedish members what was going on, and had them drive us to the Copenhagen airport.

The day after we flew back, I called a charter meeting. I couldn't instruct members what to say in front of the grand jury. That could have been considered witness tampering. But I told them what I was going to say. Testifying before a grand jury is simple. The answer to any question is always the same: "I decline to answer and invoke my Fifth Amendment right." I told everyone that Moriya was offering free consultation. Unfortunately, some guys just can't master ten words. Nineteen grand jurors stare at the witness from a large gallery. The DA parades around making veiled threats. The grand jury courtroom is a somber place with wood paneling and thick carpets that lends a reverent hush to the proceedings. Everyone involved is deadly serious, and it's easy to get overwhelmed.

As it turned out, Leonardo Martinis could not get his head around ten words. For someone who seemed to have so much difficulty speaking English, he could not shut up. He testified the day after I did. His testimony went on for page after page. This member had boasted about beating someone up. He'd heard that guy talk about a big drug deal. He had watched members snorting a white powder in the clubhouse, but, gee, he didn't know what the powder could be. The testimony was a gift to Bradbury. The jury returned a true bill. Twenty-eight people were indicted, almost all of them Ventura Hells Angels.

It was a grim Friday night when we got the news. Most of the members sat around the clubhouse in a foul mood. The TV was on, but nobody was watching. The phone rang and I answered it.

"George, it's Pat. It's time."

Pat Miller was the Ventura assistant police chief. He was one of the most decent cops and human beings I had ever come across. He told me he had warrants in hand and named off the people he was going to arrest. I was at the top of the list. Most of the targets were sitting in the clubhouse.

"George, it would be best if you sent those guys out and came out last yourself. I don't want a standoff with them."

I told the guys to go out and meet the cops. I waited until they were all on their way, and then I followed them out. The cops cuffed me and put me, alone, in the back of a cruiser. I assumed my bail would be around $200,000, and that I'd be out in twenty-four hours. I was wrong on both counts.

We were arraigned as a group. The bails were astronomical. It was $1 million for me, Georgie, Cheryl, and half a dozen other members including Martinis. Several had $500,000 bails, and nobody was less than $250,000. Bradbury was determined to squeeze us until we rolled or pled guilty. I hired Barry Tarlow again. He and I met with the DA's chief deputy in charge of special prosecutions, Jeff Bennett. I assumed that Bradbury wanted me and me alone, and that he realized what Barry had already determined, that the case had lots of holes. We offered to take a plea in exchange for dropping the charges against the other defendants. Bennett wouldn't even consider it. Bradbury didn't just want my head, he wanted to bring down the whole charter.

Bail is supposed to be a simple concept. Put up collateral, get a bonds-man to carry the bond, and walk out. On bigger, more complex cases, it doesn't work that way. Bail is a tool the prosecution uses to manipulate defendants, so that people who have yet to be tried or convicted are forced to choose between sitting in jail and taking a bad plea deal. The prosecu-tion in my case filed motions to exclude the use of the Ink House and other collateral as assets tainted by association with the charges. The ar-gument was circular. They were accusing us of having used the business in support of criminal acts that they had yet to prove had been commit-ted. My most substantial assets were ruled ineligible to be used as bond collateral. They worked the same trick on other members. The DA ar-gued that motorcycles, houses, and other assets could have been used in the furtherance of the crimes in the indictment, so those assets couldn't be considered for bail. The court went along with it.

The trial was going to be far more complicated and time-consuming than the first case had been. The large number of counts and defendants meant that pretrial preparation was going to be incredibly complex. With over a hundred counts, it was going to take a long time to sort through them. Essentially denied bail, I was forced to sit in Ventura County jail until the resolution of the trial. That too was part of the DA's strategy.

When I got booked into pretrial detention, I was told that as a high-profile prisoner with potential power among inmates, my presence in general population would be disruptive to jail procedures. Against my requests, I was put in the SHU (segregated housing unit). Anyone who has never been in solitary may think they're tougher than the SHU, but nobody is. The SHU is how the authorities get stand-up hardened crimi-nals to fold. Most people call it by the generic terms *isolation* or *solitary*. I learned the hard way that it has another, more accurate name: hell on earth.

13

Solitary confinement is one of the worst things one man can do to another. By any measure, it is cruel and unusual punishment. A year in isolation does psychological damage that experts relate to post-traumatic stress disorder. Call it what you will. I only know that the experience leaves a gaping psychic wound that you carry with you for the rest of your life. From the moment they put you in the SHU, it begins to eat away at you, to destroy who you are as a person. That's what makes it so effective for prosecutors. They know that eventually a prisoner might do almost anything to get out. Barry Tarlow and his associate Mark Haney worked hard to get me bail. Meanwhile, I struggled to stay sane.

Solitary is sensory torture. The lights are always on, dimmed at night, but still strong enough to read by. Sleep is never restful. The air-conditioning runs nonstop, creating a low-level hum that drills into your head. At times, the cell got so cold I thought I'd never feel warm again. I'd make a cloak out of my scratchy prison blanket, the only substantial piece of fabric in the cell. It was never enough.

The discomfort was just the physical part of solitary. The mental part was much, much worse. Solitary is boredom. They sent around a book cart every week, stocked with beaten-up middle-school books, most missing pages. I was allowed a subscription to the local newspaper, but it came to me days late, the pages dog-eared, and brown coffee-mug rings delivering a message from the guards about who was in charge. It was one of many ways the guards tried to wear you down.

Some guards were just doing their job. Others were sadists. I got one hour a day out of my cell. It became the most valuable time in the world. I could call my lawyers or Nikki. I could shower. But the guards would often take too long doing something else, and my one-hour window would close, gone until the next day. They didn't care. You don't matter. They would listen in on the cell, the quiet crackle of the aging speaker system giving them away. The one consolation was that I could ignore their authority. When the cell was warm enough, I'd stay in my underwear. The guards would bark through the tiny window in my heavy steel cell door or shout over the speaker, "Dress out." It never grew old, saying, "Or what? You'll put me in solitary?"

You try anything to preoccupy yourself, to make time move faster. On average, two thousand steps make a mile. My cell was four steps in one direction, four steps back. I'd try to walk a mile without losing count.

Worse than anything else were the tricks my own mind played on me. Without stimulation or human contact, the mind makes things up. I could find myself having a conversation with a wall, a rough surface scrawled with the rantings of other prisoners who had gone down the same rabbit hole. After four months, they pulled me out and told me I was eligible for a course of psych meds. I turned them down. I didn't trust them. If they were callous enough to put me in this place, who knew what kind of drugs they would feed me?

That's the system. They knew perfectly well that solitary could drive a prisoner mad. They were admitting that it would be better to lie on your rack, vacant-eyed and numb, than to be pacing your cell questioning your own sanity. And you will come to question your sanity. Those were the worst moments, a few seconds of pure panic, thinking that I might actually go crazy. What would it be like to go over the edge and lose my grip on reality? Would I come back? Would I ever be normal again?

Steve Tausen was a San Jose member who spent a year in solitary awaiting a murder trial. He beat his case, came home, and promptly quit the club. I believe he never wanted to risk repeating the experience. But I used him for inspiration. I told myself, if Steve Tausen could make it through, so could I.

A Mexican Mafia associate was in the cell next to mine. He had been ordered to kill someone and had refused. Now there was a contract on his head. He was doing the last year of a five-year bid. Solitary was the only way to protect him against his former gang. I could talk to him by lying on the floor of the cell and putting my mouth near a small vent at the base of the wall.

"How long have you been in isolation?"

"This is my fifth year."

"How do you do it? How do you keep going?"

"Same as you, man. One day at a time. But I'll tell you, George, you'll never be the same."

"What do you mean?"

There was a long pause. I thought maybe he'd walked away from the conversation.

Then: "You'll find out."

I got up slowly from the floor, shaken. I worried that he was right.

Things were happening beyond my cold four-by-eight-foot concrete world that would make solitary even more painful. Right before I had been arrested, Nikki had told me that she thought my mom was sick. My mom had lost weight and looked tired and old. I wrote it off to stress and told Nikki she didn't need to worry, my mom was tough. But Nikki turned out to be right.

One day the speaker in my cell crackled to life.

"Christie, dress out. The Red Cross is here to see you."

I walked into the interview room to find a priest sitting on the other side of the table. He looked like a distinguished college professor, with neatly trimmed gray hair and perfect posture. He was thin, with delicate hands that had probably never been made into a fist. He had sad brown eyes, and he looked unusually pale, as if he spent as much time in the SHU as the prisoners did. He introduced himself and then hesitated. He had unpleasant news to pass on.

"George, I know you know that your mom's not feeling well, but I don't think you know how sick she really is. I'm sorry to tell you this, but she has advanced cancer. In all likelihood, she's not going to be alive when you get out of here."

I thought I understood the worst things the SHU could do to me. I thought breaking me down, trying to drive me insane minute by minute, was rock bottom. But no. There was this. Now, every minute I spent in this inhumane shithole was a minute with my mother that I would lose forever. A black rage washed over me.

"I'm very sorry to have to tell you that. Do you want to pray with me?"

"You know what, Father? I appreciate you coming here. But I don't want religion in here. Everybody gets religion in here. It's easy. It's like a drug to stop you from being scared. If I get religion, I want to get religion out there. I want to get it surrounded by the drugs, the booze, the money. I want to get it honestly, not because it's convenient. So, no, I'm not going to pray. But you go ahead if you want to."

He was a kind, thoughtful man. He wasn't offended, and we talked about belief and prison and our two worlds in honest terms. I think we both came away fairly considering what the other person had said. But I was still angry. It made me seethe, the inhumanity of a system that wouldn't allow a man not yet convicted of a crime to see his mother before she died. I might never have had the chance to say good-bye if not for friends. Several supporters and associates had agreed to put up their properties against my bail, and Tarlow and Haney got the assets approved. After almost a year in the SHU, I was bailed out on house arrest. It was restrictive, but I was free of solitary.

Outlaws don't ponder mental damage. But acknowledge it or not, it makes itself known. The first night home, I was strangely anxious rather than relieved. At three in the morning, Nikki woke up to find I wasn't in bed. She looked around for me in the gray darkness, then checked the living-room couch. Finally, she came downstairs and discovered me curled up asleep on the bathroom floor with the light on. It had overwhelmed me, the space. The many different rooms. Windows that opened. That was how badly solitary had twisted my mind. In this large, rambling house with its big soft bed, I found comfort in the smallest, coldest space. She woke me up and we went back upstairs. I got into bed and she wrapped herself around me.

I heard her whispering softly in my ear.

"It's okay, George, I'm here with you."

It was an answer, even if it wasn't *the* answer. Like so many times since then, I thought, "What if I had never met Nikki?" And the truth is, I think I would have been in a different type of isolation. I would have come home, but I would never have left the SHU. As it was, I brought that horrible place with me, like a fragment of a bullet lodged too close to your heart to be removed without killing you.

Not even God should underestimate the power of a Greek mother. My mom had waited. The court would not initially approve a visit to the hospice, so she had the nurses unhook her IV tubes, got out of her deathbed, tucked her drab-green canister of oxygen into the webbed pouch on the back of her wheelchair, and came to see me. She weighed less than ninety pounds. But it was still her, her humor, her warmth. The laughter of a woman who had tricked a living room full of six-year-olds into believing a Christmas tree could talk still lit up her eyes. We had an hour together before she grew too tired and had to go back. Afterward, I sat in my living room replaying the sound of her voice: "I love you, Georgie."

A few days later I received a call that my mother was near the end.

Tarlow got the court to agree to a supervised hospice visit. The prosecutors fought the visit, floating the theory that my mom was faking her cancer. But it was all too real. I sat by her bed, watching her struggle to breathe and grimacing with pain that morphine couldn't touch. Nikki promised my mom that she would take care of me. Then I took my mother's frail hand in mine.

"Mom, you can let go. Go ahead. I love you."

Her breathing slowed, and within a few minutes she was gone. The DA investigators who had chaperoned the visit hustled me out before the body was cold.

It seemed as if the prosecutors had an endless supply of dirty tricks. When I had first gone into solitary, they had sent an informant to talk to Robert Sheahen. I had turned to Sheahen as a less expensive alternative to Barry Tarlow, who I could only afford to have work on my bail. The recorded interaction made Sheahen a material witness and ineligible to represent me. On Sheahen's recommendation, I hired Tony Serra. The subject of the movie *True Believer,* he was an unabashed hippie, a civil rights expert, and a tenacious defense lawyer who had defended high-profile clients such as the Black Panthers. Tony was always laughing and smiling. He had intense black eyes, long, stringy white hair, and wire-rimmed Ben Franklin glasses that made him look like a wizard. He always wore secondhand clothes and used his rumpled appearance to fool prosecutors into underestimating him. In reality, Tony was incredibly smart and a savage courtroom opponent. I think prosecutors feared him every bit as much as they did Barry Tarlow.

While Tony negotiated with the government, Barry got permission for me to attend my mom's funeral. The stipulations included no displays of affection. Nikki and I couldn't hold hands, and nobody could hug me. The court even limited conversations. Prosecutors recorded the funeral. No member could say more than "My condolences, sorry for your loss."

The prosecution was getting increasingly prickly. With me out of solitary, Tony was now in control. He slowed everything down, filing motion after motion. He forced the district attorney's hand by jacking up costs in what had already become the most expensive trial in Ventura County history. District attorneys are subject to the winds of public sentiment. Bradbury had justified the expense by peddling the line that Ventura Hells Angels were selling drugs to schoolchildren, pointing to the Outfit and the support gear they wore. It didn't matter that no evidence supported that claim. The problem was, the media ran with that juicy angle and it sold papers. Even members up north would grouse to me about Ventura's missteps and "selling drugs to schoolchildren."

In March 2002, we finally struck a deal. At least we thought we had. I agreed to plead no contest to tax evasion and guilty to conspiracy. In exchange, charges against Cheryl would be dropped, and the charges against Georgie and the other members would be reduced, with sentences of time served plus probation. One member decided to go his own way, gladly agreeing to a nonassociation clause as part of his plea, so that he'd have a way out of the club without appearing to quit. He was a coward and no loss to the charter.

It's very rare that prosecutors go back on a plea deal. The system works on trust. If defense lawyers didn't agree to plea deals, the courts would be overwhelmed. The defendants in the trial made their pleas in court in March. The sentencing hearings were set for April. Cheryl, Georgie, and I were sentenced on April 19. At the hearing, we were stunned to hear the prosecutors refuse to drop the charges against Cheryl and recommend that I do seven years.

My legal team jumped up. We had already entered pleas, so we were stuck. My lawyers protested to the judge that the sentence recommendation violated a preexisting agreement. Fortunately, there are still noble, decent people in the judicial system. Judge Bruce Clark said, "Mr. Christie, I'd like to hold off on your sentencing and pronounce your sentence last. Would you allow me to do that?"

It was a huge leap of faith. He would either do the right thing or I was going away for a long time. I reluctantly agreed. He sentenced

Cheryl and Georgie to time served and probation. Then he asked me to rise. He began by saying, "It's clear to me that Mr. Christie is the least culpable in all this. . . ." Everyone in the courtroom knew what was coming. He sentenced me to time served and probation with severe restrictions.

Jeff Bennett argued for a nonassociation clause, based on the government's assertion that the Hells Angels was a criminal enterprise. Judge Clark wasn't having it. He ruled that none of the convictions in the case would carry a nonassociation clause. I was free to go home and back to the clubhouse.

Although Bradbury technically had his convictions, it could hardly be called a win. Nobody was going to prison. The charter was intact, and all but one of us had walked away free to ride with our patches. Ventura County was in an uproar. Half the voters were disgusted at the waste of taxpayer money—some estimates pegged it at $30 million—and the other half wanted to know why I wasn't behind bars. District attorneys are nothing if not masters of spin. Bradbury released a statement after the trial: "An organized criminal enterprise has been stopped from selling drugs to our children and victimizing other citizens through violence, theft, fraud and intimidation." He'd never get that statewide office. Within months, he'd retire.

Your world stands still when you go into solitary. But outside the prison walls, the world moves on. In Ventura, it was moving in destructive and disappointing directions. In the early days, charters and members behaved in predictable ways. When Sonny Barger went to prison, he passed the baton of leadership to other strong personalities. Irish or Cisco. Although all of them had their faults, they kept true to Sonny's vision for the Oakland charter. Oakland remained a power base, and Sonny's seat was always kept warm. When Guy Castiglione had done time, Dago stayed just as he'd left it. Members watched out for his family and his financial interests. This was supposed to be a brotherhood after all. Respect was the foundation of it all.

But in Ventura, respect had been the first victim of my stint in solitary. My absence had created a hole and started a disgusting scrum of members trying to grab what they could for themselves. Coming home to the clubhouse was disheartening and was the first sign to me that perhaps the club and I were growing out of sync. People had tried to take advantage of my situation. Members made moves. Some were predictable. Others were unpleasant surprises.

Tom Heath had counted on my going away for a long time. I had never been totally comfortable with Tom. Even though he hadn't violated the code or club rules, he had always been a little too much of a sociopath for my taste. Ever since the Frame-Up bombing—and Tom's happy gloating about it—I had worried about what he was capable of doing at any given moment. He was a loose cannon. So it should have been no surprise that a month after I went into solitary, he decided to collect on the imaginary $3,000 debt he thought I owed him. He walked into the Ink House one afternoon with a silent David Ortega trailing two steps behind him. He told Nikki that while she could keep the salon business, the tattoo shop was now his.

Nikki wasn't the type to be intimidated. She had spent enough time with me to know how the outlaw world worked. She could also think circles around Tom. She understood that if you don't show strength, you're showing weakness. She told Tom to pound sand, knowing that even though I had stepped down as West Coast chairman right before going inside, the weight of the club would come down on a member who tried to steamroll any charter president. Tom was furious. He told anyone who would listen about the many flaws in my leadership.

Tom was far from the only one playing games. Ventura member Scott Sutton had lobbied the charter for a vote, hoping to take my place as president. But the club doesn't replace officers who are awaiting trial. If someone could be voted out of office as soon as he was arrested, the cops could dictate the leadership. Guy Castiglione had been keeping tabs on Ventura. He knew what Scott was up to and heard other members running their mouths about how I was done as a leader. Guy was an old-school outlaw, loyal to a fault. He and I shared an understanding of the "code." That didn't include betraying a brother who was facing prosecution. The scheming pissed him off. He let me know what was going on. A few days after my sentencing hearing, I called a charter meeting. My first order of business was to call out Tom Heath.

"I heard you got something to say to me."

"I don't know what you're talking about."

"You're a fucking liar."

Jimmy "Tiny" Shankles was a friend of Heath's, so it was surprising to hear him push Tom to man up: "Hey, Tom, you've said some things about George. You need to speak up."

"I don't know what you're talking about. I got nothing to say."

After the meeting, I cornered Heath outside the clubhouse.

"This is how it is. Either you go, or I go. And I'm not going anywhere. Do we understand each other?"

He just looked at his boots and didn't answer.

Tiny ended up brokering an agreement. Tom would transfer to Berdoo, and I wouldn't look for revenge. David was a more difficult issue. I was devastated that he had backed Tom's play. We would have come to blows in that meeting except that he was visibly ill. Years of hard living had caught up with him. He was in the early stages of respiratory failure and looked like hell, with gray skin and a dull glaze in his eyes. Much as I hated to see him sick, there was no easy way to repair the rift. We couldn't comfortably be in the same room. He would eventually leave to start a new charter in Santa Barbara. Many of the troublemakers in Ventura would follow him at my insistence.

I had a lot of other housekeeping to do. A source at the courthouse had sent me a copy of the third grand jury's testimony. I was stunned to read Leonardo Martinis's detailed answers. He had put members out on

Front Street—exposing them to prosecution. The rules were clear, Martinis had to go. I pushed him out at the next meeting. Ed Gregory, the man who had been convicted of drug charges with the help of Martinis's testimony, was also out because he had agreed to a "gang enhancement" on his sentence. Gang enhancements are special conditions meant to stop gang members convicted of crimes from associating with other gang members inside or outside of prison. The Hells Angels aren't a gang, and the club doesn't allow members to plea to gang enhancement charges.

We kicked out another member for smoking crack and breaking into coin-operated vending machines. He wanted quarters to go gambling on the slots. It wasn't the way Hells Angels behaved. Other members were scheming to get over on the club itself, something that is both dangerous and stupid, a good way to wind up in a fifty-five-gallon drum. A Ventura member had taken $10,000 of the defense fund allocated to the charter for the trial. We pushed him out of the club and read the riot act to two other members who urged me to steal the $40,000 that was left over in the defense fund. Instead, I took the money up to the next West Coast Officers' Meeting and returned it to the West Coast treasurer.

Out of all the patches I took back in that time, the hardest was the one closest to home. Cheryl had been given a club nonassociation clause in her plea deal. That meant the charter could no longer be a source of power for her. She pushed Georgie to quit, and he was disillusioned enough by everything that had happened to listen to her. He had been accepted to a culinary school in Reno, Nevada. I told him he should go ahead and go and come back to the charter when he finished school. There was no need to quit—he could have some distance and time to think. But he surrendered his patch and indicia at the most painful charter meeting I had ever presided over. His closest friends were angry. I was just deeply saddened. It added to what was a growing wall between us.

Painful as those few months were, I managed to square away the charter. But Ventura wasn't the only corner of the outlaw world out of whack. As I had paced a tiny windowless cell, the Mongols had expanded. They had opened new charters in Camarillo, Hollister, and San Jose, renewing the tension between the two clubs. The Camarillo charter was approachable, with only a few members and peaceful leaders. It wouldn't have been a problem. But the San Jose charter was openly encroaching on established Hells Angels territory. I wanted to talk with the Mongols and get them to at least close the San Jose charter.

I saw my opportunity in the annual multiclub Laughlin River Run. Laughlin, Nevada, is a casino town about eighty miles south of Las Vegas. The city looks like a little Las Vegas, built around a main strip packed with casinos. The difference is that Laughlin is perched on the picturesque banks of the wide, slow Colorado River. It's a pretty place, and every major West Coast outlaw club shows up to the run. It would be an ideal place for a sit-down with the Mongol president, Roger Pinney. I asked my parole officer to approve the trip. He refused. It was my birthday weekend, so I decided to take Nikki to Pismo Beach instead.

The Mongols brought a huge contingent to Laughlin, and almost a hundred members were camped out at Harrah's. I was told a few Mongols harassed vendors selling Hells Angels merchandise in a booth in the Golden Nugget. They headed back to Harrah's, where a small group of Angels were gambling on the casino floor. A cop took it upon himself to alert the rest of the Hells Angels at their usual base of operations on the other side of town, the Flamingo. Reinforcements raced to Harrah's. Massing around the slot machines, the Mongols and Hells Angels exchanged words. Suddenly, an Angel front-kicked a Mongol and all hell broke loose.

Unlike the Great Western fight, this wasn't just fists and motorcycle parts. There were guns. In seconds, that casino floor looked like a war zone. The only thing more surprising than the Wild West nature of the fight was that only three outlaws were killed. No citizens were shot.

Nikki and I had just turned in for the night when the motel phone rang. Ventura member Mike Kapp told me what had happened. It was a disaster and would bring more law enforcement heat and attention to both clubs. Mongol Anthony Barrera died from stab wounds, while Hells Angels Jeramie Bell and Robert Tumelty were dead at the scene from multiple gunshot wounds. State troopers would later come across the body of Dago member Christian Tate, sprawled on the gravel shoulder of Interstate 40. He had been shot off his bike as he rode home from Laughlin. We were at war with the Mongols once again.

The Arizona Angels charters called a meeting in Cave Creek to discuss Laughlin. My parole officer denied my request to travel to that meeting. That meant the Ventura vice president, Scott Sutton, would be taking the charter to Cave Creek. I had a bad feeling about the trip. Too much was going on, and I didn't think anybody was safe on the road.

"Why don't you guys just fly to Arizona?"

"Don't worry, we're taking the van. We're not scared of anything happening."

Caution isn't an outlaw trait.

"Okay. But listen, as soon as that meeting is over, get everyone in the van and get home. Don't get caught out in that desert at night."

My words fell on deaf ears. Scott Sutton had no intention of hurrying home. He planned on spending the night because he had a woman in Arizona. The other five Ventura members partied in a Cave Creek bar called Coyote Wild Bar and Grill. A twenty-five-year-old member named Josh Harber had just stepped outside the bar for a smoke, while Nate "Hobo" Varela played a video game. Hobo had a clear line of sight through the front door and watched as a man walked up to Josh. The two exchanged words but didn't seem to be arguing. Suddenly, the guy pulled out a pistol, shoved it up under Josh's chin, and pulled the trigger. As Josh lay on the ground, mortally wounded, the shooter drove away in a red Honda.

This wasn't a case law enforcement was going to solve. Nobody was talking. I didn't care about arrests, I wanted to know what happened. Josh was a good kid, and in some ways I saw him as a protégé. I felt like Hobo was holding out. He told me he couldn't identify the shooter. That didn't make sense. I knew the bar. The front was well lit and Hobo had a clear view out the door. In piecing it together, I discovered a backstory that made everything more complicated and increased the list of suspects.

The 2001 News Year's Eve party at the San Fernando Valley clubhouse had been a wild affair. While I had been in solitary, some Ventura members had gotten into an argument with an Arizona member. They wound up rat-packing the out-of-state Angel and stripping him of his patch. This was a serious insult and just wasn't done. You don't fuck with a brother's patch. It wasn't the only violation of protocol the charter made while I was behind bars. Another Ventura member sold Robert "Chico" Mora a stolen Harley—a huge problem. Chico had been a leader of the Dirty Dozen, the powerful Arizona one-percenter club that had patched over to become Hells Angels. Chico discovered that the bike was hot. I can only imagine how angry that made him. Mad enough to kill, maybe.

A lot of people put the shooting on the Mongols after what had happened in Laughlin. I didn't believe it for a second. There were no cries for retribution, and no intel placed Mongols in Arizona. I think Hobo saw someone he knew approach Josh that night, and I think it shook him up. After the shooting, he developed some problems, and he left the club. I was questioned by law enforcement, who asked me if Sonny had set up the hit to teach me and Ventura a lesson. The rift between Sonny and me was growing worse by the month. It was now something much larger than a beef about leadership style or the unwritten rules. I think Sonny felt that I was an actual threat to him, to his power, and even to his membership. Sonny saw the world in terms of admirers or enemies. You were one or the other. I had stopped admiring him a long time ago, and now I was becoming an enemy that he began to hate. The club—especially the charters on the West Coast—was slowly separating into factions supporting one or the other of us.

You never get used to burying a brother, but it's always worse when it's a young man. Josh Harber had his whole life ahead of him. My own son was older than Josh. It was incredibly painful to watch that casket go into the ground, more so because his parents blamed me for his death.

There is always chaos in the outlaw world. That's because of the constant tension between strong-minded, willful individuals and a code that applies to everyone in a club. But something about the way members were acting seemed to violate the fundamental notions of brotherhood. I think a Hells Angel shot Josh Harber. I think it was a misguided beef that I could easily have solved, and one that would never have happened if I hadn't been sunk into the dark hole of the SHU. But a charter is more than the president. The members need to do the right thing on their own, not because somebody's riding them.

There seemed to be a lot less partying and much more fighting in the Angels—against the authorities, against other clubs, and within our own. The one person who really had my back, who understood being in it together, was Nikki. She was the exact opposite of Cheryl. Nikki was always there, always supportive, always strong. Nikki never took an angle with me. I could trust her, which was not something I could say anymore about the people I saw sitting around the table in the clubhouse. That was a sobering realization.

Nikki was an anchor through tough times. She had waited a year for me while I fought the darkness of solitary. It made me want to commit to her, as I had committed to the club and the patch decades before. It was time for us to formalize that commitment, to get married. Ventura was so much a part of our lives that it was only natural we would have the ceremony in town. But I underestimated the pure, spiteful hatred law enforcement had for the club and for me.

We wanted to have the reception at the Ventura Theater. I'd done a lot of business with the theater, and the charter was a fixture at concerts there. The manager got back to me a few days later.

"George, I'm sorry about this, but the cops don't want you having the thing here."

"What does that mean?"

"Look, man, we really don't want to get in the middle of it. They're threatening to shut us down if you have it here. You know how it is, we got to stay in business."

"Yeah, I know how it is."

It baffled me. It was another part of the changing outlaw landscape. Back in the day, Carl Handy would gladly have arrested me if he had found evidence of a crime. He had no problem pulling Hells Angels over for traffic violations. But he didn't invent infractions. He didn't plant evidence. He dealt with me as a human. If I could help solve a problem in Ventura, he didn't hesitate to turn to me. He was never confused about our respective roles, but he never gave up his ethics and his humanity. Carl would never have interfered with something so personal as a wedding. On the contrary, he would have wished me the best. But by the end of 2002, the Carl Handys of the world were off the street. They sat behind desks or were retired. Law enforcement at that point was a zero-sum game. If an outlaw was enjoying life, the cops thought they were losing something.

I took a breath, got a leash on my temper, regrouped, and tried again. I reached out to a nightclub the Ventura charter frequented, a place called Nicholby's. The charter had given them a lot of business over the years, and the bouncer that ran the door was a martial arts student of mine. He was right on board when I talked to him, but two days later he called and said they couldn't do it. The cops had threatened the nightclub's liquor license.

Nikki and I decided to hell with everybody—we would do a truly outlaw wedding. There was a hip coffee shop downtown called Zoey's that we loved. It was like an updated beatnik coffeehouse, with a small stage where they'd have acoustic musicians play and host poetry readings. The entry was in a cool little alley paved in brick and wreathed in white string lights. The shop was upstairs, with a window that looked out over the alley. The owner was totally into the idea.

A local pastor with full-sleeve tattoos married us in the middle of the coffee shop, at midnight, December 29, 2002. Nikki looked stunning, in a simple white dress with black trim. I wore a black suit, and Aubree wore a suit that matched mine. There was only room enough for immediate family and a few close friends, but well over five hundred people crowded the alley outside and the street beyond. Friends circulated through the coffeehouse. Inside, we cut slices of chocolate cake decorated with dark red rose petals for anybody who wanted it and handed out plastic glasses of champagne. We had spread the word to everyone we knew: the whole town was invited. If you wanted to come, come.

Ironically, the police ended up providing security because they had no choice. There were simply too many people. It turned out to be a beautiful wedding with a crowd ranging from decked-out celebrities like Mickey Rourke to patch-wearing members from Berdoo and Dago. We partied until four in the morning and then got a ride to LAX, where we caught a flight to New York. We spent our honeymoon at the chic Soho Grand Hotel, enjoying a city we loved and seeing the sights.

That trip made me realize that spending time with Nikki and Aubree gave me the feeling I once got from spending time at the clubhouse. They were the joy in my life. Although I wasn't ready to admit it to myself, I was growing tired of the endless hornet's nest the club had become. The brotherhood was strained to the breaking point, and nothing would make that clearer to me than the increasingly serious conflicts I'd have with Sonny Barger.

'14

While I wrestled with the fast-moving changes in Ventura, Sonny was building a nice life for himself in Cave Creek. He had partnered with Daniel "Hoover" Seybert, the president of the Cave Creek charter, in a North Phoenix motorcycle shop called Sonny Barger's Cave Creek Cycles. By all accounts, Sonny considered Hoover a protégé and treated him like a son, but they couldn't have looked more different. Sonny was a compact, wiry, clean-shaven walking scowl; Hoover was short and unassuming with scraggly dirty-blond hair, matching untrimmed beard, and a bit of a paunch. I think Hoover was conflicted between his fierce loyalty to Sonny and trying to carve out his own identity as a Hells Angels leader. It had to be hard standing in the darkest part of Sonny's shadow.

Hoover became Sonny's cutout anytime Sonny wanted to send a message to me. The first time he was stuck in that position was after I had arranged a sit-down in Ventura with the Bandidos. I assured George Wegers safe passage for his group to come from Texas and ride through Arizona. In an admittedly petty move, I didn't alert the Arizona charters. When Sonny realized what was going on, he had Hoover call me. Not only was he opposed to hashing out peace with other clubs, I'd broken protocol. I could hear Sonny's rasp in the background, almost dictating to Hoover.

"Look, Hoover, I'll do anything that I think is appropriate to end this war. If you're having a problem with that, I don't know what to tell you. If you're upset that they rode through Arizona and you weren't notified, I apologize."

"We should have gotten a call, out of respect."

"I'm trying to stop the war in Europe from bleeding over into the States. I'm sure you can understand that."

"I can."

Sometimes, though, I just can't help being a wiseass. "Okay. Anything else Sonny wants you to tell me?" With that, I hung up.

It wasn't just the Bandidos. After Laughlin, it became clear that the Mongols were once again going to be a problem. We had two options—sit across a table or deal with them at one end or another of a gun. I was surprised to find out that Hoover actually wanted to try diplomacy. We ran into each other at a West Coast Officers' Meeting in February 2003.

"George, I have to tell you something. I have a big problem."

"I'm listening."

"We found out that Noel is a paid FBI informant." Noel was Sonny's wife. They were separated, but it was still shocking. Sonny had been living with an FBI informant.

"Jesus, Hoover."

"I know. I have to eighty-six her. I've got no choice, right?"

"You don't have to ask me that. You know what the right thing is."

"Yeah. And listen, George, there's something else. You know this thing with the Mongols? They want a sit-down. I want to go to Colorado and talk to them."

"Who's stopping you? You know what, man? You want to make an impact, you got to do something. If you're asking me, I think you should go."

"Do I have your support?"

"Absolutely, all the way."

Decades after the brawl at the Great Western, we were going over the same old ground with the Mongols. We had tried bullets and bombs. I was glad to hear someone else in the club wanted to try a dialogue. But Hoover never made it to a sit-down. Less than a month later, he would be dead. After a night of drinking with members from the Cave Creek charter at a bar called Bridget's Last Laugh, Hoover walked out with several other members and mounted their bikes. The bikes would have been parked cocked at identical angles, less than arm's length apart. The official story was that Hoover just slumped over his handlebars as everyone was starting their bikes. When he didn't move, they checked on him and found a bullet hole in his head.

That made no sense. Even with the noise of Harleys firing up, a gunshot makes a distinctive crack. And even a skilled marksman would have had a hell of a time making a head shot from a nearby vantage point in the deep dark of early morning while the target moved around trying to start a bike. It was much more likely that someone shot him up close and personal. Which begged the question, how would his brothers have missed someone walking up and shooting their president in the head at point-blank range? That, in turn, begged a lot of other troubling questions. None of them would ever be answered.

The word among law enforcement was that I put a hit on Hoover in retaliation for Josh's murder. Some Hells Angels thought the same thing. But even if I had that power, I wouldn't have used it. Hoover was headed in the right direction. He wanted to be a peacemaker and the club badly needed someone besides me to step up to fill that role. I think the real killer was closer to home. But I also believe that the murder will never be solved because too many people don't want it to be. As always, law enforcement didn't care. A dead Hells Angel was just one less problem as far as the cops were concerned.

In the outlaw world as everywhere else, birth and death follow one another like kids playing tag. Months after Hoover met his violent end in front of a dive bar in North Phoenix, I'd welcome my second son into the world. That child would radically rearrange my priorities and draw me further away from club life, toward a new and different future.

Nikki had gotten pregnant the first time we tried. At twelve weeks, she went for her first sonogram. I couldn't make it because I had an appointment with my probation officer. I told her I'd see her at home. I was surprised to pick up the phone a couple hours later and hear her voice.

"George, you're not going to believe it."

"What? What's wrong?"

"Nothing's wrong. Meet me at home. I have something that you have to see."

I raced home to meet her. She was grinning ear to ear, that beautiful, slightly devilish smile that I loved. She showed me the sonogram. The fetus was a white-noise form, but it was a recognizable shape—the Death Head. It was as if someone had altered the scan. Sometimes when you're a little lost, you look for signs. It was only natural that I saw that black-and-white sonogram as divine signal. I foolishly let my imagination run wild. What could it mean? Maybe the club would go in a new, better direction. Maybe I could still make peace in the outlaw world and bring back the focus on brotherhood in the Hells Angels. Maybe Sonny and I would get back on the same page. Standing there in my living room holding this flimsy piece of photographic paper, I wove myself a tale. This child would become a man. That man would take over the charter and carry on with my vision. Peace among outlaw clubs. Peace in our own. A unified front against law enforcement's overreach and abuse. It was wishful thinking. My second son would become the furthest thing from a Hells Angel.

In the seventh month of the pregnancy, Nikki began bleeding. The doctor told us she had placenta previa, a condition in which the placenta detaches and covers the cervix. As I listened to the doctor explain it, I saw the worry etched on his face and understood that this was bad news.

Nikki and the baby were in serious danger. The doctor scheduled an emergency C-section.

I was in the operating room when the doctor ran into trouble getting the baby out of Nikki. The child wasn't breathing, and the doctor worked hard to get the lungs going. The tension was thick. I stood there in my oversize scrubs, feeling lost. I hate being helpless. It feels too much like prison to me. That feeling only got worse hours later as I looked through the window into the neonatal room of the intensive care unit. The little boy Nikki and I had named Finn, after Mark Twain's free-spirited hallmark character, seemed so small and weak. He lay there in his plastic box, tubes and wires snaking from his doll-size chest and arms—a gut-wrenching sight. Suddenly, Nikki's doctor was standing at my shoulder.

"George, listen to me. My own son was in the ICU. I know this looks bad. But the day he gets out—and Finn will get out and come home—you're going to forget all this. It's just going to be a distant memory. He's going to be okay."

I didn't believe him. But doctors see the big picture the rest of us often miss. In my shock and pain, it seemed impossible that my son would ever come home. But the doctor was right. Two weeks later I carried Finn through our front door. Within a month, you wouldn't have known our healthy, smiling baby was ever in ICU. Going through all the turmoil with Finn pulled Nikki and I even closer. Aubree loved him like crazy. This little boy made our house seem more happy and joyful than ever before. It was the opposite of what I was getting from the club. By 2003, every month seemed to bring some new bad news, most of it from Sonny. It was like a hammer smashing what was left of our relationship. Unlike Moriya and Georgie, Aubree and Finn would never know an "Uncle Sonny."

Arizona had been ground zero for a long ATF undercover operation named Black Biscuit. A bald, buff ATF agent named Jay Dobyns had posed, along with a small, scraggly band of like-minded agents, as members of the Solo Angels. The Solo Angels were an actual outlaw club, a tiny offshoot of a Mexican club based in Tijuana and Southern California. Dobyns pretended to be a serious gunrunner who wasn't above trading drugs for guns, and getting his hands dirty when the need arose. He played the part well. Tall, muscular, and heavily tattooed, Dobyns had the nerve to pull off maybe the most famous law-enforcement bluff ever. He convinced the Mesa Hells Angels charter that he was a legitimate hard-core outlaw. Over time he got tight with the Mesa president, Robert "Bad Bob" Johnston, going so far as to set up the fake murder of a Mongol that led Bad Bob to tell Dobyns, "You're one of us now." The undercover Solo Angels charter was actually about to patch over as Hells Angels when the ATF brought the operation to a close and started making arrests. This ragtag group had infiltrated the Hells Angels to a degree that no law enforcement had ever done. And they did it right under Sonny's nose.

The club was still reeling from Black Biscuit at the end of 2003 when Chico Mora sent the New York City charter a copy of a *Phoenix* magazine profile of Sonny. New York sent it to Richard "Smilin' Rick" Fabel, the president of the Spokane, Washington, charter and a former West Coast chairman. He faxed it to me. The article was unbelievably damning. It had started out as a puff piece on Sonny's low-key life in Cave Creek. Kind of a "wild outlaw mellows into country life" human-interest article. But while the writer was working on the piece, everything fell apart in Sonny's life. Not only was Hoover murdered, but Sonny was arrested for domestic violence, accused of beating his wife, Noel, and her daughter, Sarrah. The charges were ultimately dropped following a closed proceeding. The writer quickly changed direction. The profile became an exposé full of dirty laundry. I'd always known that Noel was a troubled woman, and everything she told the writer confirmed it. She admitted to being bipolar and a drug user. The writer also revealed that Sonny had gotten into an earlier argument with Noel after she tried to run him off the road as he rode home one night with another woman on his bike. He had beaten Noel and then called 911 when it looked like she was seriously injured.

The article raised all kinds of problems. It verified what Hoover had told me, that Noel was a paid FBI informant. The writer also described Sonny's health problems, including conditions that might have affected brain function. It wrapped up with a stunning description of what could only be described as a nervous breakdown on the day of Hoover's funeral. A concerned neighbor had come by to ask if Sonny was going to the funeral. Sonny denied that Hoover was dead and simply lost touch with reality. He was subsequently hospitalized.

Putting aside everything else, there was the 911 call. After it was created in the seventies, the nationwide 911 system was a lifesaver for citizens. But to outlaws, calling 911 was considered the same as testifying, unless you made the call to save someone's life. But otherwise, an outlaw didn't dial those three numbers.

Sonny's 911 call wouldn't have been a problem if he had just told the operator that Noel needed an ambulance and left it at that. Instead, his dialogue with the operator went on and on. He revealed that Noel had tried to run him off the road and much more—that she had a handgun in the car, putting her out on Front Street. He knew that if the cops searched and found the gun, he could be on the hook for a felon-in-possession charge. But the code is clear—you don't throw anybody under the bus in a 911 call. I sat at my kitchen table, looking down at the curled fax paper copy of the article, wishing it were a fake. It felt like somebody had stabbed me in the heart. Even through all our clashes, I still respected Sonny. He had been the model of the wild, unbending outlaw. But living with an informant? Beating a fourteen-year-old girl? Calling 911? Those weren't things outlaws did. Those weren't things Hells Angels did. I understood why Rick had put it on me. It wasn't just bad news for Sonny, it was terrible news for the club. Before I could think everything through, Rick called.

"What are we going to do about it?"

We?

I had stepped down as West Coast chairman in 2000 precisely because of grief like this. As chairman you were always in the middle of conflicts. I often felt like I was one of the few adults in the room. Somebody was always pissed off at me. It got old. Rick had just stepped down as chairman and passed the position to Mark "Papa" Guardado. Rick had figured I'd have no problem bringing this to the officers' meeting and putting Sonny on notice. Rick was wrong. He didn't have it in him, though, so it was left up to me. You can't let something like that slide. I felt that as club leaders we had to be accountable, or what kind of examples were we setting for the membership?

The next West Coast Officers' Meeting was held in Berdoo. I rode down with a leather satchel strapped to my passenger seat. The satchel was full of black-and-white copies of the magazine article and transcripts of the 911 call. I'd ordered the tape and a transcript, which were public records, through Moriya's law office. As soon as all the officers took their places, I passed out the copies. It took a few minutes for people to scan the article and look through the call transcript. The more they read, the quieter the room got. Smilin' Rick said nothing. He acted like it was the first time he'd seen the article. I didn't make any motion behind the materials. I didn't want Sonny kicked out, and it would have been bizarre to suggest it. I wanted it out there so that we could address it, and so that Sonny could eventually explain his side. He wasn't at the meeting, so it ended without much discussion or other business. In the days that followed, a lot of members called me to tell me they were blown away by the article and disappointed in Sonny. None would ever come forward publicly.

Sonny Barger has always had an amazing talent for cultivating his own mystique. That talent is the root of the power he's held within the Hells Angels for more than half a century. It's puzzling to people inside and outside the club because it's not based on a reputation for violence, or being physically dangerous. It comes from nothing more than an image he's carefully developed, and Sonny's own charisma and willpower. In Oakland during the seventies and eighties, Sonny navigated power struggles with physically stronger men, power-hungry personalities who wouldn't have hesitated to kill someone in their way. Yet he was never, to my knowledge, targeted for a hit. He's always held a peculiar sway over members, especially weaker-minded Angels. Those people—his flock—have listened to him and done his bidding even when what he was saying made no sense or contradicted what he had said before or the letter of club rules. It's a talent that I can't entirely explain or understand. But one thing I'm certain of: Sonny's "minions," his congregation of zealous supporters inside and outside the club, are at the core of how he maintains control even to this day.

Knowing that, I wasn't surprised when some Oakland members circled the wagons. They accused me of fabricating the transcripts. To them, Sonny's word was gospel, no matter how much it defied facts or logic. As the campaign to discredit me gained steam, I realized Sonny and I were done. He hated being questioned. He believed it was his club. Anybody who said differently was a threat that had to be eliminated.

The club splintered. As many people as Sonny might have had in his camp, just as many wanted the issue resolved. They remained silent. Nobody else was willing to face him down. There was no point in bringing up the issue at a general meeting again, but l held out hope for a reasonable resolution. I thought we could put it to bed, get past it, and somehow get back to being a brotherhood.

I called Papa to set up a meeting. As president of Frisco, he held a lot of sway in the club. Papa was his own man, and a stand-up outlaw. He was a built in the biker mold, squat and barrel-chested. Quick with a smile, he had a broad, honest face, with close-cropped brown hair and a trim goatee. His charter was tight, and everyone in the club respected him. I sat down with him at the bar in the Frisco clubhouse.

"I'm telling you, Papa, you've got to step in and stop this problem between me and Sonny. It's going to tear the club apart."

"What do you want me to do?"

"Broker something. We need to get him to the table, admit what he did, and move on. Otherwise, sooner or later we're going to come to blows. I don't want to fight him. It would be like fighting my father."

Papa shook his head. "Well, you might have to." It was a cold assessment of the outlaw-world realities.

"You're the West Coast chairman. You need to resolve this."

"What can I do, George? He's saying you made the transcript up."

"I can get the actual recording, Papa."

He looked at me like even he didn't quite believe it.

"Well, okay. You get the tape and I'll set up a sit-down with him to iron it out."

We agreed to get together at the next officers' meeting in Oakland. Papa suggested that the three of us sit down in the back room of the Oakland clubhouse, while the officers held their meeting in the large front room.

Sonny was on the offensive from the moment he entered the room. "Those transcripts are bullshit. That's not what I said. People are saying you made them up."

"I've got the actual 911 tape, Sonny. It's fucking word for word."

That stopped him cold. He looked shocked, like a kid caught with his hand in the cookie jar.

"Why do you have the tape?"

Good to his word, Papa backed my play. "I thought it was a good idea to bring it, Sonny."

Sonny knew he was caught. But Sonny doesn't back down, even when he's wrong. We argued in circles for almost thirty minutes, Sonny getting madder and madder. His back was against the wall. I realized if we kept going, it was going to get physical. We were going to come to blows in the back of the Oakland clubhouse.

"Okay, we're never going to agree. You think what you did was right, I think what you did was wrong. Why don't we do this? Let's go out there.

I'll tell everybody I never thought for one minute that you were going to give anybody up to the cops. You can just say, 'Hey, I was angry, I made a mistake. What started out as an emergency medical call transgressed into a police call.' Or say it however you want. But the message has to go out to the club that calling 911 is wrong."

Sonny looked from me, to Papa, and back again.

"I'm not saying a goddamned thing. I don't answer to anyone." With that, he got up and walked out of the room and out of the clubhouse.

From that day forward, Sonny told everyone that I wanted him kicked out of the club. But if I had wanted him kicked out, I would have brought the 911 recording to an officers' meeting, played it for everybody, and then brought it up for a vote. I have no doubt that somebody would have seconded it. Sonny had as many enemies as friends inside the club. Instead, I never played the tape in public.

Hells Angels' fiftieth anniversaries are special celebrations. It's a long time for anyone, but an eternity for outlaws, who tend to die young or wind up in prison. So in July 2004, I looked forward to putting Nikki on the back of my blacked-out Ultra Classic Harley and making the five-hour ride up to Frisco for the charter's fiftieth. Nikki's parents had agreed to babysit Finn, and the weather was forecast to be perfect in the Bay Area. It was a hot, bright Friday afternoon when I stopped by Nikki's new place in Ventura, a salon she had moved to after growing tired of dealing with the circus the Ink House had become. Loud music and rowdy outlaws had been driving her clientele away. I told her that I was going to ride up to Santa Barbara to make sure everything was right with the bike, and that I'd be back by six to take her out to dinner.

The two lanes heading north on U.S. 101 were predictably packed. I was lane-splitting, riding my bike along the white dotted line between the lanes of traffic. Lane-splitting is legal in California, and it's one of the advantages of riding a motorcycle. As I rode to the right of the fast lane,

I saw an opening and decided to slot into it. A driver in the right lane saw the opening too. He pulled across the dotted line not bothering to check his rearview mirror. His tire clipped my front brake rotor. The collision snapped my handlebars to the left and out of my hands. I was catapulted over the bars at forty miles an hour. I hit the blacktop hard enough to knock me out even though I was wearing a helmet. When I came to, my first thought was that I might have been paralyzed. I mentally told myself to wiggle my toes. Everything seemed to be working, although I was in incredible pain. Blood streamed down my face and I was dazed. I was obviously hurt, but had no idea how bad. I tried to get up by rolling to my side. I couldn't. My hips were so damaged that I couldn't move at all.

The ambulance arrived within minutes. As they loaded me onto the stretcher, I felt like I was about to pass out again. I was having a lot of trouble focusing. The pain was intense. The ambulance drove along the shoulder to the next exit, making good time to Santa Barbara Cottage Hospital. In the trauma room, the nurses cut off my pants and tried to do the same with my jacket. I told them to pull it off instead. I wasn't going to see my patch damaged, and I held out an unreasonable hope that I'd still be okay to make the ride north.

The trauma room flooded with a dozen Santa Barbara cops. They fired questions at me. The nurses couldn't get them out of the room. A cop asked me if it had been an attempted hit. Where was I riding to? What did I remember? I didn't answer any questions. The last thing I wanted to do was talk to cops. I had a serious concussion, and a nurse had just given me a shot of morphine. I wasn't thinking straight. I told the nurses I wanted to go home. It seemed like a far safer place than this chaotic, brightly lit, curtained-off section of the emergency room. Nobody seemed to be in charge, and the cops were crowding me and filming the entire scene. I should have been sedated and checked into the hospital for tests and an overnight stay. Instead, one of the cops brought me a clipboard with my release forms and stood over me as I signed them. Nikki was waiting to drive me home.

At home, I got worse. My short-term memory was shot. I couldn't even watch a movie all the way through without losing the plot. The morphine wore off and the pain was killing me. I couldn't walk from the couch to the bathroom without Nikki's help. My head felt like it was going to explode. Nikki called a doctor whose kid had been one of my martial arts students. He came by and did a short exam. He was shocked that I wasn't in the hospital. Thanks to a preexisting condition and the accident, my hips were destroyed and I had a concussion. He called and set me up for an appointment at USC Medical Center.

They gave me a CAT scan, confirming that I had a brain trauma and a concussion. That would heal over time. The damage to my hips wouldn't. The doctors told me I'd need hip replacements for both hips, but they couldn't schedule surgery until my concussion symptoms cleared up (it would be almost five months). They sent me home with strict instructions not to ride a motorcycle or exert myself. That meant camping out in my front room, constantly dizzy and nauseated.

My bike-building business had stalled, and the injuries meant that I couldn't keep the martial arts studio open. My martial arts supplies sales had come to a standstill. The Ink House was a mess as well. Cash flow got tighter and tighter. Out of the blue, what seemed like an answer walked through the steel front door of the Ventura clubhouse.

Ventura member Archie Schaffer had met Robert Blessing through a mutual friend. Blessing presented himself as a real estate investor who was buying and flipping properties throughout Southern California. The real estate market was white-hot. Blessing was convincing. He had the bland good looks of a suburban dad in a car ad. He was trim and easygoing, with a gleaming Hollywood smile you could only get with whitening treatments. Everything about him screamed money, from his $200 haircut to his high-end BMW to his Ermenegildo Zegna shoes and Hugo Boss suit. His watch alone cost more than any bike parked outside the Ventura clubhouse. His pitch was simple. If the charter let him take an equity loan out against the clubhouse, he would use the money to buy property, flip it, and return a $50,000 profit in ninety days.

My name had originally been on the clubhouse deed because I'd paid the down payment. But my probation opened the door for law enforcement to search any property I owned without warning. So I signed a quit-claim deed, transferring the clubhouse to Marty Kada. Marty was the Ventura member I trusted most next to Georgie. In my mind, the building belonged to the club in any case, although Cheryl strongly disagreed with me on that point.

Blessing's proposal sounded like quick, easy, and legal money. The charter voted to support the deal, and Marty signed the papers for the equity loan. Ninety days later, Blessing walked into the clubhouse and laid a $50,000 check on the varnished surface of the bar. He asked the charter if they wanted to do it again. It was easy to believe that Blessing could make the deals happen indefinitely. I owned the Oak View house, another property, and my grandparents' Ventura house. After twice returning $50,000 to the charter, Blessing seemed legit. I agreed to meet with him at my house.

"George, I've got this condo town house I want to flip. Let me take an equity loan on your house and I'll get you one hundred thousand dollars in six months."

Staring down the barrel of an expensive hip replacement with no health insurance, it was an easy call. It was the first time Nikki and I disagreed on a big decision.

"I don't trust that guy, George."

"Nikki, look, he's already done it more than once. And we need the money."

It was hard to argue. We set up the equity loan and scheduled my hip replacement. I didn't understand how traumatic a hip replacement would be, much less two. Riding a motorcycle would never again be easy, and riding cross-country would be a painful challenge. I would struggle to accept this new reality, along with other realities. Like a lot of people,

I had an illusion in my head, an ideal, a vision of what true outlaws were, and how they should conduct themselves. Like many ideals, it was outdated and didn't line up with reality. Time changes everything. It changes us, and everyone we know. Nobody likes change, but we ignore it at our own risk. My biggest mistake of all might have been not acknowledging that simple fact.

15

Something was wrong with Finn. As that sank in, it scared the hell out of me. Everything had been so easy with Moriya, Georgie, and Aubree. I was there sometimes, sometimes I wasn't. They were always healthy. I was so focused on being a Hells Angel that I had put my family second. But now, my son had to come first.

Finn had started talking like any other child. He was making noises that sounded like "Daddy." Then nothing. He just stopped altogether. Even stranger, he would fall into a trancelike thousand-yard stare. As if he were locked inside himself. We took him to the doctor, but these things are hard to explain. You live with a child day to day, and you pick up on what's normal and what's not. The doctor asked, "Is he progressing?"

"He quit talking." I thought maybe kids did that sometimes. I felt silly even mentioning it. But the doctor looked worried. He asked us a series of specific questions, then said, "Let's keep an eye on him." It wasn't what you wanted to hear about your toddler. Nikki and I didn't know what to think. Then we visited her aunt and uncle in Fresno. Her aunt was a pediatric nurse and confirmed our worst fears. She told us that something was definitely off with Finn.

"You need to check up on this. I think he might be autistic. As soon as you get home, call the Easter Seals. Ask them to come out and do an evaluation."

Autistic. I had no idea what that meant. Was it like diabetes, or like a reading disorder? Would Finn grow out of it? Would he get worse? All we had was questions when the Easter Seals adviser showed up. The Easter Seals is a great organization that provides services and support to kids dealing with disabilities and their families. The adviser assessed Finn. My heart sank when she told us that Nikki's aunt was right. My little boy was autistic. She described what autism was, what the outlook would be, and told us to contact Tri-Counties Regional Center in Oxnard. Tri-Counties offered all kinds of support programs. Although it took me a while to get my head around Finn's condition, the support from Easter Seals and Tri-Counties turned out to be a lifesaver.

The worst part of autism is that your child can't communicate with you. Finn would get so frustrated. He'd start screaming over the slightest thing—if we told him he couldn't have a cookie or if the wheel bent on a Matchbox car. I didn't realize how stressed I was about it until we took Finn with us on a trip to the Bay Area.

Nikki's parents were driving her sister up to the School of Fashion Design in San Francisco, and I had to be in Oakland for a West Coast Officers' Meeting. We all decided to have lunch at a fifties-themed diner in San Francisco's Tenderloin district. As soon as we walked in, Finn fixated on a candy machine by the front door. We tried to move him along so that we could sit down and have lunch. He went ballistic. Nikki and I tried everything we could to calm him down, but he just kept pulling on the knobs, banging on the glass, and screaming. I was embarrassed and completely at a loss.

I always tried to be cordial when wearing my patch. I enjoyed surprising people who thought all outlaws were rude. But even I had my limits. It was a mistake for anyone to think that just because I was well-spoken or shorter and leaner than the average outlaw, I wasn't capable of violence. I felt my temper rise when a jackass sitting in a nearby booth made a loud comment about how certain people let their kids run wild and probably shouldn't be parents. The frustration of being unable to help Finn, of trying to understand autism and realizing it was a problem I couldn't fix, came to a head. This guy thought he could mouth off to a Hells Angel and somehow, because the diner was crowded, he'd be safe. He thought wrong. I stood over him, looking down on this soft little suburban citizen with his dumpy little wife, and I motherfucked him as only a Hells Angel can. He went sheet white and shut his mouth. I called him out, telling him to get his ass up and we'd settle it in the parking lot. But he just sat stock-still, staring down at the table, quiet as a mouse. Nikki's father and mother were shocked. I couldn't have cared less.

I don't know what would have happened to Finn and to us if not for Tri-Counties. They spent so much time, effort, and devotion working with Finn. It was a relief that somebody seemed to know something to do to help our son. We got him into a local preschool program for kids with disabilities. We worked with him at home, doing everything the doctors and professionals recommended, and he began to improve. One afternoon, as he turned five, Finn was playing with his action figures when he just started blurting out words and forming sentence fragments. It felt like we had won the lottery. Our son suddenly seemed normal. We took him to the doctor a couple weeks later, and the pediatrician couldn't believe the progress.

"Oh my God, he's come out the other side. This is a miracle, George."

The struggle to help Finn only made being home that much more important. At the clubhouse, I'd find myself thinking about Nikki and Finn. Georgie had come back to the charter at his mother's urging. I should have been overjoyed, but I was conflicted. He had a chip on his shoulder. He resented Nikki and Finn because his mother resented Nikki and Finn. I couldn't understand how he could still be so blindly under her sway. It felt strange to walk into the clubhouse and not have my son say, "Hello." We wore the same patch but I had no idea how to close the vast distance between us.

It was a symptom of a larger condition. The Hells Angels had changed. The charter had changed. Georgie had changed. His enthusiasm was gone. He never smiled. He hadn't come back because he wanted to ride with me, or because he loved being an outlaw. He'd come back because he didn't have anywhere else to go, no other identity. I felt like I had let him down. But he was a full-grown man. Men have to work these things out for themselves. You can't tell a man what he needs to be, or what he should do next. I couldn't hand Georgie the answers. I could see Cheryl's influence, and I only hoped he would make his own decisions, whatever they might be.

Georgie called Cheryl every day. The last Sunday in January 2006, she didn't answer. He tried again and again. Then he got worried. The charter had just ridden back from breakfast, a Sunday ritual, when Georgie decided to go check on Cheryl. He let himself into the condo and found his mom in her bedroom, sprawled on her bed. The room was in shambles, like she had only just managed to stumble to the bed before collapsing. He thought she was dead, but she was in a coma. He called for an ambulance and the EMTs transported her to Ventura County Medical Center, where she was admitted to the intensive care unit.

The doctors did a CAT scan and discovered that Cheryl had a brain tumor the size of a baseball pushing her brain stem down into her spine. Moriya met Georgie at the hospital and called to let me know what was going on. They put Cheryl on life support; clearly, she was never leaving the hospital. I left the clubhouse and headed home to have dinner with Nikki and Finn and told Nikki what had happened.

"Are you going to the hospital?"

Cheryl had been a constant source of irritation once Nikki and I decided to get married. Cheryl never missed an opportunity to harp on the age difference or talk shit about Nikki. When Finn was born, Cheryl flipped out. You could feel the hate coming off her anytime we were in the same room.

"Ain't no reason for me to go to that hospital."

Nikki has a certain grace. One of the things I've always loved about her is the sheer size of her heart, and her compassion. She can be tough as an angry pit bull, but you won't find a kinder person. She doesn't have a malicious bone in her body.

"George, I can't decide for you. But you need to go to the hospital, and you need to reconcile with that woman. Especially if she's . . ." Nikki sat down at our kitchen table and took my hand in hers. "Put everything else aside. Your kids need you. You need to go over to the hospital."

She was right. Even an outlaw is a fool to let hate guide him. I got in my white van and drove to the hospital. I had a knot in my stomach. I knew what type of scene I was heading into. I found my oldest children standing outside Cheryl's room. Moriya's eyes were red and swollen from crying. She was on the outs with her mother because Moriya had taken my side against Cheryl in an argument. Georgie looked shell-shocked. I hugged them both for a long time, then told them I needed some time alone with Cheryl.

The only sound in the room was the soft rush of air from the ventilator that kept Cheryl breathing. She looked as if she were asleep. The nurses had combed her hair and tucked the sheets and blanket neatly around her. She was still a pretty woman. I stared at her for the longest time. We had such a history, Cheryl and I. We had two children together. We had sat on the *60 Minutes* set, and she had flirted with Mike Wallace. I had been her protector in high school, not knowing that I could never protect her from herself. I had loved her. I had never figured out the demons that haunted her, and now I never would. But now, those demons didn't matter. I leaned over her.

"I'm so sorry the way all this turned out. I never meant to hurt you, Cheryl. It's just the way it is. But I wish you could have been happy."

I bent down and kissed her on the forehead and whispered, "Goodbye."

Cheryl had specified in her will that she didn't want to remain on life support. The doctors were clear there was no hope of recovery. All that was left was to literally pull the plug. Georgie, Moriya, and I stood around the bed looking down at this woman who had been such a force in our lives. The nurse told us we could disconnect the ventilator whenever we were ready. The kids were in no condition to handle that responsibility.

"Do you want me to do it?"

They both nodded. I pulled the plug. Slowly, the rise and fall of Cheryl's chest became shallower and shallower. After ten minutes, the nurse checked for a pulse.

"She's gone."

I felt I'd made some kind of peace with Cheryl. Moriya had always been tough as nails, and although she was devastated, I knew she'd recover. But Georgie looked ruined. In a way, I don't believe he ever got over losing his mother. Without her voice in his ear he would struggle to find any direction.

Less than a year later, I'd say good-bye to yet another connection to my past. I received calls from several members that David Ortega was asking to see me. David had been admitted to that same hospital as Cheryl because his organs were failing. He had been a hard-living partyer for as long as I knew him, and his lifestyle had finally caught up with him. I was still stung from David's support of Tom Heath, but David was a brother. The members who called all said pretty much the same thing.

"It doesn't look like he's going to get out of there, and I know he'd like to talk to you."

I found myself walking down the same fluorescent-lit corridors of the hospital, breathing through my mouth to avoid the smell of disinfectant and prepping myself for whatever I'd find in David's room. I walked into a crowd of Santa Barbara and Berdoo Hells Angels, clocking time with a respected veteran. David asked everyone to clear the room so that we could talk.

I sat on the foot of his bed and tried not to give away how shocked I was. His skin was ashen, and he had lost so much weight that his eyes looked unnaturally big in their sockets. He might as well have been wearing a death mask. But he was full of life when he spoke. He admitted that he had always had a problem with me being in charge, even when he knew I was making the right calls. He couldn't explain why he had gone with Tom to the Ink House. He had no particular respect for Tom. We let it be and made our peace.

"Do you want to come back to Ventura?" I meant it as something hopeful, a sign that we were good. It wasn't a realistic proposal given the ghost I was talking to.

"No, I'm going to go to San Luis Obispo. I'm going to finish getting these guys established in Santa Barbara, and then going up to San Luis Obispo and get a new charter going there. But I'll be back. I'll come to Ventura then."

He was so sure of it, so definite, that I believed him—regardless of how he looked or what I had been told. He seemed so lucid and confident. I thought, "The doctors have to be wrong."

"Okay, man. I can't wait to ride with you again."

We said our good-byes, hugged, and I left much happier than when I'd arrived. Outlaws beat the odds all the time. But time mocks plans. David had done all the living he could fit into one life. He died the next day. For me, an era of old-school Southern California outlaws died with him. I felt like the last man standing.

There is a peaceful place in the foothills above Ventura, called Serra Cross. It's a concrete circle jutting out from the slope of the foothills, surrounded by a low stone wall and dominated by a large, crude wooden cross. The view is stunning. You can see the whole town. You can trace the entire length of Ventura's iconic wooden pier jutting out past the foaming breakers, like a finger pointing straight on toward Hawaii. Whenever I was struggling with a decision or a problem, I'd always ride up there. In our better days, David liked to tag along.

I rode up that night and sat on the stone wall, at its leading edge. I listened to the far-off whisper of waves I couldn't see in the dark. I thought about the Question Marks, how simple it was to be in that group of guys.

Way back then, even before I wore a patch, I could roar into Ventura and feel like I owned the place. As outlaws, we were gods. David was the first of my brothers. He was a true outlaw, like Old Man John. Any of us might fight another in the sketchy flickering light of a bonfire. But afterward, you dusted each other off and shared a drink and a laugh. We forgave each other our small offenses and were brothers once again. Like most young men, we didn't believe we'd ever die. We thought we were invincible and that those days would last forever.

Look backward too long when you're riding a motorcycle and you'll wreck. It's a lesson for life as well. But sitting there that night, the beautiful lights of Ventura sparkling at my feet, I couldn't help but indulge a bit of nostalgia. Riding down from Serra Cross, though, I realized I had to accept those days were gone for good.

Daydreaming about the past was a luxury I couldn't afford, along with a lot of other luxuries. I watched the miracle money from Robert Blessing's deals evaporate almost overnight as the real estate bubble burst. The market was crashing across the country, but the losses in Los Angeles property speculation were staggering. By the end of January 2008, the financial train wreck was obvious in the daily news stories. The government had no idea what to do. Robert Blessing called me to tell me that his investments had tanked. The scramble was on to save what we could.

After Cheryl died, I had given Georgie and Moriya early inheritance in the form of property, and they'd hooked up with Blessing like the rest of us. Blessing had used different sources for each note. In Georgie's case, a traditional bank foreclosed as soon as the equity loan was overdue. The note on the clubhouse was held by a guy who owned a flooring company in Los Angeles. The paper on my house was held by Velocity Investment Group. For the time being, we were able to meet the payments on my house and the clubhouse.

Things were no less turbulent in the club. Out of the blue, Georgie and I had our bikes confiscated as part of a sheriff's investigation into stolen bikes and bike parts. My bike was clean. I'd bought it from a loan company that had reclaimed the motorcycle from the first owner for nonpayment. Georgie had bought his bike from a Fresno Hells Angel named Mike Lynch. Unfortunately, Lynch was the one under investigation. He'd been arrested after a search of his garage had turned up stolen bikes and parts.

Our bikes were worth north of $10,000 each, so I called the Ventura County Sheriff's Office to try to get them back. I spoke with a deputy who taped the conversation. He asked me what would happen if it turned out that a member was selling stolen bikes to other members. I said, "That would be a problem." The tape and that comment were the feeble hooks my club adversaries would use for a smear campaign. Lynch's attorney received the tape as part of the discovery in his case. He gave the tape to Sonny, who made sure it got delivered to charters up and down the West Coast. It was his shot at revenge for the dustup over his 911 call. I learned about the tape when I got a call from a Richmond Hells Angel.

"George, I just wanted you to know that I listened to the tape and I think it's bullshit."

"What are you talking about?"

"You don't know?"

"I have no idea what you're talking about."

"Oakland is passing out a tape of you talking to the cops."

"About what?"

"It's you talking to some cop about your bike. About Georgie's bike."

"Yeah, so? I was trying to get our bikes back."

Oakland was doing Sonny's bidding, but it was all smoke, no fire. Oakland was the only charter getting worked up. Everyone else who called me thought it was a whole lot of nothing. Sonny wasn't going to let it go, though. Oakland member Sam Botchvaroff was a nothing in the club. He elected himself point person on the attack, but I wasn't about to let some Sonny wannabe talk shit about me. I called him to see what he would say directly to me.

"I heard you got a problem with me."

"Yeah, I do. I think you should quit the club. You talked to the cops, man. It's right there on the tape."

"Yeah. So?"

"So you got to quit. We don't talk to the cops. You need to go."

"That topic's not open for discussion. You want to talk to me about this, get your ass to Ventura."

"I got another call. I gotta go."

Several months later, a Ventura member went up to the Bay Area for a party. Botchvaroff handed him a letter and told him to deliver it to me. I wasn't about to start accepting hand-delivered letters. Outlaws don't send each other letters.

"Take it back to Sam and tell him if he's got something to say to me, to come down and say it to my face like a man. This isn't high school. We don't pass notes."

It was 2010. I was sixty-five. I was tired. Riding a motorcycle was harder than it had ever been for me because my hips would be on fire after a hundred miles. The clubhouse wasn't fun because I had to watch everything I said knowing that it could get back to Sonny and get twisted. West Coast Officers' Meetings were brutal, with some bizarre new accusation popping up from Sonny almost every month. I trusted few people and I wanted to spend time around fewer still. Money worries dogged everyone. The club was at war everywhere. The year started with a group of Santa Cruz Hells Angels brawling with several Vagos outside a Starbucks. In April, Hells Angels on a run in Minneapolis got into a huge fight with a large group of Outlaws. In August, a small band of Hells Angels exchanged gunfire with some Vagos outside a Circle K in Chino Valley, Arizona. September saw the arrests of nineteen Pagans in Long Island and New Jersey on charges of plotting to blow up Hells Angels with grenades. Any illusion I had ever had about brokering peace among outlaw motorcycle clubs was thoroughly dispelled.

I felt ineffective. If I was the outlaw world's peacemaker, I hadn't been successful. I realized that most—and the most powerful—outlaws simply didn't want peace. They needed enemies. I'd missed the memo that the life was no longer about partying and brotherhood, or living on your own terms. Somewhere along the line it had become about chest puffing and power grabs, and every man for himself. I was ready for something different when documentary filmmaker Nick Mead approached me about a project. I had known Nick since 1989 when I was doing all kinds of press for the club. Nick had approached me about participating in a documentary called *Black Leather Jacket*. I turned him down because it would have taken forever to get approval through the club for the patch to appear on-screen.

Now he wanted to do a movie called *American Ride*. The idea was that I'd ride my bike to meet eclectic subjects around the country (the title would eventually be changed to *The Last American Outlaw*). I'd interview each person about the state of America and what freedom meant in modern times. Nick wanted me to do the project as a Hells Angel. But given how difficult it would be to get approval through the club, we agreed to film two versions of every scene, one with the patch and one without. That way, he could produce the film no matter what the club thought. Given how at odds Sonny and I were, it seemed a smart move.

A month after we filmed the first interview with Michael Blake, the author of *Dances with Wolves*, I rode up to a West Coast Officers' Meeting in Oakland. The hot issue was the Vagos. The Vagos were one of the Big Four outlaw motorcycle clubs. Founded in San Bernardino in 1965, the club's logo was neon-green lettering on a black background, held up by Loki, the Norse god of mischief. The Vagos called themselves the Green Nation. They had coexisted with the Angels in California and other states for decades. But by 2010, they were regularly clashing with the Hells Angels. I'd been having informal back-channel talks with the Vagos' leadership, trying to find middle ground.

The younger Hells Angels officers were pushing hard against the Vagos. I got up in the meeting to say my piece, knowing full well it wasn't going to be a popular point of view.

"Listen, we're fighting the Outlaws, the Pagans, the Mongols, and the Bandidos. Now you want to go to war with the Vagos. We're fighting wars on five fronts. This is a problem for us. We keep looking for enemies, and eventually we'll find them inside. If fighting is all we do, we'll end up fighting each other."

But we already were.

"You know what, man, why are you getting involved with this? This is our problem."

I couldn't believe what I was hearing. "Our problem?" Like we were in different clubs? After the meeting wrapped up, I headed out to my bike. I was parked next to an older member who had patched in a couple of years after I had. He shook his head as we said our good-byes.

"These young guys, they don't want to hear what you've got to say, George."

That one comment gave me pause. I meditated on it for the ride home and long after. Words had always been my weapons, and I had fought so hard for so long. That simple sentence meant all my fighting was for nothing. Because in the end, I was good with a gun, and great with a knife, but I was always best with my words. If words had stopped working for me, I had damn well run out of road. You don't get peace with a gun, you get it with words. But most members never wanted peace. Maybe my message had always been doomed to fall on deaf ears.

That meeting lit the fuse. Whatever I was part of, it wasn't the life I recognized. Outlaw culture had changed. Or the Hells Angels had changed. Or I did. Likely, it was all three. Whatever the case, you have to know when you're in the wrong place.

When I joined the Hells Angels, I'd become a member of an exclusive one-percent fraternity. It wasn't just a club, it was a unique lifestyle. Difficult to get in, and difficult to be accepted. Now *Sons of Anarchy* was a hit show. Anybody could go to a bike shop, plunk down a wad of cash, and roll out on a custom Harley—no work or dedication required. Everyone had tattoos. Everybody was wearing faux cutoffs. It started to dawn on me that maybe the outlaw thing to do was to not be in a club.

A couple weeks after the officers' meeting, the thoughts were still rattling around in my head. I pulled into a gas station in Ventura, wearing my cut. As I got off my bike, I glanced around and saw looks of fear, and something else. Revulsion. For the first time in my life, I was ashamed to be wearing my patch. I felt sick. It was like a great big neon arrow pointing to what I needed to do.

At the next charter meeting, I stood up for what would be my last time in the clubhouse. "Guys, I've thought a lot about this. I'm done. I'm out." As members started talking around the table, I realized that they thought I meant I was just stepping down as president. "No, guys, I'm not talking about the office. I'm through as a Hells Angel. I'm quitting the club."

After a moment of shocked silence, one member after another came up and hugged me. In this sentimental moment, they all seemed to be genuinely blown away that I would quit. They said all the right things, all the things brothers would say.

"Hey, can we come to you for counsel?"

"Sure, yeah, I'm always available. I'll never turn my back on you guys."

I turned in my Death Head rings, flags, and other indicia. I took off my cut, folded it neatly, and put it in the center of the table. I got up, hugged my son last, and rode home without my colors for the first time in more than thirty years. I thought it would feel like a hole, like something was missing. But instead, it felt like a weight had been lifted. I knew that I'd made the right decision.

I called Nick Mead. I assumed it would kill the documentary.

"I'm sorry to jam you up, Nick. It was something I had to do. The club and I were just going in different directions."

"It's not a problem, George. It was never about the Hells Angels. We can still do it. We've got the scenes without the patch and we'll film the rest without them."

So we made plans to keep on filming. But if I thought walking away from the club was going to be as easy as standing up in a meeting and hugging a few guys on the way out the door, I was sadly mistaken. I should have been smart enough to know that Sonny wasn't going to be content to let me fade into a comfortable retirement.

My vice president, Shane Moeller, had been voted in as president. A few days later, Shane called and asked me to come over to talk to him. I'd agreed to give counsel whenever someone needed it. He lived a block away, so I walked over.

"What's going on?"

"The guys from Santa Barbara called me. They told me they're coming and taking over in Ventura."

The guys, like Scott Sutton, that I had pushed out of Ventura for one reason or another had all landed in the Santa Barbara charter. My quitting created a power void they wanted to fill.

"You need to tell them they can come back, but nobody's taking over anything. You're going to have to make a stand with these guys. First of all, you're going to have to vote them into the charter. Make them stick to the rules."

We talked for about an hour and then I left. Four days later, a friend called and told me that Shane had quit the club. Rob Smith became the Ventura president. He called me shortly after.

"Look, George, I'm sorry but this is the way it is. The club doesn't like the message it sends, you quitting. We're changing your status to out bad, no contact."

"Let me get this straight. You guys put me on trial and made a decision, without me even being there?"

"We voted on it and it's a done deal, all over the world. And another thing. They're saying you need to settle with Tom. He says you owe him. He wants you to think about a figure. I'm going to give you a couple days to think on it, and I'll call you back."

"I don't need to think about it, I've got a figure in mind right now. Nothing. I don't owe that guy anything. You can tell him to fucking come get his money if he thinks I owe him something. And here's something else you guys need to keep in mind. I'm not any different than I ever was. I'm that same guy. If you approach me, or anyone approaches me, I'm going to take the offensive. I'm not going to wait. I'm going to assume you're coming to hurt me. We understand each other?"

"Yeah."

"Then this is the last conversation we're ever going to have."

I knew Sonny and I had disagreed on just about everything for more than a decade. But in quitting, I thought I was leaving those battles behind. I underestimated Sonny's ability to hold a grudge and his ongoing influence within the club. In his mind we now were and would always be mortal enemies. It came from a basic difference in our personal beliefs. I had always felt I belonged to the club. Sonny would always believe that the club belonged to him. That I had ever threatened that perceived ownership was simply a sin he could not forgive.

'16

You don't just stop being an outlaw. You can quit a club and lose friends you've had your whole adult life, but that doesn't change who you were, or who you really are. In fact, I had walked away because everyone in the club was acting just like the people we rebelled against in the first place. Quitting wasn't leaving the life. Quitting the Hells Angels, with their conformity and me-first philosophy of 2011, was the most outlaw thing I could do.

Law enforcement certainly still saw me as an outlaw, and a valuable one. The feds think an out-bad ex–Hells Angel would have good reason to roll. They assume the right amount of pressure can make you give up high-value targets and whole charters. That pressure always comes in the form of an indictment. Mine would rise out of a toxic mess of tattoo shops, firebombs, and rats.

It was all about the Ink House. When I'd started the business after cutting loose from Tom Heath, it was Ventura's only tattoo shop. Tattoos were still taboo in mainstream society. The only people with body art in 1979 were servicemen, outlaws, strippers, and others on the fringe. You didn't see ink on any of the soft, pasty bodies lying around the country club pool.

As I built the business, society slowly changed. Suburban kids who wanted to look tough would get a flaming skull or a tiny piece of World War II fighter-plane-nose art on their biceps. Even reputable women would splurge on an ankle band or shoulder rose. Along the way, two other ink shops opened up on the outskirts of town. They weren't competition. They were off the beaten path and kept irregular hours. Nobody gave them a second thought. Meanwhile, the Ink House became a Ventura institution. The charter claimed it. Angels worked there, hung out there, and got inked there. It was a point of pride among the members that they had this anchor in the community. It was a way of saying that Ventura was a Hells Angels town.

In 2002, a guy from Camarillo set up Slingers Tattoo Shop on the east end of Ventura. He didn't tell anybody he was coming and didn't ask permission. Even worse, he boasted about his connections to Oxnard's Colonia Chiques, a vicious gang with ties to La Eme. The young guys in the charter didn't take it well. Neither did the local gang members. Two months after the shop opened, it was torched. I had nothing to do with the fire. The cops had a long list of suspects, but the crime was never solved.

By 2006, tattoos were in vogue (and in *Vogue*—literally on the models in the magazine). They were everywhere. TV shows such as *Inked* and *Miami Ink* made getting and giving tattoos hip. Librarians wanted half sleeves that they could show off on the weekends. Accountants put full-color flags on their chests. Soccer moms got elaborate tramp stamps to prove to themselves that they hadn't lost their edge. Business boomed, which attracted competition. Scratch the Surface opened up a half mile down Main Street. Twisted Ink followed, located another half mile down the street. Elbowing into established Hells Angels territory would have been enough of an insult. But the people behind those shops came with a lot of baggage that made everything worse.

Scratch the Surface was started by guys who had worked in a Mongols tattoo shop in Camarillo. The Angels thought the shop was backed by the Mongols. The Mongols, it turned out, thought I had offered the shop protection. The artists in Twisted Ink had originally worked in Fresno, where they ran into trouble with the Fresno Hells Angels. But as soon as they got to town, they spread the word that they were protected by the Fresno charter. That created friction between Ventura and Fresno. The shops became a heated topic at every charter meeting. Ventura members were pissed that anyone would dare creep onto their turf. People constantly spouted off about the shops.

"These dirty sons of bitches. What are we going to do about them?"

I saw a setup. I had to keep a lid on my guys.

"We're not going to do anything. You guys need to stay away. Besides, it's not 1985. It's 2007. The industry has changed. Everyone wants into the tattoo business. Everybody wants to be an artist. We had a good run, but there's no way we're going to keep people from coming in here."

I was doing my best to keep the situation cool. But controlling Hells Angels is a challenge. Jared "Crash" Plomell was the last member I thought would cause me problems. I liked Jared. He was a tall, lean, good-looking, soft-spoken kid with a shaved head. He was popular with the ladies but certainly not the sharpest tool in the shed. He was raising hell late one night in the alley behind Scratch the Surface when a small group of guys from the shop knocked him off his bike and rat-packed him. Take on one Hells Angel, you take on all of them. They called me to apologize, but I told them, "You don't understand. You were his problem, now you're my problem." They disappeared and we never found them again. I was pissed at Crash for jamming me up. I told my members, in meeting after meeting, to let it be. But like little kids told they can't touch something, it only made them want it more.

Crash wasn't the only one ignoring my orders. James Ivans took it upon himself to send a message to Twisted Ink. The Demons were a Hells Angels support club. Ivans met with a small group of them—Kyle Gilbertson, brothers Brian and Richard Russell, and Benito Hurtado, a longtime friend of Georgie's. Ivans told them to go into the shop and tell whoever was working there that they had two weeks to move or be moved. What they didn't realize was that the FBI was, for all intents and purposes, running the shop. The Bureau had the place wired for audio and video. The feds were just biding their time and gathering evidence.

On the night of July 6, 2007, Molotov cocktails shattered the plate-glass windows of both Scratch the Surface and Twisted Ink. The firebombs exploded, spraying flammable liquid over the floors, walls, and fixtures, but it was a flashout. As bad as the word *firebombing* sounds, the shops sustained modest fire and water damage that was largely cosmetic, although it would be expensive to fix. Regardless of my orders to stay away from the shops, Crash Plomell had hired two guys he'd done time with to bomb the places. The feds began their investigation, which would take years. All along they were looking for a connection to me. If they couldn't find it, they'd manufacture it.

Crash Plomell became that connection. After I quit the club in 2011, Crash got busted on drug and gun charges. The two guys he had hired to torch the shops had given him up, and now the feds had a way to turn him. He was looking at a long time in prison. The FBI made him an offer. Give me up, and he'd do no time. Ultimately, they'd even pay him thousands of dollars for his cooperation.

The feds came knocking on Friday, August 12, 2011. It was just after six in the morning. Ruby, my pit bull, started barking her stranger bark. I went outside in my bathrobe and heard my neighbor's voice floating over my fortified front gate. "Are you really from the FBI?" It was no way to start a morning. The feds pounded on the steel gate, trying to get through.

"Stop pounding on my gate."

"FBI. We have a warrant."

"Fine. Just stop pounding on the gate. The sheriffs already broke it once. Give me a minute to open it and I'll let you in."

I was arraigned later that day, part of a small group of "coconspirators." The indictment included me, Kyle Gilbertson, Benito Hurtado,

James Ivans, and the Russell brothers. At some point in the process, Ivans quietly flipped and became a prosecution witness. Benito Hurtado pled to a minor charge—effectively the equivalent of looking the other way during a felony—and walked away with probation.

The arrest could not have come at a worse time. I was essentially broke. When Nikki had left the Ink House, I had nobody I could trust inside. That meant spending as much time as possible at the shop and ignoring my other businesses. Everything I made went into paying the high-interest equity note on my house. There was no buffer of savings. So even though Robert Sheahen and Mark Haney offered to take the case for $100,000, a figure that would have lost them money, I told them no. Even that amount was out of my range.

I drew Michael Mayock from the public defender lottery. Mayock was a respected former federal prosecutor. Tall, distinguished, with close-cropped gray hair and perfectly straight posture, Mayock knew all of the government's tricks. He had sat at the feds' table and was a seasoned trial attorney who knew how to argue a case. He wasn't available the day of my bail hearing, so one of the lead public defenders, an astute defense lawyer named Angel Navarro, represented me.

"Mike's in court right now, George. But I'm confident I can get you bail with this judge."

It was exactly what I wanted to hear. I didn't want to spend another year inside waiting to fight a bogus federal trial. I couldn't keep the Ink House going from jail. The judge gave the Russell brothers $50,000 bail each. I thought, "Okay, this is going to be pretty reasonable." When it came to me, Angel Navarro stood up.

"Mr. Christie quit the Hells Angels in 2011. This firebombing took place in 2007. Why did they wait until 2011 to indict him? Because they want Mr. Christie to flip. Mr. Christie is not prepared to do that. Mr. Christie needs an appropriate bail. He needs to fight this case from his home."

The judge agreed, and set a $200,000 bail. But the government has ways of undercutting bail even after it's granted. Assistant U.S. Attorney Jay Robinson told the court that the prosecution would appeal my bail. The magistrate had no choice but to entertain the motion and keep me in custody until the appeal was resolved. It would take two weeks to get a hearing. But sometimes the system works. The judge who drew the trial, Judge Jacqueline Nguyen, ruled in my favor. I bailed out, under house arrest. I had just got home, when Nick Mead stopped by. I felt bad because Nick had stuck with *The Last American Outlaw* project when I quit the Angels and hadn't flinched when I told him the club had changed my status. He had said we'd do it without any Hells Angels association. But now I was going to be fighting a trial and would have no time or opportunity to ride out for interviews.

"I'm sorry, Nick. I know you've invested a lot in this. I had no way of knowing this was coming. I'm sorry that we can't finish the film."

He didn't miss a beat. "No, let's let the government drive the project forward. Whatever they do, we'll document it. This will make a brilliant documentary."

"You sure?"

"Absolutely."

"But I can't even leave here."

"It doesn't matter. We'll shoot it all from your house, and we've got the other background stuff that we've already done."

From then on, Nick showed up at court every time I did. And he often had company. A local blogger who wrote about the outlaw motorcycle club culture showed up with him. The guy had written about me before and was regularly posting about my arrest and pretrial hearings. He'd be more than an observer. He would play a part in the trial.

One Wednesday night I was sitting in my favorite easy chair reading a motion that Mike Mayock had filed when the phone rang. It was Vince Scott, the moneyman who held the paper on the Ventura clubhouse. The loan was months in arrears.

"George, can you talk to these guys? They're not making their payments."

"Vince, I'm no longer involved with the club. I have legal problems and I'm not even allowed to interact with any of those guys."

"Man, I can't keep holding this paper if they're not going to pay on it."

"That's something you're going to have to take up with them."

Within a few months, he would be forced to foreclose. I had to watch from a distance as the charter I had built lost its home. The sheriffs showed up and evicted the charter. It was a mess. Scott Sutton, the new president, was not managing the charter well. I couldn't figure out if I was more angry or sad. In any case, I had bigger worries.

People read about a trial in the news, and they think that's where all the drama is. But the gamesmanship and maneuvering in the lead-up to a complex trial are often more intense than the actual trial. Discovery is the process in which both sides are required to reveal evidence that is pertinent to the case. It's one of the key ways feds screw with a defendant who has limited funds and a small defense team. Prosecutors drag their feet releasing relevant documents. They provide a modest stream of evidence right up to the last week or so before the trial. Then they do an "evidence dump," swamping the defense with more material than anybody could reasonably get through. The defense is left asking the court for more time and is out of luck if they don't get it. The U.S. attorneys were holding back discovery materials, and Mike Mayock cried foul time and time again.

But even the modest documents we got painted the picture of a seriously flawed case. Plomell and Ivans were telling distinctly different versions. Some of the conflicts in the testimony would have been comical if they weren't so absurd. The bombers had agreed to testify. In their first interviews with the feds, they said I met them with Crash Plomell at a doughnut shop and gave them $200 in a bag. At their second interview, they claimed I hadn't been at that meeting, but that they had met me at the Ink House. The third time around, they admitted they had never met me. I had never laid eyes on them. By the time we began selecting a jury, the government would have rounded up no less than seven informants, each one less reliable than the last.

All along the way, Nick Mead filmed me. The blogger continued writing updates. Those blog posts became the focus of contention when the U.S. attorney got around to reading them. Anyone who was the least bit sophisticated could have accessed most of the discovery documents. They were part of the public record. A simple PACER (Public Access to Court Electronic Records) account would have allowed anyone to figure out that the government's unindicted "co-conspirator #1" and "co-conspirator #2" were Plomell and Ivans. When the blogger named the two, the prosecutors wanted sanctions. In quick succession, Robinson accused me, Nikki, and Moriya of being the blogger. He wanted whoever had published the information identified. Little did he realize the blogger was sitting three rows back, watching and listening just as anyone else in the general public could.

Judge Nguyen came up with her own solution. She sealed the case. All records from that point forward would be sealed. All the principals were ordered not to speak to bloggers or the media. It was ridiculous. That the government, with all the resources it was using, couldn't figure out who the blogger was seemed like satire. Robinson was visibly angry at the end of the day's proceedings when he waved Mike Mayock over to the prosecution's table. The courtroom was empty and quiet, so I could hear everything from where I was seated at the defense table. Robinson wanted me to hear.

"You tell Christie to get his ass upstairs and start talking or I'm coming with a superseding indictment."

Superseding indictments are amended to either reduce or—more often—increase the charges in existing indictments. It was an angry threat, plain and simple.

Mike Mayock sat back down next to me at the defense table. "Well, you heard him." Mike knew me well enough by then to know what my response would be.

"I'm not going to flip. I'm not debriefing, I'm not giving them shit. Let 'em come."

Several weeks later, the U.S. attorney filed a superseding indictment carrying mandatory minimums and life sentences on three of the counts. The Russell brothers folded that day and got their own unindicted "co-conspirator" numbers. As if things weren't chaotic enough, we had to change judges a month before we were set to go to trial. Judge Nguyen had been nominated to the federal Court of Appeals. In May 2012, she was confirmed and two days later vacated her seat on the district court. In a case already full of surprises, we faced a new unknown.

The judge selected was Judge George Wu. He was respected, fair, and reasonable. Almost from the moment he took over the trial, he pushed for the two sides to make a deal. Judge Wu could see that the prosecution's case had critical flaws, but he also felt that Robinson was never going to give up. It seemed to me it had become personal for the assistant U.S. attorney.

Choosing a jury was every bit as troublesome as the rest of the trial. *Sons of Anarchy* was wildly popular. We couldn't find a juror who hadn't seen the over-the-top TV drama about a fictional outlaw motorcycle club. We used the jury voir dire to determine how what they saw on TV affected their perception of what really went on in the charter. The answers weren't encouraging.

"Well, of course Mr. Christie knows what's going on."

"How do you know that?"

"I watch *Sons of Anarchy*. Everything's done in the meeting. And the president tells the members what to do."

I wasn't thrilled with the jury we chose. Putting the rest of your life in the hands of twelve strangers is scary. But it's even more so when you think those strangers might have a hard time telling the difference between television drama and real life. It didn't take long for more concerns to crop up. On the first day of the trial, the prosecution put expert witness Jorge Gil-Blanco on the stand to establish his credibility. Gil-Blanco started his career with the LAPD and moved from one law enforcement agency to another up and down California. By 2012, he was a consultant for rent, a supposed expert on outlaw motorcycle clubs, and the Hells Angels in particular. He gave the impression of anything but expertise. He sat uncomfortably on the stand, wearing a cheap, off-the-rack suit and rimless glasses that I suppose were meant to make him look more learned, but just made him look bookish. Under cross-examination by Kyle Gilbertson's public defender, Larry Bakman, Gil-Blanco dropped a bombshell.

"What makes you an expert on the Ventura Hells Angels? You've never testified in a case about them before. You've never investigated them. Why should we think you're capable of testifying against Mr. Christie and Mr. Gilbertson?"

Gil-Blanco said he had a source inside the Ventura charter who was giving him information. Bakman exploded, demanding the name. Judge Wu quickly clamped down, rejecting Bakman's request and excusing Gil-Blanco.

By the end of day two, everybody in the courtroom knew that the trial was going to be an utter circus. The indictments had problems, the jury was questionable, and the proceedings were a mess. Judges don't like to be overturned on appeal. By day two, we already had grounds for multiple appeals. For my part, I didn't want to sit in jail waiting on appellate court rulings. Judge Wu found a receptive audience when he dismissed the jury for the day and took yet another shot at bringing the two sides to a deal.

"Mr. Robinson, this case isn't what you think it is. There are a lot of issues with this case."

I felt smug as he scolded the prosecution. But then it was my turn. "And you, Mr. Christie, God only knows what you've gotten away with in the last forty years." Judge Wu sat back and looked from one table to the other.

"I would like both parties to go down to Judge Walters's court. I'd like Judge Walters to try to negotiate a compromise. Can we do that?"

Mayock and Bakman nodded. "Yes, Your Honor."

Robinson agreed.

"Good. Come to a deal today, and I'll bake you a cake."

This was frustrating, all-too-familiar territory. The feds had a weak case full of holes. If Barry Tarlow had been sitting next to me, it would have been a slam dunk. He would have fought and won. Hell, the feds would have given up the fight. But with a public defender—even a good one such as Mike Mayock—the prosecution might be able to persuade the jury. I was faced with rolling the dice and risking three life sentences, even though I knew I was innocent, or taking a plea.

We all headed to Judge Walters's chambers. I had heard he was a hard-nosed judge, so I was a little surprised when he asked me if I'd be willing to talk to him alone so we could speak candidly. I agreed, and he sent everyone else out in the hallway.

"Look, George, counts six, seven, and eight are mandatory minimums. If you get found guilty on any of them, you're going to go to prison for the rest of your life. I'd like to bring the U.S. attorney back in here and negotiate something that will satisfy everyone. But you may have to do some time. Can we agree that I'll negotiate a five-year ceiling on the sentence? After that, it's up to Judge Wu. You'll walk out of here looking at zero to five years. All right?"

I agreed and he brought everyone back in. Mayock, Bakman, and Robinson discussed pleas for Kyle and me. They ironed out the terms and we met again in Judge Wu's courtroom the next morning. We entered our pleas. Weeks later, at sentencing, I was given a chance to make a statement. The prosecution prefers an allocution of the crimes in the plea. Instead, I used the opportunity to make a statement that summed up my life at that moment.

"The man that law enforcement is pursuing no longer exists. Like the

Western outlaws of old, he walked into a new century and vanished. He is gone, and I ask you to let him rest in peace.

"It's true, for forty years I rode with the Hells Angels. Thirty-five of those as one of its leaders and spokesmen. Although I am no longer a member or participant in that lifestyle, it is hard to separate my past from the present for many people, as well as the man from the myth, and that includes myself at times.

"Over time I have tried to become smarter, wiser, and more tempered. I've not always taken the correct turns in life, but when I have realized I was off course, I have always tried my best to once again find true north.

"Several years ago I made a decision to not just relinquish my office, but to end my tenure as a club member. It was a difficult personal decision I knew would arouse suspicion in many. But I found myself on a road down which I was no longer willing to take my wife and young son.

"As a leader, you can either fish each day for your men or teach them to fish for themselves. I thought I had taught them the art of fishing. I made a mistake in judgment as their leader. And, as I slowly let go of power, it created a vacuum. That set off a power struggle that created a series of events that brings me before the court.

"Although I did not personally direct anyone, I accept that if I am truly guilty of anything, it is a lack of leadership. So I stand here before you ready to accept the punishment for the crimes I've pled guilty to and once again find true north."

The prosecution agreed to probation for Kyle. They recommended I be given three years. Mike Mayock took one last Hail Mary.

"The defense requests house arrest for the duration of Mr. Christie's sentence."

Judge Wu wasn't having it. "Counselor, you know this is a custody case. Mr. Christie has to go into custody."

"Your Honor, there are rumors that my client is an informant. His life would be in jeopardy in prison."

"I'm going to dispel that rumor because I'm going to send him to prison. Informants don't go to prison. Anyone in the Hells Angels will know that."

He sentenced me to a year and a day. It was a nod to both sides. I had done almost two years on house arrest. But in federal court, pretrial detention cannot be considered part of the sentence. So actually, Judge Wu was giving the prosecution what they wanted—three years of detention—while still being fair to me.

Unfortunately, judges don't have any say in where you do your time. If Judge Wu had been able to influence the Bureau of Prisons, I would have been sent to the logical place—Terminal Island. He gave me two months to get my affairs in order and then report for incarceration. After a week, I got a call from my pretrial service officer.

"George, I'm going out on a limb here. You didn't hear this from me, but they're sending you to Texas."

"You're kidding."

"No, it's official."

"Why? Why not Terminal Island?"

"You know why."

It was one last shot from the feds. There's only one reason why the Federal Bureau of Prisons would send a California resident to La Tuna prison rather than Terminal Island. Payback. A little extra punishment. Instead of doing a year where my family could visit, I was being sent to dust-bowl Texas, ten miles from the Mexican border. To a place known as the "armpit of the federal corrections system."

At the end of the trial, Nick Mead wrapped up the documentary, now titled *The Last American Outlaw*. It premiered at Ventura's Bell Arts Factory right before I surrendered to prison. I liked the movie, and we agreed that we would pursue distribution when I got out of prison.

My personal lawyer, James Devine, offered to drive with me to Texas. I showed up at the prison intake office with nothing more than the clothes on my back. They interviewed me to see if I had any problems or special conditions such as diabetes that they would need to deal with. After having pictures taken of my tattoos, I was told to wait in a holding cell. An hour later, a lieutenant showed up, concern etched on his face.

"We have a group of Bandidos inside."

"So?"

"Come on, George, we know what's going on."

"Look, I'm retired from the club. If there are Bandidos in here, in all likelihood I know them. I'm the guy that was negotiating peace throughout the outlaw bike world."

"Sit tight. I'm going out to talk to them."

The Bandidos knew it was me because they had read about my trial in the papers. But the lieutenant was worried about trouble in the yard. He and two guards walked me out. He looked shocked when the Bandidos' leader waved, smiled, came over, and gave me a big hug. I'd known the guy for almost thirty years.

"George, it's good to see you, man. You're with me. I got clothes for you, and we'll hook you up with everything you need." We would be cellmates for the duration of my stay. Outlaw life makes for strange bedfellows.

It was odd being back behind bars at sixty-eight. I had my reputation and friends inside, but that didn't mean I wasn't subject to the same pressures as other inmates. It was still prison.

I had gone in with a pair of prescription bifocal Ray-Ban sunglasses. I owned an expensive pair of polarized reading glasses, but was concerned that they would be stolen or destroyed in prison. The Ray-Bans led to a stressful misunderstanding.

I became friends with an old-school Mexican gangster from New Mexico. Nobody knew if I was an active Hells Angel or not. People didn't ask, and I didn't explain it. But this guy was cool with me and gave me respect. One day I went into the mess hall and he wasn't sitting at the New Mexico table. I thought, "Uh-oh, trouble. Something's not right." Later, he was found in his cell, covered in his own blood. He had been stabbed fifty times. Two guys in his gang had come in and jumped him. He was still alive when the authorities found him. In a show of toughness, he refused the gurney and walked to the hospital wing. He disappeared after that. That was the system. They got him out of there and then he was just a ghost.

After he left, I noticed that all the New Mexico associates were eyeballing me in the yard. You get paranoid in prison because, more often than not, someone really is after you. I convinced myself that the Mexicans in the yard thought the guy they stabbed had been giving me intel. I came to the conclusion that these gangsters were worried that I had information about them. They stared at me, day after day.

Then a new guy showed up in their crew. He was dangerous-looking, well over 250 pounds of pure muscle. His head was shaved and his body, face, and head were all tattooed. Initially, he was put into unit four. Over time, he transferred again and again until he was in unit six, my unit. I put two and two together, and they added up to trouble. I didn't like his eyes. I didn't like how he watched me.

I had a week left when he approached me in the yard. I thought, "Well, if this is it, this is it." I squared up for battle. I might have been the old guy, but I had some gas left in the tank.

"Hey, man, I'm Toony."

We nodded at each other.

"Would you be offended if I got the info off those glasses. We really dig them. We want to get us some of those." All these guys from New Mexico, they had been staring at my glasses all along.

"Sure, no problem," I said. But I thought, "Jesus, what could have happened over a misunderstanding?"

Federal probation is a transitional process. So I left La Tuna for a quick flight to California and on to a halfway house in Hollywood. Even though I wasn't thrilled to be there, at least I could see Nikki and Finn. They had been living with Nikki's sister. Right before I went to La Tuna, Velocity

Investment Group had called in the loan on my house. I made them a short sale offer, but instead of taking it, they foreclosed and put the house up for auction. They ended up selling it for the amount I offered. The bitter irony was that Velocity's principals were indicted a few weeks later on charges of running a Ponzi scheme.

Leaving the halfway house meant coming home to a blow-up mattress in Moriya's home office while Nikki and I looked for a place of our own. We found a tidy little two-bedroom rental near Finn's school. I wasn't in love with it, but it was convenient and we needed a base of operations where we could start to rebuild.

Unfortunately, law enforcement isn't alone in harboring an unreasonable hatred of outlaws. Many citizens hold the same bias. It comes from fear. Fear of the "other," of anybody who might look or act different or hold different views. Narrow-minded people always fear someone who challenges their norms.

The Ozzie-and-Harriet couple that lived next door decided a sixty-eight-year-old ex–Hells Angel, his beautiful hairstyling wife, and their quiet preteen with the constant smile were a blight on the neighborhood. They began a campaign of harassment that would have made the ATF proud. They called the police to report disturbances. We were the quietest house on the block, so they just made shit up. We were blasting our stereo, even though we didn't own one. Motorcycles were racing up and down the block at all hours of the night, even though I didn't own a motorcycle and club members weren't allowed to contact me. It went on and on, until the landlord paid us to move. Much as the temperamental Greek in me wanted to dig in my heels, the new house she found us was much more our style. In a quiet neighborhood, it was within walking distance of everything, with Hispanic neighbors who couldn't care less who I was or what we did.

After settling in, I began to form a plan for the future. The History Channel came to me with the idea for a short series on my life in the Hells Angels. I've always been comfortable in front of the camera, and it seemed like a History Channel series could lead to good places. We would film the six-part series, *Outlaw Chronicles: Hells Angels*, two years later.

I hadn't heard from Nick Mead so I asked him out to lunch. Sitting across from him in a Vietnamese restaurant, I sensed something was wrong. Nick was sullen and silent. It was strange, but I assumed that he was having problems at home or in business. I figured he'd talk when he was ready.

It would be the last time I would ever see Nick Mead. I was told by an associate who had become friends with Nick that the club threatened both Nick Mead and the blogger who had been such an avid supporter throughout my trial. Out of the blue, the two began a campaign against me that continues to this day. Nick was paraphrased on the blog saying that he no longer believed in *The Last American Outlaw* and would not promote it. He accused me of lying to him. Sonny himself repeatedly posted on the blog when *Outlaw Chronicles* aired, in a petty attempt to discredit anything and everything I said on-screen. It was a bizarre moment.

Sonny's troops went on the attack. Facebook pages went up promoting the idea that I was a "rat," even though nobody ever said who I betrayed, or who had gone to prison in back of my betrayal. There was no logic, sense, or truth to any of it. But blind followers are just that, blind. I realized I had to let it go. You can't argue with people who are willing to freely lie. They're delusional. The only thing I could do was the outlaw thing, just keep marching to my own drummer. These days, I consult with the media, and I'm working on a prison meditation program. I give speeches and interviews. Members reach out to me by e-mail or text message with words of support. I have a hard time trusting them. Anyone who tries to engage me always looks like a shill for the club or a trap waiting to be sprung. Anybody with a patch on his back, and even those who have given theirs up, could be one of Sonny's minions.

Things turned around. Nikki is a busy and happy yoga teacher and hairstylist. Finn is a normal teenager, but still endearingly sweet and always smiling. Other proposals have come in behind *Outlaw Chronicles*. Still, even now, life hands me the occasional reality check. On August 5, 2015, Georgie went to sleep in his bed. Just a normal night after a normal day. He never woke up. The medical examiner found that he died from a diabetic coma. Georgie hadn't taken care of himself in recent years, and as far as Moriya or I knew, he was never diagnosed as diabetic.

His death hit me harder than I expected. No parent wants to bury a child. It's a perversion of the natural order of things. It was worse with Georgie because I hadn't seen him in almost six months. He had quit the club right after I did, in protest of how they'd treated me. But then he was unmoored. I foolishly waited for him to find his new path, to find happiness. I assumed that he would sort things out and reach out to me, and that we would sit down for a heart-to-heart. That we would work everything out. Instead, that part of my life remains a chapter not finished. So much left unsaid.

I focus on the good times, on the two of us riding side by side, when he was my vice president. More and more, I choose to remember the club like that. I remember riding free and fast, hard against the wind. I remember brothers laughing around a tumbledown clubhouse, not worried about anything. I remember the man who my kids called Uncle Sonny, a man I called Ralph. A man I looked up to and respected and called friend.

Hand it to Sonny. He's outlived a lot of people. But I pity him. Being the oldest outlaw in the room can be as much a curse as a blessing. That he still spends so much time and energy worrying about what I'm doing and saying is sad. It's like an itch he can't scratch, and it seems to drive him a little crazy. I can't help but wonder if it's a type of fear. The fear that one morning he'll wake up and everyone will see through his façade. That everyone will figure out he's just plain old Ralph Hubert Barger, a man with more skeletons in the closet than most people. Or maybe it's the fear of a bitter old man, irrelevant and scared of dying, and wishing he were young again. Whatever it is, I honestly hope he finds peace.

I found mine. In the end, I didn't find it on the open road. I learned that being an outlaw isn't something you find "out there," it's inside you. You don't have to own a motorcycle or wear a patch on your back to be an outlaw. You just have to live life on your terms, and to be true to whatever you believe in even when it's hard to stand up for those beliefs. So many people are lost in this world, and especially in America. They're so worried about what others think, letting themselves be defined by what they buy, own, wear, drive, or ride. Given what the masses are doing, if you follow your own compass and know where you're going, you're already an outlaw.

I had a saying for when guys in the pack were worried that we were lost. My philosophy was that, no matter what, you'll get where you're going. Maybe you take the road you didn't expect, and it turns out to be the long way. That doesn't matter. You keep your head because you're an outlaw. You get there traveling whatever road you need to take. I'm not on the path I thought I'd ride. I thought I'd be leading a column of brothers, but the pack went in different directions, not really a pack at all. Now, I'm getting there, my way, the outlaw way. As I said to my brothers in the pack so long ago, all roads lead to where I'm going.

ACKNOWLEDGMENTS

A first book is a big challenge for any writer. I owe my gratitude to several people for helping me meet that challenge. Thanks to my representation at Flutie Entertainment, including Robert Flutie, Shab Azama, and Jesse Kirk. I'm also grateful to Jane Dystel and Miriam Goderich at Dystel & Goderich, who believed in and supported the book, finding it a great home even in a tough publishing market. Thank you to editor Peter Joseph, always diplomatic and careful with my words. And a tip of the hat to freelance editor and beta reader Chris Peterson, whose gentle critiques and suggestions for cuts were invaluable in making the final product as good as it could be. A heartfelt thank-you to the talented legal minds that helped me get through my legal trials: Barry Tarlow, Robert Sheahen, Tony Serra, Mark Haney, and Michael Mayock. Last, but certainly not least, much love, honor, and respect to those of my brothers who were or are members and who have quietly voiced their support to me even at risk to themselves. It means a lot.